VEGETABLE

FATS AND OILS

THEIR PRACTICAL PREPARATION, PURIFICATION, PROPERTIES, ADULTERATION AND EXAMINATION

BY

LOUIS EDGAR ANDÉS

AUTHOR OF "ANIMAL FATS AND OILS," "DRYING OILS, BOILED OIL
AND DRIERS," ETC.

TRANSLATED FROM THE GERMAN BY

CHARLES SALTER

SECOND EDITION, ENLARGED

94 ILLUSTRATIONS

LONDON

SCOTT, GREENWOOD & CO.

19 LUDGATE HILL, E.C.

1902

FIRST ENGLISH EDITION, 1897.
REPRINTED WITH THE ADDITION OF APPENDICES, AUGUST, 1902.

Printing Statement:

Due to the very old age and scarcity of this book, many of the pages may be hard to read due to the blurring of the original text, possible missing pages, missing text, dark backgrounds and other issues beyond our control.

Because this is such an important and rare work, we believe it is best to reproduce this book regardless of its original condition.

Thank you for your understanding.

PREFACE.

VEGETABLE fats and oils play an important part in many modern industries, a circumstance associated with great improvements effected in the processes of manufacturing and refining and an increase in the number of purposes for which oils and fats are now employed, as compared with former times.

In place of the old primitive presses many establishments are now fitted with all the appliances suggested by the development of technical knowledge, both for expressing the oil from the seeds by mechanical means and for obtaining it by extraction, whereby the yield is greatly increased. In the case of certain fats, Palm Oil for instance, bleaching processes have been introduced whereby the fats are rendered pure white, their sphere of application being thus more widely extended. From distant lands, by reason of increased commerce and the opening up of hitherto unknown territories, rich in nut-bearing trees, we obtain supplies of oils and fats that were formerly met with in European commercial centres but rarely, if at all, and which are now the sources of new and valuable products.

Full cognisance is taken in the present treatise of all modern improvements in the production, purification, and manipulation of vegetable oils and fats, so that the author hopes that all engaged in this industry will be able to derive from his work not only direct information but also the stimulus to further improvement in their processes of manufacture.

LOUIS EDGAR ANDÉS.

TRANSLATOR'S PREFACE.

As the author rightly observes in his prefatory remarks, the industrial application of the vegetable fats and oils has now attained a greater magnitude than in any other period of history, and the balance of probability tends towards its still further extension, since the opening up of new—and especially tropical —countries enlarges the sources of supply at a much more rapid rate than can possibly be attained in the case of animal fats, and that, too, at less cost.

These considerations fully justify the production of a work like the present, which deals in a concise manner with the origin of the various raw materials for the production of vegetable oils ; their preparation and manipulation for extracting their oleaginous treasures ; and the subsequent processes of refining and purifying the product. The qualities and uses of the latter are indicated, and the machinery employed is also dealt with comprehensively, the whole book reflecting the author's wide experience in his subject.

A few additions have been made to the index, with a view to facilitate search, and it is hoped that the retention, in this translated edition, of the French and German names of the various oils will be of value both to the student and practical man.

LONDON, *January*, 1897.

TABLE OF CONTENTS.

LIST OF ILLUSTRATIONS.

VEGETABLE FATS AND OILS.

CHAPTER I.

INTRODUCTION.

THE vegetable fats and oils constitute a group of bodies exhibiting strongly marked characteristics, both as concerns their physical properties and their chemical composition. They consist of compounds of one or more fatty acids with glycerin ethers, are fluid or solid at ordinary temperatures, leave a permanent oily mark on paper, dissolve in boiling alcohol or in cold or warm ether, and are universally of lower specific gravity than water.

Fats and oils are among the most widely distributed of vegetable substances, and are met with in large quantity as stores of nutritive material in fruits and seeds; more rarely in the underground parts of plants, *e.g.*, Cyperus grass. In small quantities they occur in almost all the tissues of phanerogamic and cryptogamic plants, which explains why the proximate analysis of plant leaves, starchy seeds (legumes), starch-bearing fruits (grain), etc., reveals, almost without exception, the presence of at least small amounts of fat. As a rule the fat is contained within the cells and but seldom in the cell wall; an example of the latter is, however, afforded in the tissue of the beet. Usually the fat remains where it is elaborated, and is therefore almost always found imbedded in the tissue, in rare cases escaping thence, by some means at present unknown, and forming a covering of greater or less thickness upon the organs of the plant, as is seen, for example, in the seed of Stillingia sebifera, from which the Chinese tallow of commerce is derived.

Fat occurs in minute quantities in the protoplasm of young cells. It figures in larger amounts as a constituent of cellular sap, in the shape of small drops or. globules, along with the fine granules or slimy mass of protoplasmic residue also suspended in the liquid. Other bodies associated with fats in the vegetable cell are : Starch grains (nutmegs), aleuron granules (cacao beans), chlorophyll (flesh of the olive), granular colouring matters (tissue of the seed of Virola sebifera), resin granules (cotton seed), colouring matter dissolved in fat (palm fat), etc.

In the majority of instances the globules and balls of fat occur in a state of free suspension in the fluid contents of the cell; in many cases, as in the flesh of the olive, they appear as though enveloped by a peculiar soft membrane (fat bubbles). According to the investigations of J. Sachs, the aleuron granules occurring so frequently in oily seeds are mixtures of fat and albuminoid substances.

Next to nothing is yet known of the method by which fat is elaborated in the vegetable cell, whether it proceeds direct from the granules of the plasma or is formed from globular matters suspended in the sap, not having hitherto been ascertained.

The fruits and seeds containing oil or fat must be subjected to special treatment for the extraction of their valuable matter. The means whereby this is effected have, although only in very primitive form, been known from the remotest periods, since we find in the defective traditions handed down to us mention made of the employment of oils. The ancient Egyptians and Phœnicians were acquainted with oil and made use of it for purposes of nutrition, but scarcely ever for lighting, and from them its applications were learned by the Hebrews and subsequently the Greeks. The former possessed oil mills, which their prisoners were set to " tread," and oil lamps are frequently referred to in the Scriptures.

Such of our forefathers as dwelt in lands where the olive is indigenous and grows luxuriantly, derived their supplies of oil almost exclusively from this tree, and only began in later times to extract oil from seeds.

It is to Pliny that we owe the earliest description of an oil mill. That in use by the Romans, and named by them a "turpetum," resembled ordinary edge runners, the stones being horizontal on the inner and convex on the outer side. The base was formed by a circular vessel of hard volcanic stone, a short pillar in the centre constituting the pivot round which the stones were made to revolve by the united efforts of two men pushing at the projecting axles. In this mill the olives were crushed but the kernels remained intact, an important factor in the preservation of the pure flavour of the oil.

The crushed olives were packed into rush bags and pressed under heavy stones, raised by levers while the bags were placed in position and then allowed to descend, their power being increased by hand pressure on the levers.

The preparation of fatty oils in China was thus described by the Swedish sailor Captain Eckeberg in 1767 :—

The oil-producing seeds are ground in an iron mill, consisting of a circular roller with wedge-shaped periphery, running in a similarly shaped groove with sharp rough sides, in which it is easily moved back and forwards. The base in which the groove for the reception and grinding of the seed is situated resembles the sharp keel of a boat. The ground seed is spread on a mat, and warmed over a vessel of boiling water. The steam permeates the meal, and (as Eckeberg expressly remarks) prevents the seed from becoming scorched and the oil from turning rancid. The hot seed is put into bamboo vessels and pressed in wedge presses, identical with the ordinary form, with the single exception that the wedges are driven by hammers wielded by hand. According to Schädler, this communication of Eckeberg's fills up a gap in the historical record of oil mills, nothing new having been recorded between the time of the Romans and the sixteenth century, although it is said that in the tenth century a beginning was made in Germany to use stamping mills for pulverising hard-shelled oil seeds.

Zeisig, in the *Teatrum Machinarum*, published in Leipzig from 1607 to 1612, mentions a German oil mill, the description being accompanied by an unsatisfactory drawing. The mill consisted of three chief parts—a seed stamper, a heating pan, and a wedge press.

In the seventeenth century the Dutch mills driven by wind power came into vogue. The seed was ground by edge runners, and the presses, which were fitted with vertical wedges, were stationed in separate press rooms. The stamps descended perpendicularly.

In France and England improvements were only effected at a much later date. In the former country the industry was for a long time confined to the extraction of olive oil, and that in a very primitive manner. Upright mill stones (edge runners) were employed for grinding or crushing the fruit, and ordinary screw presses with a vertical wooden spindle set in the centre of a frame were used, the screw being rotated either directly by leverage or by means of a kind of windlass.

The invention of the hydraulic press in 1795 marked an important advance in the oil industry. In 1815 these new presses were introduced into France and Germany, where they rapidly spread and are still in use in the majority of oil works, attempts to supersede them by presses working without noise having been unsuccessful. At first only vertical hydraulic presses were made, but later on the horizontal form was introduced ; nevertheless the vertical shape is still the most widely used. A further advance resulted from the employment of steam-heating pans for the seed meal, but although these met with extended application they were not able to entirely drive the old pans, heated by direct fire, out of the field.

As in other branches of industry, unremitting efforts are being made for the improvement of the machinery, especially in the direction of increasing the yield of oil by suitable modifications in the construction of the presses, plates, etc., as well as to arrange the various apparatus in such relative positions as conduce to economy of labour and the continuity of the work. In view of the unreliability generally attendant on labour in the countries where oil seeds are grown, and with the idea of abolishing the long-distance carriage of the seeds, English makers construct mills containing all the necessary apparatus within a limited space and easily portable. Several of these will be described later.

A highly interesting picture of the backward condition of the vegetable oil industry, in respect of the number of oil-producing plant seeds and fruits in technical use twenty years back, is afforded by the report of Professor Julius Wiesner on the "Foreign Plant Stuffs in Industrial Use," in the Vienna Universal Exhibition, 1873. It reads as follows :—

" The exhibition affords us proof of the existence of a large number of hitherto unknown vegetable materials capable of yielding fluid and solid fats, and the importance of fatty bodies for many industrial purposes is such as to imperatively demand the thorough investigation of these crude materials and their products.

"England, France and Holland have already made use of a large number of tropical oil fruits and seeds, whereas we in Austria have remained behind the times, using only such home-grown materials as rape, colza, linseed, hemp-seed, almonds, etc., and, among fruits, merely the olive, for the production of oil, the only foreign vegetable material employed to any extent for that purpose in Austria, as far as we know, being cotton-seed. It therefore seems necessary to make the Austrian oil pressers aware of the fact that their English and French *confrères* work up enormous quantities of castor oil, sesame, and ground-nut kernels. The first-named oil is known in Austria as a medicament only, but is well adapted for many industrial uses, *e.g.*, in the preparation of softening oil for leather, in soap making, etc. Sesame oil is employed in soap making, and may, in common with ground-nut oil, be used to replace olive oil for many purposes. Castor-oil seeds (from Ricinus communis, viridis, Americanus) are to be met with in the exhibits from Martinique, Guiana, Senegal, Reunion, Gaboon, Algiers, India, and other countries, Italy making a very good show. Sesame is exhibited to an even greater extent, and the fruit of the ground-nut displayed in the exhibits of all warm countries shows the development the cultivation of this plant for nutrient purposes has attained in the tropics, especially in the West African colonies, Congo and Senegal annually exporting about 80,000 tons (1873) of ground-nuts, the bulk of which is consumed in the manufacture of Marseilles soap. From Madras and Calcutta there also come important quantities of this substance, chiefly to England.

"A source of oil not hitherto regarded by the European oil industry is the Bankul nut (from Aleurites triloba), which deserves to be brought into use, on account not only of the low price of the raw material, but also from the high quality of the oil. It belongs to the category of 'drying' oils, of which there are none too many, and is occasionally met with in commerce as 'huile de Bancoul' or kekune oil.

According to the Catalogue of the French Colonies this oil is highly suitable for the manufacture of paints, but even if this be not so, and it should only be fit for printers' ink—for which at present linseed oil is almost exclusively used—the introduction of this oil could not be otherwise than advantageous, provided the price remained low." (This is not now the case at all, as will be seen later.)

The utilisation of the oil of the Calaba nut (from Calophyllum calaba) so frequently encountered in the tropics, of the Owala seeds (from Pentaclethra macrophylla, common on the East Coast of Africa) which yield 50 per cent. of a fat resembling olive oil, of the Bera seed (from a kind of Citrullus, growing extensively on the West African Coast), must also be regarded as indicative of progress. Everywhere in warm and hot countries there exist plants producing enormous quantities of oily fruits and seeds which, pending their introduction into European industries, are simply wasted.

It should be further remarked that already some fats are brought as such to Europe from tropical countries. Some of them occupy a foremost place among the fatty bodies we utilise; such, for example, are palm fat, palm kernel oil, and cocoanut fat. The English industry was the first to seize upon them, an example followed by the Continent. The case will no doubt be the same with other fats now used in England alone, e.g., Shea butter (from the seed of the Indian Bassia butyracea), Crab oil (from the seed of the South American tree Carapa guyanensis), Borneo tallow, Piney tallow, etc. There are also several fats utilised in France, e.g., Galam butter, Djare fat, Mahwah butter, Benailé oil (from Moringa pterygosperma), Dika fat (which resembles Cacao butter), Aouaro oil, etc., which will probably later on be turned to account by other countries.

The statistics of production of the various oils and fats are very defective, but the subjoined figures, although insufficient to do justice to the extent of the industry, will never-theless afford some indication of its development.

Olive oil is chiefly produced in the Mediterranean countries and the East. In 1877, 317,800 acres were planted with olives in France, yielding 7,318,352 bushels of fruit and 392,018 cwts. of oil. Spain devoted 2,500,000 acres (468,335 in the province of Cordova) to this object, and produced 2,750,000 gallons of oil. In 1874, Italy had 1,223,768 acres under olives, yielding 9,310,375 bushels of fruit. The total amount of olive oil exported from Italy was, in 1878, 51,413 tons, and in 1879, 88,655 tons. Greece exported 12,244,665 oke (the oke is equal to 22 fluid ounces) in 1875. Algeria produced in 1877, 55,239 tons of olives, which yielded 1,543,400 hectolitres (of 22 gallons) of oil. Turkey exports 90,000 tons per annum. French imports are estimated at 20,000 tons per annum, and the exports at 5,000 tons. England imported:—

	1887.	1888.	1889.	1890.
Olive oil (tons) .	20,756	18,580	22,954	20,187
Value in £ sterling	757,040	674,472	818,352	785,787

The production of olive oil in California is estimated at 1,000 gallons.

German imports and exports amounted to :—

	1890.		1891.	
	Import.	Export.	Import.	Export.
Edible oils .	27,648	1,252	34,989	1,328 *
Denaturised .	71,044	—	88,748	—

Rape or colza oil is produced in Germany, France, Australia, Hungary, Russia, and Roumania. In Germany 445,000 acres were planted with Brassica in 1882 ; the crop amounted to 188,290 tons, of a total value of about £252,500. In 1882, 68,100 tons of rape-seed were imported into Germany, and 115,429 tons in 1883. Deducting the amount reserved for seed, 250,000 tons were used for oil pressing,

---

* *Translator's Note.*—Basis of weight not given ; probably tons are meant.

from which were obtained some 90,000 to 100,000 tons of oil, worth between 48,000,000 and 56,000,000 marks (1 mark equals 1 shilling). In 1891, Germany imported 228 tons of rape oil and exported 10,062 tons.

England's yearly imports of rape oil amount to 80,000 tons. Australia manipulates 55,000 tons of rape-seed every year, and obtains 20,000 to 22,500 tons of oil. The total consumption of this oil throughout Europe is estimated at 280,000 to 300,000 tons per annum, valued at £8,500,000 to £8,750,000 sterling.

Russia exported in 1879, 1,294,798 bushels; Roumania, 938,376 bushels in 1878. From India 3,193,488 cwts. were shipped in the years 1877 and 1878.

SESAME OIL. The seed is chiefly derived from the East Indies and the Levant, and is worked up in Marseilles and Trieste. British India exports 130,000 tons; Turkey, 12,000; Siam, 3,000 tons. France imports more than 10,000 tons; England, 25,000; Italy, 15,000; and Germany, 14,000 tons.

COTTON-SEED OIL. In the United States the yield of seed is estimated at 3 lb. from each lb. of husked cotton. Since the cotton crop of 1889-90 amounted to 7,313,926 bales (3,437,451,220 lb.), some 10,000,000 lb. of seed must have been obtained. The weight of spent seed from the press amounted to 1,058,200 tons.

The amount and value of the produce of cotton-seed in 1889-90 were as follows:—

Crude oil	.	.	.	.	gallons,	41,287,300	= £12,386,355
Oilcake .	.	.	.	.	tons,	383,759	= 7,867,054
Bast	.	.	.	bales of 470 lb.,	63,519	= 1,905,570
Husks .	.	.	.	.	tons,	529,375	= 1,587,970

Of the above quantity, 9,000,000 gallons were used for making "compound lard," the remainder being either exported or used for mixing with drying oil or for soap making.

The exports of cotton-seed oil during recent years amounted to :—

	1885-6.	1886-7.	1887-8.	1888-9.	1889-90.
Oil (gallons)	6,240,139	4,067,138	4,458,597	2,690,700	13,384,385
Value £ stlg.	2,115,674	1,578,935	1,925,739	1,298,609	5,291,178

England is the chief centre of the cotton-seed oil pressing industry in Europe, the seed being mainly derived from Egypt. In 1881, the imports amounted to 230,000 tons, valued at £1,783,100; in 1882, 210,000 tons, worth £1,585,850; and in 1883, 250,000 tons, equal to £1,845,000. France imported in 1882, 20,575 tons; 1883, 23,480 tons. Italy, 20,050 tons in 1881 and 25,283½ tons in 1882. In 1890 the imports into Germany amounted to 19,458 tons, and 21,365¾ tons in 1891.

Hemp-seed oil is chiefly produced in Russia. The export of seed from Riga amounted to 629,520 bushels in 1878, and 725,809 poods (of 36 lb.) in 1879.

LINSEED OIL. Linseed is produced in all countries, but chiefly in Russia and India. In 1890, 3,783,000 acres were planted with flax in Russia in Europe, yielding a total crop of 21,000,000 bushels. The exports were, 1887, 13,000,000 bushels; 1888, 14,000,000; 1889, 13,500,000; 1890 (estimated), 12,000,000. From India the total exports to the end of the year (31st March) amounted to 7,146,896 cwts., of which 4,342,962 were sent to Great Britain (U.S. Consular Reports, 1891). In Germany 292,500 acres are devoted to the production of linseed, and yield 50,000 tons of seed. The last-named country imported in 1885, 38,313 tons; 1886, 39,743; 1887, 41,493; 1888, 44,070; 1889, 43,973; 1890, 35,708; 1891, 37,381½ tons of linseed oil.

IMPORTS OF LINSEED OIL INTO THE UNITED STATES.

	1888.	1889.	1890.
Linseed oil *	1,461,480	3,259,460	2,391,175
Value in £ sterling .	1,505,499	3,851,685	2,839,057

* *Translator's Note.*—Basis not stated; probably metercentners of 2 cwts.

The home production in America reached 9,000,000 bushels of seed from 1880 to 1890 ; the 1890-91 crop was taxed at 12,000,000 bushels.

OILCAKES AND OILCAKE MEAL. AMERICAN EXPORTS.

	1886.	1887.	1888.	1889.	1890.
Oilcake (lb.)	585,947,181	622,295,233	562,744,209	588,317,880	711,704,373
Value £	7,053,714	7,309,691	6,423,930	6,927,612	7,999,926

CHAPTER II.

GENERAL PROPERTIES OF THE VEGETABLE FATS AND OILS.

The fats are either fluid or solid at the ordinary temperature. In the former event they are termed oils (Oel, huile),
in the latter tallow (Talg, suif) or butter (Butter, beurre).
The vegetable tallows usually melt below 50° C., and the fats
generally boil at about 300° C. If heated further they vola-
tilise, one part being decomposed and another evolved entire
(fatty acids). At high temperatures the glycerin of the fat
undergoes decomposition into acrolein, a substance having a
powerful, penetrating, unpleasant smell. The production of
acrolein vapours affords a valuable means of detecting fats.

The specific gravity of the oils and fats is less than that
of water, and can in many cases be relied on to furnish a
characteristic indication of their purity.

The melting and setting points are also characteristic,
and the refractive index is a valuable adjunct in the analytical differentiation of oils of various origin.

When fresh the vegetable oils frequently possess a very
agreeable odour. Fresh palm oil has the pleasant smell of
violet root, cacao butter the odour of the cacao bean, nutmeg
butter the smell of the nutmeg, and so on. With age, however, in most cases a disagreeable smell is developed, due to
the liberation of fatty acids.

In flavour the fresh fats are, as a rule, agreeable and
mild, the instances being rare where fresh fat (*e.g.* ; carapa fat,
which is decidedly bitter) has a penetrating taste. The unpleasant flavour of rancid fats is well known. Taste and

smell afford highly characteristic indications of most fats, and decided colour is also characteristic, being only present in few instances. Palm oil when fresh is orange yellow, but the colour flies with age, and, when rancidity is at its height, turns to dirty white. Fresh palm fat from Astrocaryum vulgare is vermilion red in colour, and fades but little, even after the lapse of years. Ordinarily the fats are yellowish, greenish or dirty white; seldom colourless (several kinds of olive oil) or pure white (cocoanut or vateria fat). The appearance and lustre of the fats are so well known as to need merely passing mention.

Nearly all fats leave (at ordinary temperatures) on paper greasy marks that do not disappear on the application of heat, and even those of comparatively high melting point leave similar marks when heated. When absorbed by a wick all fats will burn with a more or less bright or smoky flame.

Under the microscope at ordinary temperatures the solid fats are seen to consist of mixed solid and liquid matters, the former existing mostly as crystals, almost always of acicular form, either single or congregated into tufts or spherical masses. In some instances, such as in nutmeg butter or many rancid fats, the aggregations are so large as to be visible to the unassisted eye. These crystals are nothing more than free fatty acids. If the fat be warmed on the microscope slide to the melting point, some solid amorphous granules will be found still remaining on the mass; on cooling, the fatty acids will crystallise out again, mostly in acicular form, but a portion of the fatty acid in the fat from Astrocaryum vulgare separates out, after fusion, as tabular crystals, a form not present in the original fat. It is remarkable that the fatty acids in many fused fats, rich in crystals in their original condition, do not separate out again, even after standing for some hours at a temperature at which the original fat was semi-solid and rich in crystals, the crystals only forming after some days or exposure to a low temperature. An example of this is afforded by cocoanut butter. In solid fats containing little olein, the liquid portion appears in globular form, but where much olein is present it forms the matrix in which the crystalline and amorphous granules are suspended. Frequently the fluid exhibits a lack of homogeneity under the microscope, bearing globules of different refractive power from the rest. In palm fat and fat from Astrocaryum vulgare these globules show (optically) a red coloration somewhat like the vacuoles in yeast cells. When examined microscopically the colouring matters appear either to be dissolved in the fluid oil (palm fat, fat from Astrocaryum vulgare), or as granules lying interstitially between the crystals (Virola fat), or enclosed in cells (Bassia fat). The occurrence of entire cells or portions of tissue is no rarity in fats, particularly those obtained by boiling, and such foreign bodies contain either fat, starch granules (Myristica fat), or colouring matter.

With regard to solubility, it is mostly stated that fats are insoluble in water. It would appear, however, that this is not so, although the degree of solubility is very small, since if fat be shaken up with water a very slight amount can be afterwards extracted from the latter by means of ether. As a rule, fats are but slightly soluble in alcohol in the cold, with the exception of ricinus oil, which is completely dissolved. Ether, bisulphide of carbon, ethereal oils, benzol, canadol, acetone, and wood spirit dissolve nearly all of them with ease. Sulphur and phosphorus are dissolved by fats, and some oils form with chlorine and chloride of sulphur compounds resembling caoutchouc, which may be used instead of that body.

The vegetable fats and oils consist principally of neutral glycerides of the fatty acids, and are therefore expressed by the general formula $C_3H_5(O\ OC\ R^1)$, wherein R^1 indicates a monovalent hydrocarbon. In addition they may also contain free fatty acids.

The " Waxes," on the other hand, consist of fatty acid ethers of monatomic alcohols, whereas glycerin is a triatomic alcohol. The difference between fats and waxes is, however, not very sharply defined, " Japanese wax " containing almost exclusively glycerides; whilst, for example, spermaceti, which is generally designated as (animal) fat, consists for the most part of cetyl palmitate, and should properly be classed with the waxes. The following acids and alcohols have up to the present been detected in fats and waxes :—

A. ACIDS.

1. Saturated acids of the general formula $C_nH_{2n}O_2$.

$C_4H_8O_2$	Butyric acid.
$C_5H_{10}O_2$	Isovaleric acid.
$C_6H_{12}O_2$	Caproic acid.
$C_8H_{16}O_2$	Caprylic acid.
$C_9H_{18}O_2$	Pelargonic acid.
$C_{10}H_{20}O_2$	Capric acid.
$C_{12}H_{24}O_2$	Lauric acid.
$C_{14}H_{28}O_2$	Myristic acid.
$C_{15}H_{30}O_2$	Isocetic acid.
$C_{16}H_{32}O_2$	Palmitic acid.
$C_{17}H_{34}O_2$	Margaric acid.
$C_{18}H_{36}O_2$	Stearic acid.
$C_{20}H_{40}O_2$	Arachidic acid.
$C_{21}H_{42}O_2$	Medullic acid.
$C_{22}H_{44}O_2$	Behenic acid.
$C_{24}H_{48}O_2$	Carnaubic acid.
$C_{25}H_{50}O_2$	Hyaenic acid.
$C_{27}H_{54}O_2$	Cerotic acid.
$C_{30}H_{60}O_2$	Melissic acid.
$C_{64}H_{128}O_2$	Theobromic acid.

2. Unsaturated acids with double carbon bonds of the general formula $C_nH_{2n\ 2}O_2$.

$C_5H_8O_2$	Tiglic acid.
$C_{16}H_{30}O_2$	Hypogaeic acid.
$C_{16}H_{30}O_2$	Physetolic acid.

$C_{18}H_{34}O_2$ Oleic acid.
$C_{19}H_{36}O_2$ Doeglic acid.
$C_{22}H_{42}O_2$ Erucic (Brassic) acid.

3. Acids with triple carbon bonds of the general formula $C_nH_{2n-4}O_2$.

$C_{17}H_{30}O_2$ Elaeomargaric acid.
$C_{16}H_{28}O_2$ Linolic acid.

4. Acids with the general formula $C_nH_{2n-6}O_2$.

$C_{18}H_{30}O_2$ Linolenic acid.
$C_{18}H_{30}O_2$ Isolinolenic acid.

5. Ketone acids of the general formula $C_nH_{2n-2}O_3$.

$C_{18}H_{34}O_3$ Ricinoleic acid.
$C_{18}H_{34}O_3$ Rapic acid.

B. ALCOHOLS.

1. Triatomic alcohol, with the composition $C_nH_{2n+2}O_3$.

$C_3H_8O_3$ Glycerin (glycerol).

2. Monatomic alcohols of the fatty series, with the composition $C_nH_{2n+2}O$.

$C_{16}H_{34}O$ Cetyl alcohol.
$C_{18}H_{38}O$ Octodecyl alcohol.
$C_{27}H_{56}O$ Ceryl alcohol (Isoceryl alcohol).
$C_{30}H_{62}O$ Myricyl alcohol (Melissyl alcohol).

3. Monatomic aromatic alcohols.

$C_{26}H_{44}O$ Cholesterin (cholesterol).
$C_{26}H_{44}O$ Isocholesterin (isocholesterol).
$C_{26}H_{44}O$ Phytostearin (phytosterol).

Most frequently the fats consist of glycerides of the fatty acids ; palmitic—as palmitin, tripalmitin, $C_3H_5(C_{15}H_{31}CO_2)_3$; stearic—as stearin, tristearin, $C_3H_5(C_{17}H_{35}CO_2)_3$; oleic—as olein, triolein, $C_3H_5(C_{17}H_{33}CO_2)_3$. A few contain the glycerides of linolic acid, $C_3H_5(C_{16}H_{29}CO_2)_3$, and of physetolic acid, $C_3H_5(C_{15}H_{29}CO_2)_3$.

In very rare cases acids with an odd number of carbon atoms are also encountered. The other acids mentioned occur in unimportant amounts, though individual fats are characterised by the presence of large quantities of the glycerides of these acids. The fats are distinguished from the fatty oils by their consistency, which is influenced by the varying proportions of the individual glycerides. Stearin and palmitin are solid at ordinary temperatures, whereas olein is liquid. A characteristic common to all fats is their ready decomposition into glycerin and fatty acids, which may be effected by absorption of water or by the action of acids, alkalis or superheated steam, and is, when the reagent is an alkali, termed " saponification ".

Palmitin, stearin and olein constitute the bulk of the fats and oils, larger or smaller quantities of linolic acid being present in the drying oils in the form of linolein. The vegetable oils may be regarded as pure triglycerides, whilst the vegetable fats contain, often before their removal from the fruit, etc., free fatty acids. All rancid fats and oils contain free fatty acids, produced, together with glycerin, by the decomposing action of the air.

The saturated fatty acids up to caproic, as well as oleic, doeglic, linolic, and ricinoleic acids are liquid at the ordinary temperature, all the others being solid. Only butyric, caproic, caprylic, and capric acids can be distilled without decomposition under ordinary pressure, and these are therefore designated " volatile " fatty acids.

When fats and oils or fatty acids are treated with caustic alkalis or lead oxide they saponify. Concentrated alkaline lyes saponify the fats with great difficulty, wherefore only dilute lyes are used. Stearin and palmitin saponify more readily than olein.

When melted with potassic hydrate oleic acid = acetopalmitic acid, erucic acid = acetoarachic acid, hypogaeic acid = acetomyristic acid, and their isomers are decomposed into palmitic, arachic, myristic and acetic acids.

Concentrated sulphuric acid in proportions between 8 and 10 per cent. forms with fats at high temperatures

2

"sulpho-acids," which on treatment with water split up again into free fatty acids, glycerin, and sulphuric acid.

On treating oils with alkali carbonates, albumen or aqueous solutions of gum arabic, or exposing them to the action of ammonium carbonate, emulsions are formed. An alcoholic solution of ammonia decomposes the fats, etc., after protracted exposure at the ordinary temperature, into acid amides and glycerin.

$$\text{Palmitamide} = C_{16}H_{31} \quad O_1H_2N.$$
$$\text{Stearamide} = C_{18}H_{35} \quad H_2N.$$
$$\text{Oleamide} = C_{18}H_{32} \quad H_2N.$$

Chlorine and bromine form substitution products with the fats, *i.e.*, fatty acids, of the methane series (lauric, myristic, palmitic, stearic, arachic, behenic, carnaubic, melissic, theobromic, cocinic, cetic, margaric, medullic, hyaenic, and cerotic acids). Iodine does not act in a similar manner, but forms—as do also the other two elements—addition products with glycerides, *i.e.*, fatty acids, of the unsaturated hydrocarbons (crotonic, hypogaeic, physetolic, erucic, tiglic, moringic, doeglic, linolic (stearolic), elaeomargaric, and ricinoleic acids).

Nitric acid exerts a powerful oxodising effect on the fats, etc., producing oxalic acid, succinic acid, adipinic acid. Nitric anhydride transforms the acids named below into their isomers:—

Hypogaeic acid into gaidic acid.
Oleic acid into elaidic acid.
Erucic acid into brassic acid.
Ricinoleic acid into ricinelaidic acid.

From the differences noted in their behaviour on exposure, especially in thin layers, to the action of air, the fats and oils have been separated into two groups: "drying" and "non-drying" (*i.e.*, drying slowly or with difficulty).

By the oxidation of linolein (the chief constituent of all drying oils) in air is formed the neutral body linoxin,

$C_{16}H_{28}O_6$, which is transformed by the action of bases into oxylinoleic acid, $C_{16}H_{25}O_4OH$. According to Bauer and Hazura, the drying oils contain in addition to olein the glycerides of linolic acid, $C_{16}H_{22}O_2$, which absorbs four atoms of iodine. From the oxidation of linolic acid there results sativic acid, $C_{18}H_{36}O_6$, tetrastearic acid; linolenic acid gives linusic acid, $C_{18}H_{36}O_6$, a heptatomic monobasic acid. The proportion of these two acids in the different drying oils varies, linseed oil, for instance, containing 6·5 of sativic acid and 20·3 of linusic acid, whilst nut oil contains 25 of sativic and 2 of linusic acid.

When exposed to the air the non-drying oils and fats develop a sharp, unpleasant flavour and odour, oxygen being apparently absorbed, without however causing "drying"; they become in fact what is termed "rancid," a change accompanied by the formation of small quantities of volatile fatty acids (butyric, caproic, etc.), the glycerin partly disappearing. Part of the non-volatile fatty acids, especially oleic acid, is liberated, and frequently, as in palm oil, complete separation of the oil into fatty acid and glycerin occurs. Rancidity occurs less extensively in the solid than in the liquid fats, and they keep better and longer in proportion as the quantity of glycerides of the solid fatty acids is larger. As to the causes of this weighty transformation, which is of great importance in many instances in respect of the employment of fats and oils (for alimental purposes, as lubricants for metallic surfaces, etc.), opinions are divided.

According to Liebig, rancidity is induced by the reaction of the foreign bodies present in the fat. Löwig assumed fermentation in the presence of water and air. Kosch, on the other hand, considers it as resulting from oxidation by atmospheric oxygen, a view shared by Duclaux; whilst Berthelot attributes the effects to moisture, the action of which is facilitated by the presence of foreign substances, oxidation being merely a concomitant reaction. Von Reichenberg, Flugge, Pachoulin, H. Schulze, and Nenecki believe that rancidity is due to the influence of structureless ferments or microbes capable of decomposing the fats. Gröger assumes that the process is one of hydrolysis followed by oxidation, which extends both to the fatty acids and to the glycerin, since the latter cannot be detected as existing in a free state. The fatty acids are converted into compounds (acids), poorer in carbon but with a higher percentage of oxygen, belonging partly to the fatty acid series and partly to the oxalic series. Among the latter azelaic acid has been detected.

Ritsert proved that rancidity is not due to bacteria, whether aerobic or anaerobic, if the fat be pure. Fat protected from air and light remains fresh, and on the other hand germs sown on pure undecomposed fat die, whereas they live if the fat is rancid. Another proof that rancidity is not due to the action of ferments is afforded by the fact that sterilised fat when heated to 140° in a closed vessel for several hours, but exposed to light and air, "turns" rancid. Neither is moisture essential, for perfectly dry fat will, under the influence of air, become more decidedly rancid than in presence of water. The phenomenon is one of oxidation, occasioned by the oxygen of the air independently of any organism, but varying directly with the light, no oxygen being absorbed in the dark ; neither has the latter reagent any power of producing rancidity by itself. Air alone, when oxygen is excluded, has no action, and pure hog fat kept in the dark remains sweet after a lapse of two months. Carbonic acid is absorbed by fats in small amount, both in the light or in the dark, the fat becoming tallowy but not rancid. In this respect the carbonic acid in the air acts precisely like the pure acid, only more faintly. Nitrogen and hydrogen are indifferent towards fat, whatever be the conditions of light, and pure butter fat behaves precisely in the same manner as pure hog fat. Aerobic and anaerobic bacteria can exist in rancid fats, but not when the proportion of free fatty acids is high (*e.g.*, rancid palm fat). In practice, the chief precaution to be adopted for preventing fat from becoming rancid is to thoroughly exclude air. This done, it is a matter of indifference whether the fat be exposed to light or not.

CHAPTER III.

ESTIMATION OF THE AMOUNT OF OIL IN SEEDS.

On account of the varying proportion of oil existing in oil seeds, it is always important to estimate the amount actually present in the seed (or other material) from which oil is to be obtained. This is most suitably effected by treating the perfectly dry, powdered substance with solvents, under conditions facilitating complete extraction. The Soxhlet apparatus (Fig. 1) is the one most frequently employed. A is the extractor, B the distilling flask, C the condenser, D the syphon tube for emptying the extractor. A is filled to two-thirds of its capacity with the powdered oil seeds, and B is half filled with petroleum ether, carbon bisulphide, or any other suitable solvent. On account of its comparative fragility, the Soxhlet apparatus may be replaced by a simpler form, *e.g.*, that devised by Thorn (Fig. 2). In order to recover the oil from the solvent, the solution is distilled over the water bath.

To remove the final traces of the solvent, the flask is heated in the water bath until of constant weight.

The method of determining the content of oil in a seed by displacement in a funnel (Figs. 3, 4) is only rarely practised nowadays. From 200 to 300 grams of the seed or fruit under examination are powdered with great care, and after being well mixed 10 to 12 grams are placed in the separating funnel, previously fitted with a plug of cotton or a filter. The solvent is poured on to the substance in a moderately warm condition, the tap of the funnel being closed, and left to act for about half an hour. On opening the tap and the stopper or lid at the top of the funnel, the extract runs into the flask below. The operation is repeated until the effluent liquid is colourless, and ceases to leave a fatty mark behind when dropped on to a sheet of white paper. When the method is properly performed, about 40 grams of ether, canadol, benzol, or other solvent will suffice for 10 grams of substance. The solvent is distilled direct from the flask,

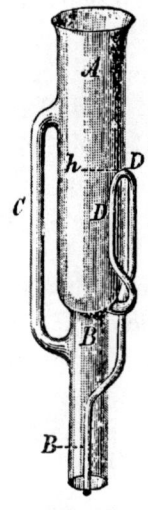

FIG. 1. Soxhlet Extractor.

FIG. 2. Thorn's Extractor.
D, Distillation Cylinder; K, Condenser; T, Funnel; a, p, Condensing Tube.

after the latter has been connected to a condenser. The residue is emptied into a tared glass beaker, the flask well rinsed out with a little of the solvent, and the contents of the beaker heated over the water bath until constant. The weight of oil thus ascertained is a little in excess of the truth, owing to the presence of colouring matter and resin in the solution.

An example of the new forms of extracting apparatus wherein the solvent is evaporated without delay, is afforded by Vohl's Oleometer. This apparatus, shown in Fig. 5, is made entirely of glass, and consists of four parts, the extractor A, the boiling flask B, the hood C, and the condenser D. The extractor is formed out of a wide tube cc, into which is fused the narrow tube b, the latter communicating with the tube o by way of the boiling flask B. At the lower extremity of cc is a side tubulus d, into which the tube o fits by means of a cork. The last-named tube terminates at the bottom of the flask B, so that its mouth is always closed by the liquid in the latter.

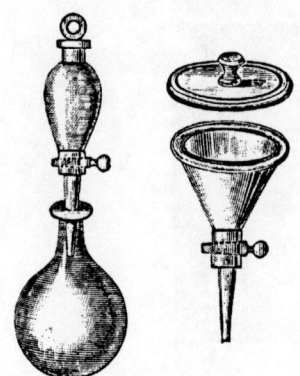

At the top of cc is a side tubulus f, containing a tube g drawn out fine. The hood C is connected with b by the tube h and with the tubulus f (*i.e.*, the wide extraction tube cc) by a tube i. It also communicates with the condenser D by means of a tube k. The tube l is constricted at n to one-third its ordinary internal diameter.

FIGS. 3, 4. Separating Funnels.

The apparatus is worked as follows: A loose wad of cotton is placed in the tubulus d, the tube o fitted in place by a cork, and the ground and weighed seed inserted in the wide tube cc through the opening in f, only enough to occupy seven-eighths of the capacity of the vessel being taken. The substance being evenly distributed, the extractor is connected with the flask B, and canadol is poured over the seed through f, until B is filled with liquid to a depth of about two centimetres. The condenser D and hood C are then placed in position, and the tube mm filled with cold water, or better, with ice. A strong retort stand is used to keep the apparatus in its place, one with two clamps, to hold A and D, being preferable. This done the liquid in B is heated to boiling, the vapours ascend through *e* into *b*, and flow back again, condensed, until the contents of *cc* have attained the boiling point of the canadol. When this is reached the vapours ascend through *h* into C, where they are condensed until this vessel also becomes heated, whereupon they rise into *l via k*, and are there liquefied by the cold water or ice, and flow back into C through the bent tube *k*, thence through *i* into the tubulus *f* in A, finally reaching B by way of the tube *o*. The tube *g* serves for the ingress and escape of air during fluctuations in the temperature of the apparatus. In the above manner a considerable quantity of seed can be extracted by a comparatively small amount of solvent. The operation may be considered complete when the solvent running back into B is colourless. The canadol impregnated with oil is subjected to distillation and the latter weighed. The specific gravity of the canadol should not exceed 0·66 to 0·68, and it should boil between 50° and 60° C. With a little practice, the estimation may be performed in one and a half to two hours. Where many estimations have to be made, the distillation of the extract takes up too much

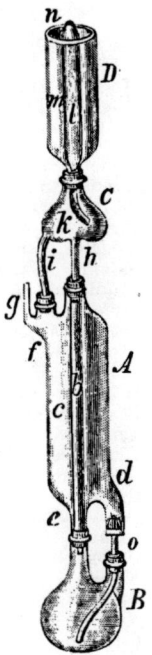

Fig. 5. Vohl's Extractor.

time, in addition to requiring great care and necessitating the provision of a separate distilling apparatus, which is not always at disposal, on which account Vohl has endeavoured to determine the oil volumetrically. The specific gravity of the fatty vegetable oils being considerably higher than that of the canadol solvent, the specific gravity of the extract must increase proportionately with the amount of oil extracted.

TABLE OF VEGETABLE FATS AND OILS, WITH FRENCH AND CENTAGE OF FAT IN THE PLANTS

English Names: Oil, Fat, Butter, Tallow of	German Names: -Oel, -Fett, -Butter, -Talg	French Names: Huile, Graisse, Beurre, Suif de
Cashew apple	Acajou	Noix de Caju
Charlock	Ackersenf-Ravison	Ravison d'Odessa
Prickly poppy	Argymone	Pavot epineux
Ailanto	Ailanthus	Ailante du Japon
Anda	Anda	Anda
Tucum	Aouara	Aouara de la Guyana
Apple kernel	Apfelkern	Pepins de pomme
Himalayan apricot	Aprikosenkern	Amandes de l'abricot
Cabbage palm	Arekanuss	Noix d'arec
Cardon	Artischokensamen	Cardon
Alligator pear	Avocado	Abacetier, Avocatier
Galam	Bambuk, Galambutter	Shée, Bambouk
Candlenuts	Bankulnuss	Noix de Bancul
Olive	Baumöl	Olives
Cotton, Cotton-seed	Baumwollsamen	Coton
Ben	Behensamen	Ben
Becuiba	Bicuyba	Ucuuba
Henbane seed	Bilsenkrautsamen	Jusquiame
Pear kernel	Birnenkern	Pepins de poire
Tangkawang	Bonducnuss	Borne
Nickerseeds, Fevernuts	Borneotalg	Noix de Bonduc
Beechnut	Buchenkern, Buchelkern	Faine
Cacao	Cacaobutter	Cacao
Calaba, Poonseed	Calaba	Calaba, Galba
Camul	Camul	Polango
Crabwood	Carapa, Krabholz	Carapa
Koëme	Castanhas	Ogadioka du Gabon
Centaury	Centaurien, Flockenblumen	Centaurie
Vegetable tallow of Chironji [China	Chinatalg Chironjetalg	Suif de la Chine Charolée
Cocoanut, Coprah	Cocos, Coprah	Noix de Coco, Coprah
Croton	Croton	Graines de Tilly
Dika, Oba	Dika	Dika
Thistle	Distelsamen	Chardon
Elupa	Ellipebutter	Mohwa
Cyperus	Erdmandel	Suchet comestible
Earthnut, Peanut	Erdnuss	Arachide, Pistache de terre
Antidote cacoon, Abilla	Feuillia	Liane contre poison, Coulevre, Noix de [serpent
Reedpine seeds	Fichtensamen	Sapin
Indian butter, Fulwara	Fulwa	Fulwara
Galam, Nungu	Galam, Djaveöl	Shée, Bambouk
Gambo, Sunn-okra	Gambohanf	Rose de chine
Cress-seed	Gartenkressensamen	Cressen alenois
Gamboge	Gamboge	Gamboge
Gilla	Gilla	Gilla
Cucumber	Gurkensamen	Pepins de concombre
Gundschitt	Gundschitt, Siva	Lallemantia

GERMAN NOMENCLATURE, SOURCE AND ORIGIN, AND PER-
FROM WHICH THEY ARE DERIVED.

Plants from which obtained.	Country of origin.	Percentage of Fat and Oil in the Seeds.
Anacardium occidentale	West Indies, Brazil	40-45
Sinapis arvensis	Europe	31-33
Argemone mexcana	West Indies, Mexico	25-30
Ailanthus glutinosa	China, Japan	54-56
Anda Gomesii	Brazil	30-35
Astrocaryum vulgare	South America	40-45
Pyrus malus	Europe	17-19
Armeniaca vulgaris	Asia	40-45
Areca catechu	East Indies	14-16
Cynara Cardunculus	Mediterranean countries	20-22
Persea gratissima	West Indies, Brazil	28-30
Aleuritis moluccana	Oceania	62-64
Olea europaea	Southern Europe	40-60
Gossypium herbaceum	Asia, Africa, America	24-36
Meringa olifera	Egypt, India	35-36
Myristica bicuhyba	Brazil	70-71
Hyoscyamus niger	Europe	35-37
Pyrus communis	Europe	18-20
Caesalpina Bonducella	Tropical countries	24-25
Hopea splendida	Islands of Sunda	45-50
Fagus sylvatica	Europe	43-45
Theobroma cacao	Central America	44-47
Calophyllum Calaba	Antilles	60-63
Malottus philippensis	Abyssinia, India	20-24
Carapa guyanensis	Brazil, Guiana	65-70
Telfairia pedata	Madagascar, Africa	33-35
Centaurea sonchifolia	W. Europe, France	27-28
Stillingia sebifera	China, Punjab	37-39
Buchanania latifolia	Malabar	40-45
Cocos nucifera	Guinea	40-45
Croton Tiglium	East Indies	53-56
Mangifera gabonensis	West Africa	60-64
Onopordan Acanthium	Europe	30-35
Bassia longifolia ·	East Indies	50-55
Cyperus esculentus	Mediterranean countries	20-23
Arachis hypogaea	West Africa, India	43-45 (50)
Feuillia cordifolia	Brazil	55-60
Pinus abies	Europe	25-30
Bassia butyracea	Himalaya	50-52
Bassia Parkii	Tropical countries, W. Africa	49-52
Hibiscus cannabinus	India ·	17-18
Lepidium sativum	Europe	23-25
Garcinia pictoria	India	24-25
Entada scandens	Bengal	70
Cucurbita pepo	Orient	20-25
Lallemantia iberica	Persia, Kurdistan	29-30

TABLE OF VEGETABLE FATS AND OILS—*continued*.

English Names: Oil, Fat, Butter, Tallow of	German Names: -Oel, -Fett, -Butter, -Talg	French Names: Huile, Graisse, Beurre, Suif de
Chaulmoogra	Gynocardia	Chalmogrée
Hemp-seed	Hanf	Graines de chanvre
Hazel nut	Haselnuss	Noisettes
Wild radish	Hederich, Ackerrettig	Ravenelle
Hickory	Hyckorynuss	Noix amère
Wood	Holzöl, chinesisches, Fir-nissbaumöl	Bois de Chine
Horned poppy	Hornmohn	Pavot cornu
Vegetable wax	Japantalg (wachs)	Cire vegetable
Java Almond	Javamandel	Canari
Mahwah	Illipe	Illipe, Mahwah
Inga	Inga	Inga
Kapok	Kapok	Graines de capoquier
Scotch fir seeds	Kiefersamen	Pin
Corn poppy	Klatchmohnsamen	Coquelicot
Bur	Klettensamen	Bardane
Cocum	Kokum (Goa) butter	Cokum, Goa
Korung, Ponga	Korungbutter	Korung
Indian cress	Kressen (Kapuziner)	Capucine
Pumpkin seed	Kürbiskern	Pepins de Citrouille
Butea, Pallas tree	Lackbaum, Kinobaum	Butea
Gundschitt	Lallemantia	Lallemantia
Lettuce seed	Lattich- (Oellattichsamen)	Laitue à l'huile
Linseed [lina	Lein	Lin
German sesame, Came-	Leindotter	Cameline
Lentisk	Lentiscus (Mastixpistacien-samen)	Lentique
Gilliflower seed	Levkosensamen	Giroflée quarantaine
Linden seed	Lindensamen	Tilleul
Lion's tooth (Dandelion)	Löwenzahnsamen	Pissenlit
Bayberry	Lorbeer	Laurier
Macaja	Macajabutter	Mocaya
Madi	Madia [Mandobi]	Madi
Peanut, Earthnut	Madrasnusse (Erdnuss,	Pistache de terre
Mafura tallow	Mafurratalg	Mafura
Maize, Indian corn	Mais	Maïs
Piney tallow	Malabar, Malabar Copal, Piney	Piney
Almond	Mandel	Amandes
Silybum	Mariendistel	Chardon Marie
Seakale	Meerkohlsamen	Chouxmarin
Cakile	Meersenf- (Meerhanf-)samen	Caquille
Nagasur	Mesua (Eisenholz) Nagasur	Nagasur, Bois de fer
Poppy	Mohn	Pavot somnifère (du pays)
Moldavian	Moldavica (Drachenkopf)	Moldavique
Nutmegs	Muskatnuss	Muscade

TABLE OF VEGETABLE FATS AND OILS—*continued*.

Plants from which obtained.	Country of origin.	Percentage of Fat and Oil in the Seeds.
Gynocardia odorata	East Indies	30-32
Cannabis sativa	Asia	30-35
Coryllus avellana	Europe	50-60
Raphanus Raphanistrum	Europe	35-40
Carya amara	North America	29-30
Aleurites cordata	China, Cochin China	54-56
Glaucium luteum	Central Europe	30-35
Rhus succedana	China, Japan	22-23
Bursera paniculata	Moluccas	40-42
Bassia latifolia	East Indies	50-55
Parkia biglandulosa	West Africa	18-20
Bombax pentandrum	India	30-32
Pinus sylvestris	Europe	20-30
Papaver Rhoeas	Europe	61-65
Arctium Lappa	Europe	14-20
Garcinia (Brindonia) indica	Lower India	22-25
Pongamia glabra	India	34-36
Tropaelium majus	South America	46-50
Cucurbita Pepo	Orient	20-25
Butea frondosa	India	24-26
Lallemantia iberica	Persia, Kurdistan	29-30
Lactua oleifera	Europe	37-38
Linum usitatissimum	Orient	38-40
Camelina sativa	Europe	31-34
Pistacia lentiscus	Italy, Greece	44-45
Matthiola annua	Southern Europe	22-23
Tilia macrophylla	Germany	25-28
Leontodon taraxacum	Germany	—
Laurus nobilis	Southern Europe	24-26
Cocus aculeata	West Indies, Brazil	60-65
Madia sativa	Chili	32-33
Arachis hypogaea	West Africa, India	43-45
Mafureira oleifera	Mozambique	60-65
Zea Mais	America	6-10
Vateria indica	East Indies	—
Amygdalus communis	Mediterranean countries	48-50
Silybum Marianum	Europe	25-26
Crambe maritima	Europe	40-42
Kakile maritima	Europe	52-55
Mesua ferrea	Java, Ceylon	39-40
Papaver somniferum	Asia Minor	48-50 blue 41-45 white
Dracocephalum moldavicum	South-east Europe	21-23
Myristica muscata	Brazil	38-40 ?

TABLE OF VEGETABLE FATS AND OILS—*continued.*

English Names : Oil, Fat, Butter, Tallow of	German Names : -Oel, -Fett, -Butter, -Talg	French Names : Huile, Graisse, Beurre, Suif de
Nettleseeds	Nesselsamen	Ortie
Niam	Niam	Niam
Ramtil	Niger	Ramtille
Ochoco	Ochoco	Ochoco de Gabon
Ocuba	Ocuba (Wachs)	Ocuba
Olive	Olive	Olives
Otoba	Otoba	Otoba
Cobnut, Quabenut	Quabenuss	Noix d'Omphalier
Owala	Owala	Owala
Palm	Palm	Palme
Palm kernel	Palmkern	Palmish
Brazil nut	Paranuss (Juvianuss)	Noix de Brésil
Peach palm	Paripou	Paripou
Peach	Pfirsichkern	Amandes de la Peche
Plum kernel	Pflaumkern	Amandes de Prune
Pinion nut	Piniennuss	Pignons
Pistachia	Pistacien	Pistaches
Orange seed	Pommeranzenkern	Pepin d'Orange
Epurge	Purgirkern (Purgirwolfsamen)	Epurge
Purgir nut	Purgirnuss (Curcas)	Pignon d'Inde
Rambutan	Rambutan	Ramboutan
Rapeseed	Raps	Navette
Radish seed	Rettich (Chin. Oelrettich)	Raisorts
Weld seed	Reseda (Wau)	Gaude
Castor	Ricinus	Ricin
Honesty	Rothraps	Julienne
Horsenut oil	Rosskastanien	Marron d'Inde, Fécule
Rubsen seed	Rübsen	Navet (turneps)
Rutabage	Rutabaga	Rutabaga
Safflower	Safflor	Carthames [pucaja
Sapucaja	Sapucaya	Marmite de singe, Sa-
Soap berry	Seifenbeeren	Noix à savon
Silk cotton, Kapok	Seidenwollsamen	Graines de Capoquier
Sesame, Till, Benné	Sesam	Sesame
Black mustard	Senf, schwartz	Moutarde noire
White mustard	Senf, weiss	Moutarde blanche
Sierra Leone	Sierra Leone butter	Sierra Leone
Sunflower	Sonnenblumen	Tournesol

TABLE OF VEGETABLE FATS AND OILS—*continued.*

Plants from which obtained.	Country of origin.	Percentage of Fat and Oil in the Seeds.
Urtica divica	Europe	30-32
Lophira alata	Africa	44-45
Guizotea oleifera	Abyssinia, India	40-45
Dryobalanus guienensis	Guiana	61-63
Myristica ocuba	Brazil	20-25
Olea europaea	Southern Europe	40-65 fruit 12-15 kernel
Myristica otoba	Columbia	35-40
Omphalea triandra	West Indies	39-41
Pentaclethra macrophylla	Guinea	48-50
Elais guinensis	West Africa	65-72
Elais guinensis	West Africa	45-50
Bertholetia excelsa	South America	66-67
Guilelmia speciosa	South America	30-32
Prunus persica	Persia	46-48
Prunus domestica	Europe	40-42
Pinus pinea	Southern Europe	44-48
Pistacia vera	Southern Europe	51-53
Citrus aurantium	Southern Europe	27-28
Euphorbia Lathyris	Southern Europe	43-46
Curcas purgans	West Indies, South America	55-57 husk'd
Nephelum lappaceum	China, Sunda Island	40-45
Brassica napus	Europe	35-43
Raphanus sativus	China	45-50
Reseda luteola	Central Europe	30-32
Ricinus communis	East Indies	51-53 Ind. 46-49 Amer.
Hesperis matronalis	Southern Europe	28-30
Aesculus hippocastanum	Southern Europe	6-8
Brassica rapa	Europe	35-40
Brassica napobrassica	Sweden	38-40
Carthamus tinctorius	Egypt, India	30-32
Lecythis Ollaria	Brazil, Guiana	40-42
Sapindus emarginatus	India	30-32
Bombax pentandrum	South America	30-32
Sesamum indicum	India	50-57
	Antilles	51-53
	Pondicherry, Bombay	50-52
	Levant	54-56
	Egypt	55-57
Sinapis nigra	Europe	31-33
Sinapis alba	Europe	25-30
Pendadesma butyracea	Sierra Leone	59-62
Helianthus annuus	Mexico, Peru	21-22

TABLE OF VEGETABLE FATS AND OILS—*continued.*

English Names: Oil, Fat, Butter, Tallow of	German Names: -Oel, -Fett, -Butter, -Talg	French Names : Huile, Graisse, Beurre, Suif de
Picaya	Souaributter	Piquia
Spindle tree	Spindelbaum	Graines de fusain
Prickly poppy	Stachelmohn	Pavot épineux
Stramonium seeds	Stechapfel	Stramoine
Hollytree seeds	Stechpalmen	Hout épineux
Stinking bean	Stinkmalven	Sterculia
Tobacco seeds	Tabaksamen	Tabac
Tacahamac	Tacahamac	Tamann
Cassweed seed	Täschelkrautsamen	Cresson, Taburet
Tallow tree	Veget. (chinesiche) Talg	Sebifère
Tangkallak	Tangkallak	Tangkallak
Tangkawang	Tangkawang	Borneo
Tea	Theesamen (Camelia)	Thé
Fir cone	Tannensamen	Epicea
Nightshade	Tollkirschen	Belladonne [gal
Toloucouna	Toloucouna (Krabholz)	Touloucouna du Séné-
Grape seeds	Traubenkern	Pepins de raisins
Ungnadia	Ungnadia	Ungnadia
Walnut	Walnuss	Noix sans coque, Noy
Nimb	Zedrach (Paternosterbaum)	Margosa

TABLE OF VEGETABLE FATS AND OILS—*continued*.

Plants from which obtained.	Country of origin.	Percentage of Fat and Oil in the Seeds.
Peckea guyanensis	Guiana, Brazil	61-63
Evonymus europaeus	Central Europe	44-45
Argemone mexicana	West Indies, Mexico	25-30
Datura stromonium	Europe	25-27
Ilex aquifolium	Europe	25-27
Sterculia foetida	W. Indies, E. Indies	28-30
Nicotiana tabacum	America	38-40
Calophyllum inophyllum	India	60-62
Thaspi bursa pastor	India	
Stillingia sebifera	China, Punjab	37-39
Cyclodaphne sebifera	Java	40-45
Hopea macrophylla	Sunda Island	45-50
Camellia oleifera	China, Japan	43-45
Pinus picea	Europe	32-33
Atropa belladonna	Europe	27-28
Carapa touloucouna	Senegal	50-60
Vitis vinifera	Asia	11-12
Ungnadia	Mexico	9-10
Juglans regia	Persia, Himalaya	68-65
Melia azedarach	India	50-60

CHAPTER IV.

THE PREPARATION OF VEGETABLE FATS AND OILS.

As we have seen in the section devoted to the general characteristics of the fats and oils, they are of varying degrees of consistency, some being more or less liquid at ordinary medium temperatures, others thicken below 10° C., forming a granular deposit, whilst others again remain buttery or set like tallow, even at high summer temperatures. These properties influence the choice of methods of preparing the fats and oils from their respective raw material. From the fleshy olive, as well as from the various oil-seeds (rape, linseed, sesame, etc.), the oil may be obtained by more or less powerful pressure, although it is not feasible to extract all the contained oil by pressure in this way, the mass having to be warmed in order to facilitate the removal of the final portions of the oil. The solid fats, which come to us from tropical countries exclusively, can only be extracted by the aid of heat, the most primitive method being to boil the fat-producing substance up with water and complete by hot pressing, which of course also assists in increasing the amount extracted. The most complete method of obtaining all the oil or fat from oily and fatty seeds or fruits is, however, by extraction with the aid of a solvent, after a cold pressing. The oils obtained by cold pressing or cold drawing are of the finest and best flavoured quality, being also of better colour than where heat has been applied. This is easy to understand, since by the mere application of pressure only a certain quantity of free running oil is forced out, which is perfectly free from other substances contained in the seeds or in the residual albuminoid and protein bodies partly expressed in the warm process.

Poppy oil and linseed oil afford good examples of this, having, when cold pressed, an agreeable sweet flavour, and being suitable for alimental purposes, as salad oil or in the baking and roasting of food; whereas the hot pressed oils are of unpleasantly bitter, irritating flavour, especially in the case of linseed oil, and are no longer fit for use as food. It therefore becomes a fundamental principle that all oils and fats of vegetable nature intended for alimental purposes should be pressed without the aid of heat, hot pressing and extraction being only applicable to fats used for technical purposes, a category comprising the bulk of the vegetable oils. The " extraction " process, whereby the oil is obtained from the seeds and fruit by the aid of a solvent, such as carbon bisulphide, benzol, petroleum ether, canadol, etc. (liquids boiling at low temperatures), is performed with finely ground raw material, the fat of which passes into solution, and is obtained as a residue when the solvent is driven off from the extract by distillation. This method took a number of years to gain favour.

Dr. Heinrich Schwarz in his report on oleaginous substances in the Vienna Universal Exhibition, 1873, referred to the "extraction" method as follows:—

"The process of extracting the remaining oil from the pressed residue (especially in the production of olive oil) by means of carbon bisulphide has rapidly developed, particularly in Italy. One firm from Bari exhibited carbon bisulphide prepared for this purpose, one-third of their yearly production of the article being employed in their own works for the extraction of oil. A similar factory has been working successfully at Leghorn for some years, and in Greece (Corfu) the same process for extracting the oil from the residues from the olive oil presses is practised. The sample products shown at the exhibition were dark green in colour, and remained of the consistency of butter even at summer temperature, pointing on the one hand to the presence of chlorophyll in solution, and on the other to the predominance of margarine in the oil, a circumstance favourable to its use in the manufacture of hard soaps."

Deiss was the first to propose the extraction method in Germany, where it was practised but without much success, and now is only employed at a few works, e.g., Heyl's factory at Moabit. The improved modern methods of pressing yield but very little less oil, and what remains in the cakes is saleable as cattle food at a good price; besides, the cakes from the pressing process are better adapted to meet the requirements of the trade as regards storage and transport than the powder remaining from the extraction method. The extra yield obtained in the latter process is about counterbalanced by the dangers of the method and the loss of solvent, and is probably only profitable when oil is worth a high price, or where the residual oil, as in the case of the fatty lumps from the olive presses, cannot be recovered in any other way. It also seems that only those factories prosper wherein, by the use of simple appliances, the escape of the carbon bisulphide is reduced to a minimum, even though they use a larger quantity for the extraction.

The chief drawback to the extraction process lies in the low feeding value of the meal—consisting of the component parts of the fruit or seed after removal of the oil—as compared with oilcake (which always retains a certain percentage of fat or oil), and the difference in price resulting therefrom. Where oilcake brings a good price, and the increased value of the extra oil obtained by the extraction method does not compensate for the lower price of the meal, this latter method will naturally be discarded and the press residue sold as cake, more especially as the erection of an extraction apparatus entails a certain minimum amount of working expenses.

Furthermore, the nature of the solvent exerts an influence on the quality, *i.e.*, flavour of the oil. Carbon bisulphide is preferable to petroleum ether, in that it dissolves a larger quantity of oil and at a lower temperature than the latter; it is also more easy to recover without, if pure, leaving behind any trace of its flavour in the oil. On the other hand, carbon bisulphide has the drawback of dissolving out resin and colouring matter, neither of which is extracted by petroleum ether, nor is there any unpleasant smell left behind by the latter, such as occurs when impure carbon bisulphide is used, so that petroleum ether is suitable even for fine edible oils. In North America this solvent is largely used, but it requires a more complicated apparatus than bisulphide on account of its tendency, due to low specific gravity, to condense on the surface of water rather than below like the carbon bisulphide. Moreover, resinified oil is only imperfectly extracted by petroleum ether.

The preliminary methods of preparation to which the materials for pressing or extracting must be subjected relate to (1) Mechanical separation (cleaning) of the seed from the seeds of other plants and organic or inorganic impurities; (2) Removal of the more or less hard shells or husks which would lower the quality of the cake or meal, or absorb oil; (3) Crushing or grinding to break down the seed cases and to convert the seed or fruit into meal or pulp, thereby facilitating the expression or extraction of the contained oil or fat.

Formerly these manipulations were performed in an exceedingly primitive fashion. For example, the seeds were bruised by stones in a stone mortar or between millstones, a practice resulting in considerable waste of valuable material. Less value was also placed on the cleaning of the seed than is now the case in the light of modern experience, so that it is easy to understand that with progressive technical improvements in the milling of oil seeds, the quality of the product has been heightened. As the storage of the raw material also naturally affects the quality of the oil or fat, it is important that this should be effected in a suitable manner.

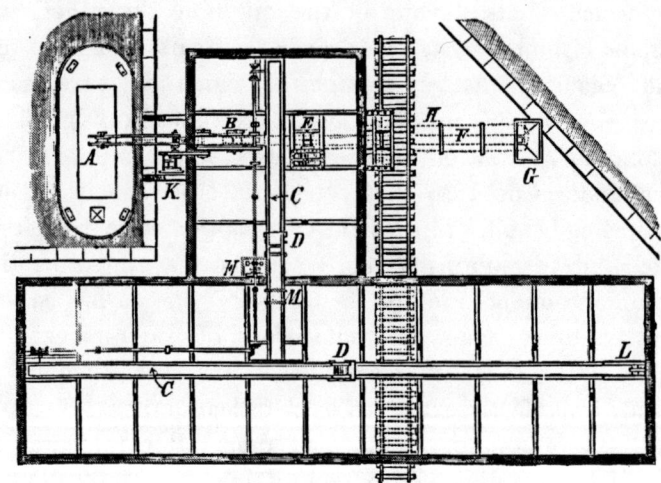

Fig. 6. Oil Seed Store (Rose, Downs & Co.).

Storing Oil Seeds.

Like all vegetable substances, oil seeds contain a certain amount of moisture, and are liable, if not frequently exposed to the air, to sustain unfavourable alterations from the attacks of fungi, mould, etc., softening the husk and deteriorating the quality of the oily kernel. Very often the seeds are externally damp when put into store, in which case they require specially careful handling, consisting of frequent turnings in dry airy store rooms by shovelling the heaps from

one position to another. This operation should be repeated
at regular intervals, and the more frequently it is performed
the less likelihood is there of loss from damage being
incurred.

Frequently, however—and this particularly applies to
stocks in large oil works where sufficient must be stored at
gathering time to last for the entire year—it is a matter of
impossibility to move the enormous mass by manual labour.
In such cases it becomes necessary to arrange the heaps so

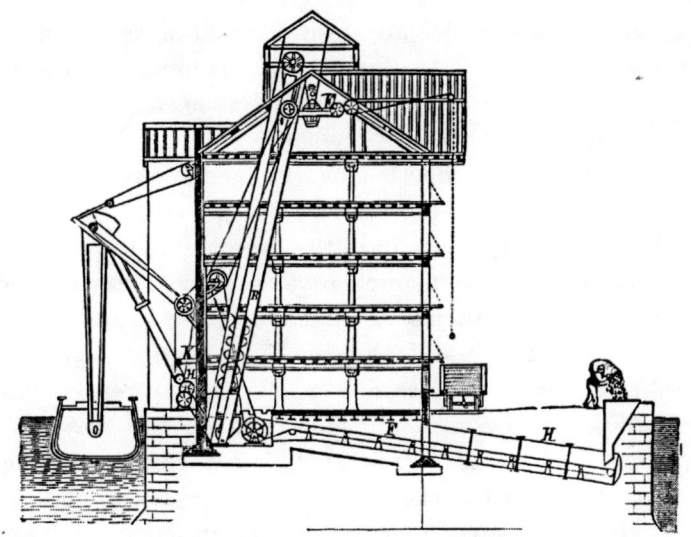

FIG. 7. Oil Seed Store (Rose, Downs & Co.).

that they may be moved by means of mechanical appliances
and thoroughly worked over to ensure the conservation of
their valuable properties for the press.

Such a storehouse has been constructed, by Grimm, of
stone and iron, similar to a granary, and perfectly fireproof.

The oil seeds are raised by means of an elevator, archimedean screw or similar appliance to the second or third
floor, where they are emptied into the hopper K (Figs. 6 and

7) and are carried up to the roof of the building by an elevator E. The domed roof, made of corrugated sheet iron, is fitted with a lantern turret for lighting the rooms, and in this turret is situated a screw which conveys the seeds in a horizontal direction and distributes them through perforated pipes on to the upper floor, the distribution being regulated by slides. The other floor spaces communicate with the first one in such a manner that each in turn can serve as a resting place for the seed. When the change from one floor to the other is to be made, the valves of 150 pipes of about two inches in diameter are opened, and the seed descends until a heap of about five feet in depth is formed, a rotatory motion being imparted to each seed by the fall. The seeds collect into conical heaps on the floor.

The valves are connected by rods, and the entire control of the transfer can be exercised by a single workman.

To transfer the seeds from the lowest to the upper floor and recommence the manipulative operations, they are conveyed by four longitudinal archimedean screws to a transverse screw, debouching into the hopper K, feeding the elevator E.

Variations in the working conditions may render other directions of movement advisable, and for this reason the columns are traversed by pipes with lateral openings through which the seeds may be passed. By this means the seed may also be lowered from the roof direct on to the lowest floor without having to traverse the others, and it is also possible to exclude any one floor from the circuit if desired. If, for example, new seed is introduced, the floor in question can be shut off without interrupting the manipulation of the remainder. The ceilings of the store rooms are of corrugated iron. A ton and a half of seed can be stored on every square metre of floor space. The pillars are connected by braces to support the lateral thrust. Motion is imparted to the elevators by shafting branching from the intermediate gearing of the oil mill, and wherever the driving belts have to pass through the seed heaps, they are protected by iron casing extending above the surface of the heap. Ventilation has received special attention. The shutters are constructed of iron, and by means of connecting rods a whole row of windows may be opened or closed at once. When necessary an extra elevator, serving three floors, can be erected ; this is advantageous when the store communicates with other storage rooms. Provision has then to be made for the horizontal transport of the seed, as screws do not act sufficiently well when the distance is long. Recently a new method of transport has come into use, consisting of a wide endless belt of caoutchouc or cotton, moving horizontally and kept on the stretch. The seed is discharged on to the one end of this 12-inch belt, and travels with it, without a single seed being spilled, until the other end is reached. Such a method of transport helps to preserve and clean the seed.

Cleaning the Seed.

The seed must be free from sand, earth, stems, etc., of plants and all other impurities, as well as from foreign seeds, otherwise the cakes may possess a disagreeable by-flavour. Again, the presence of sand or dirt tends to wear out the machinery, in addition to injuring the quality of the oilcake by increasing the proportion of non-nutritious material therein. Foreign bodies of lower density than the seed may be removed by a blower, the draught of which carries them away. Foreign seeds capable of lowering the quality of the oil seeds may conduce thereto in different ways.

1. Oil-yielding seeds will not greatly lower the percentage of the product, but may appreciably injure its quality, as, for example, when seeds yielding drying oils contain others yielding non-drying oils. Thus in linseed there are found

seeds of wild radish, mustard, or camelina, because these weeds constantly infest the linseed crop.

2. Seeds neither yielding oil when pressed nor absorbing any when in the state of meal (containing themselves already so much that they cannot take up any further quantity), but adding to the bulk of the mass. Such are fleawort and corn spurry.

3. Seeds containing little or no oil. These absorb oil during the pressing process, and thereby reduce the yield. Such are flax weed and darnel.

The earthy and other admixtures also take up oil, diminishing the yield and increasing the weight of the cake.

In the subsequent cleaning operations a great deal depends on whether the impurities are equal in size to, or greater or less than the seeds to be cleaned. If they are of the same size as the latter the difficulties

FIG. 8. Screening Cylinder (Front View).

are increased, since they remain mixed up with the seed unless sufficiently soft to be crushed in a sieve (like earth). Impurities larger or smaller than the seed are easily removed by passing the seed through a riddling machine where an oscillating motion is imparted. Such an apparatus is depicted in Figs. 8 to 11. The cylinder is of hexagonal or octagonal section 25 to 32 inches in diameter, and from 3 to 30 feet in length, sloping from C to E at a pitch of about 2 to 3 inches per running yard. The driving axis of the cylinder is hexagonal or octagonal, about 6 inches in diameter, and fitted at the ends with trunnions revolving in cast-iron bearings, a driving pulley B being affixed to the upper trunnion. The framework of the drum C, consisting of 6 or 8 wooden rods, is covered, for a

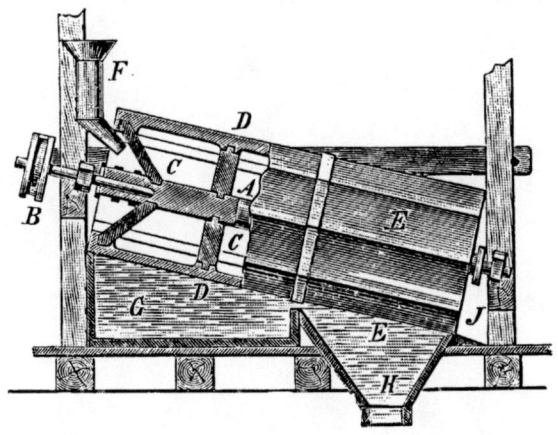

FIG. 9. Screening Cylinder (Elevation and Vertical Section).

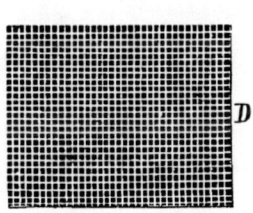

FIG. 10. Wire Screen.

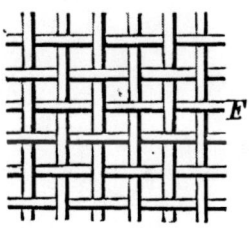

FIG. 11. Wire Screen.

distance of some 43 to 44 inches from the upper end, with a screen of fine iron gauze (Fig. 10) of $\frac{1}{25}$ inch mesh. The remainder of the frame is covered with a coarser netting (of about 5 meshes to the inch). The feed pipe F is of tin plate, and is bent in the direction in which the cylinder rotates. The latter is arranged internally in such a manner that the dust arising from the seed is removed by a blower. The apparatus requires $\frac{1}{4}$ horse-power, and makes 40 revolutions per minute, and is capable of cleaning $8\frac{1}{4}$ to 10 bushels of rape per hour. In the case of very dirty seed, the slope of the machine is reduced to about $1\frac{5}{8}$ inch per running yard, and the speed increased to double the above rate.

CHAPTER V.

THE cleaned oil seeds are next ground to meal in various kinds of apparatus, but the large oil fruits, palm kernels or cocoanuts, require to be broken up small before grinding. Certain among them, such as castor-oil beans, are first decorticated by the aid of special machines (Figs. 12, 13) to remove the leathery or cork-like seed capsules, and then ground into meal or crushed to a soft mass, whereby the oily kernel is fully exposed and obtained clean.

The cocoanut breaker, shown in Figs. 14 and 15, reduces the cocoanut (coprah) to pieces the size of palm kernels, that is to say, to such dimensions as permit their being ground in a palm kernel mill. The knives and hopper are constructed of cast steel, but the upper part of the feed box is now made of wood to facilitate removal. The machine is very strong throughout, and of extraordinary capacity.

DISINTEGRATOR FOR COCOANUTS.

This machine (Fig. 16) is largely used in Ceylon and other countries where cocoanuts are grown. It grinds by percussion, the material being introduced at the periphery of the drum, where it falls on to the end of the beater, which rotates at the rate of about 15 feet per minute. Disintegration is effected either by this contact or else by the impact of the material against the toothed internal wall of chilled iron enveloping the upper part of the drum or the steel sifting rods at the bottom. The manufacturers, Messrs. Rose, Downs & Thompson, of Hull, emphasise the difference between this mill and those grinding by friction between iron plates revolving at high speed. The beaters of the dis-integrator move at a uniform distance (1 inch) from the walls of the drum (whether the material is to be finely

FIG. 12. Cotton Seed Decorticator.

ground or merely granulated), and pulverise by beating with a flat surface instead of grinding between two corru-gated iron plates as in ordinary mills, which have to be set closer in proportion as the material is to be more finely ground, whereby increased friction results. Grooved plates are, moreover, unsuitable for pulverising, being only capable, even if enormous power be applied, of granulating the material, but never of converting it into a fine powder. The capacity of the disintegrator varies, with the size, from 10 cwt. to $4\frac{1}{2}$ tons per hour.

STAMPS AND EDGE RUNNERS.

Formerly ordinary millstones or stamps were employed for preparing oil seeds and fruits for the press. The stamps

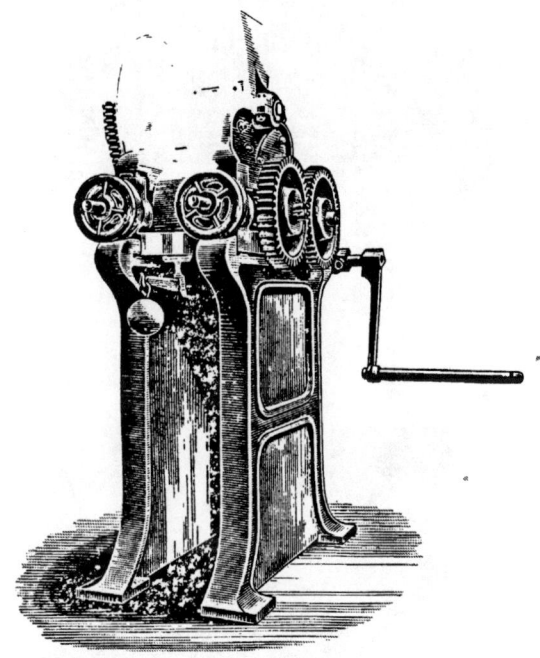

FIG. 13. Hand-power Decorticator for Castor-oil Seeds.

consisted of a trough in which the material was placed and subjected to the concussion of a row of stamps, rising and falling at regular intervals, and so gradually reducing the mass to a meal of greater or less degree of fineness, a certain amount of oil being at the same time expressed by the concussion of the stamps.

Subsequently stamps were replaced by edge runners,
which ground without concussion, and thereby prevented
the premature expression of the fat or oil.   The arrangement
of these runners is shown in Figs. 17 and 18, the former

FIG. 14. Cocoanut Breaker (Viewed from above).

FIG. 15. Cocoanut Breaker (Front View).

being fitted with overhead driving gear, and the latter driven
from below.   The choice of these two methods of arrangement will depend on the space at disposal, there being no
difference in their influence on the quality of the produce,

since the pressure is not exerted by the driving gear, but only by the weight of the stone or metal runners.

The final grinding of the seeds or disintegrated fruits is effected by

CRUSHING ROLLERS.

The arrangement of crushing roller mills is indicated in Figs. 19 and 20. A large iron roller A, either smooth or slightly grooved, of some 4 feet in diameter and 16 inches in

FIG. 16. Disintegrator for Cocoanuts.

width, is actuated by a motor. A second roller of the same width as the first but smaller diameter (about 12 inches) can be adjusted by screws to approach or recede from the face of the large roller. The feed hopper C is fixed over the rollers, and contains a grooved roller D, worked from the axle of A by a driving belt outside the hopper, and serving for the regular distribution of the seed to the latter. The feed is regulated by an adjustable board E. Scrapers FF, kept in position by weighted levers, serve to remove the adherent meal from the rollers.

4

Usually the rollers are adjusted so as to completely crush the seed falling between them, and deliver it as meal to the receiving trough below. It is, however, absolutely essential that the seed should have been previously passed through a

FIG. 17. Ordinary Edge-runner Seed Mill.

properly constructed sorting machine to remove any hard bodies (stones, etc.) which might easily damage the rollers, and necessitate their being re-turned in order to be of any use.

There are various modifications in the arrangement of crushing mills, chiefly relating to the number of rollers, which depends on the amount of material to be treated, *i.e.,* on the size of the works. The breaking machines serve not only for grinding the seed but also for re-grinding the cakes of meal from the press, and prepare them for the second pressing. Disintegrators are also frequently used for break-

FIG. 18. Edge-runner Seed Mill (Anglo-American Pattern).

ing up the oilcake, on account of their enormous capacity and the fine meal they produce.

Highly effective roller mills for seed crushing are made by Fr. Krupp, "Gruson" Works, Magdeburg-Buckau. Figs. 22 and 23 show one of these mills, with three pairs of rollers, which is chiefly used for grinding palm kernels and ground nuts. The two upper pairs of rollers are grooved, the lowest pair being smooth. On the other hand, for crushing linseed, coprah and other oil fruits, mills with smooth rollers are used; these must, however, have a soft surface. For this purpose the pattern shown in Fig. 24 (one or two pairs of adjacent rollers), or else that given in Fig. 21, is employed.

The seed meal prepared in the foregoing manner is next subjected to cold pressing, if intended for the production of finest quality alimental oils, without any further treatment. For oils of lower quality the seed meal is warmed before

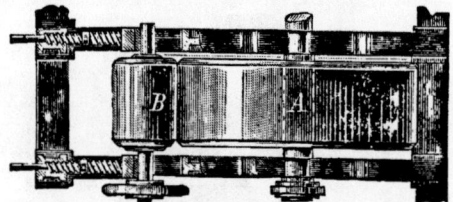

FIG. 19. Crushing Roller Mill (Top View).

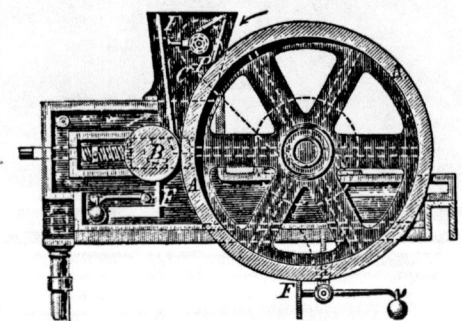

FIG. 20. Crushing Roller Mill (Section).

pressing, in order to liquefy the fats and oils and facilitate their extraction in the press. Formerly it was customary to perform this heating in a very primitive manner in iron pans warmed by direct fire or hot water, a method which exposed the meal to various contingencies, particularly the risk of overheating. On this account it not infrequently happened that instead of clear and agreeably flavoured oil, a product of decidedly empyreumatic taste and smell was obtained.

It is only of late that special

SEED-HEATING PANS

have been introduced.

These appliances are of very simple construction, as is shown in Fig. 25. The vessel *cc*, which has a highly con-

FIG. 21. Seed Crusher (Anglo-American Pattern).

cave bottom, is surrounded by an outer flat-bottomed jacket *aa*. At the centre of the cylinder C is an axis *p*, supported at *m*, and carrying arms *ll* for stirring up the contents of the pan. The warmed seeds are drawn out through an opening at the bottom of the cylinder, which is closed by a shutter k. Steam is admitted *via* f, and the condensed water run off at e.

As will be seen from the sketch, one side of the pan rests on brick setting, the other side being conveniently supported by an iron leg r. In practice a number of these pans are placed side by side, and the stirrers actuated by gearing on a single shaft suspended from the ceiling.

FIG. 22. Crushing Rollers for Palm Kernels and Ground Nuts (Fr. Krupp).

The size of the pan c depends on the capacity of the press, and it is not advisable to have the pan larger than the contents of a press will fill.

As soon as the contents of the pan are warm enough, a press bag is held before the opening at the side of the cylinder to catch the hot mass when the shutter is removed, the pan being quickly emptied by the action of the stirrer.

An improved heater is depicted in section in Fig. 26, and in ground plan in Fig. 27. It consists of two cylindrical chambers A and B, resting one above the other, and each

Fig. 23. Roller Mill (Fr. Krupp).

surrounded by a steam jacket. The meal to be warmed is placed in the central chamber, and steam is admitted at E, the exhaust steam and condensed water escaping at F. Two pairs of stirrers are fitted on to the axle G for mixing the meal in a uniform manner. The operation is begun by filling the chamber (closed by the lid T) with the meal to be warmed, which is allowed to remain for about ten minutes, the stirrers meanwhile making 300 to 350 revolutions. By opening the slide L, the warmed meal is allowed to fall into the lower part of the apparatus, where it remains until transferred to the press bag. In order to fill the latter without risk of burning the men's hands by the hot meal, wooden

Fig. 24. Two-pair Roller Mill (Fr. Krupp).

boxes M, large enough to hold a sackful of meal, are fixed under the outlet, and are fitted with a slide at the bottom.

In filling the bags the workman holds the mouth under the valve of the box M, opens the lower chamber by drawing the slide L, and allows the meal to run into M until the latter is full, whereupon he closes L and opens the valve in M to let the meal run into the bag. The apparatus may be conveniently modified by making the upper chamber considerably smaller than the lower one, which is not so much used for warming; so that by keeping the apparatus constantly at work a stock of warmed meal may be accumulated in the lower chamber, and may be drawn upon for the press at any minute. In such case a narrow pipe may be attached to the storage chamber for removing any oil that may run from the meal, and conveying it into a vessel underneath.

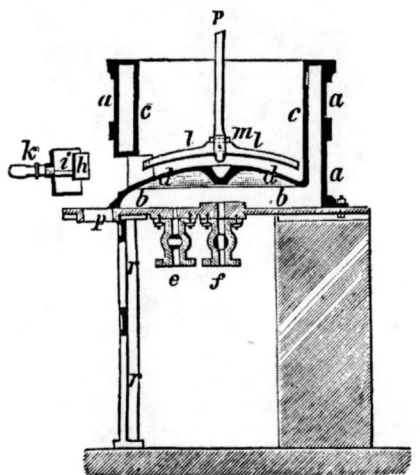

Fig. 25. Heating Pan for Oil Seed.

Fig. 28 shows a heating pan with a steam cake mould, and one of Krupp's heating vats is presented by Fig. 29. This latter is jacketed, heated by steam, and fitted with removable stirrers, steam and waste pipes and a water tap. Sometimes these vats are stationed immediately above the presses. In works where the power is supplied by water or by petroleum or gas motors, and where consequently no steam is available, the vats may be arranged for fire heat.

In the extraction process this preliminary warming is, of

course, dispensed with, the seed meal being filled direct into the extractors.

OIL PRESSES.

The cold or warmed seed meal is next delivered to the press, and for this purpose is packed in either press cloths or bags, in which it is laid between the plates of the press. The cloths as well as the bags must be made of some very strong textile fabric, capable of withstanding, without break-

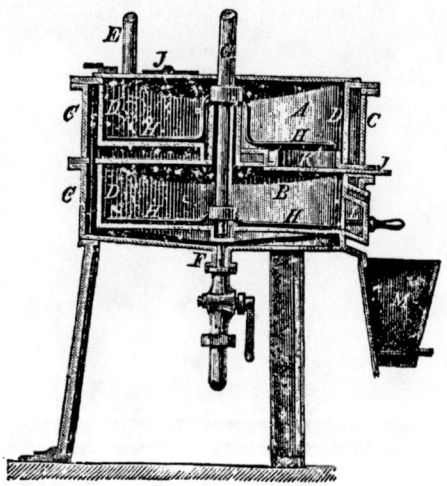

FIG. 26. Improved Heating Pan (Section).

age, the highest pressure to which it will be exposed. At the same time it must be sufficiently porous to allow the passage of the liquid, without being too absorbent. As a matter of fact it is quite impossible to find a single material combining these two qualities with any degree of perfection; the best results are obtained by using a very closely woven cotton cloth, and enclosing it, to prevent breakage whilst in the press, in a close horsehair cloth. It will be readily appreciated that the manner of handling the press bags and cloths will greatly influence their durability, and, for this reason, care should be taken not to apply the pressure suddenly, but only by degrees, until the highest power of the press is exerted, in order that with the gradual increase of the pressure the compression of the fatty mass may be effected progressively. Actually the cloths will burst only if the compression be produced too suddenly.

In order to avoid the loss of the fatty material absorbed by the bags, they are used over and over again until they get defective, the oil with which they are impregnated being then recovered by extraction or by boiling for a long time in

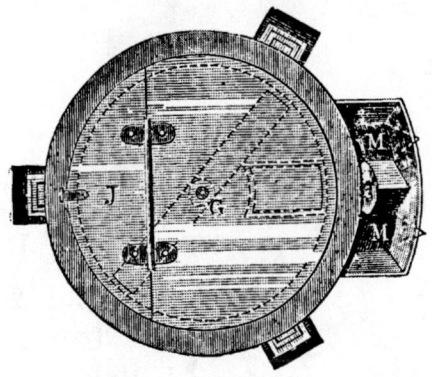

Fig. 27. Improved Heating Pan (Ground Plan).

a weak solution of alkali, which saponifies the fat and leaves the cloth clean and in a fit condition to be repaired for use anew. Press cloths and bags may be supplanted by special appliances, fitted into the press, which will be referred to later.

Naturally, the construction of the oil presses is an important factor, influencing the profitable working of a factory. The chief considerations are that the press should be able to yield a maximum amount of fat or oil with a minimum of power in the shortest time. The earlier presses in no wise fulfilled these conditions, and we have to thank the progressive developments in mechanical technology for the efficient presses now at our disposal.

The presses employed in the oil industry may be classified as :—

　　1. Wedge presses.
　　2. Hydraulic presses.

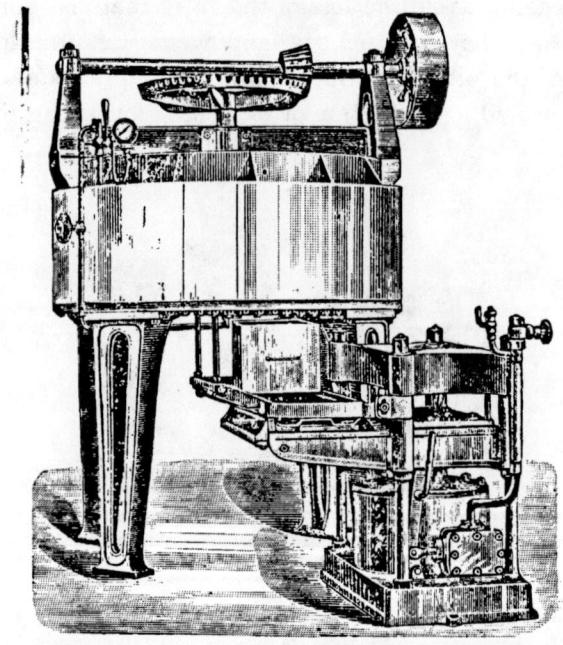

FIG. 28. Heating Pan with Steam Cake Mould.

The latter being divided into :—

　　(a) Pan presses.
　　(b) Trough presses.
　　(c) Pack presses.
　　(d) Patent hydraulic presses.
　　(e) Ring presses.
　　(f) Horizontal presses.

The wedge presses constitute the most ancient and primitive form, and are found even nowadays in many oil works, notwithstanding their numerous drawbacks; new establishments, however, should scarcely be fitted with apparatus of this description.

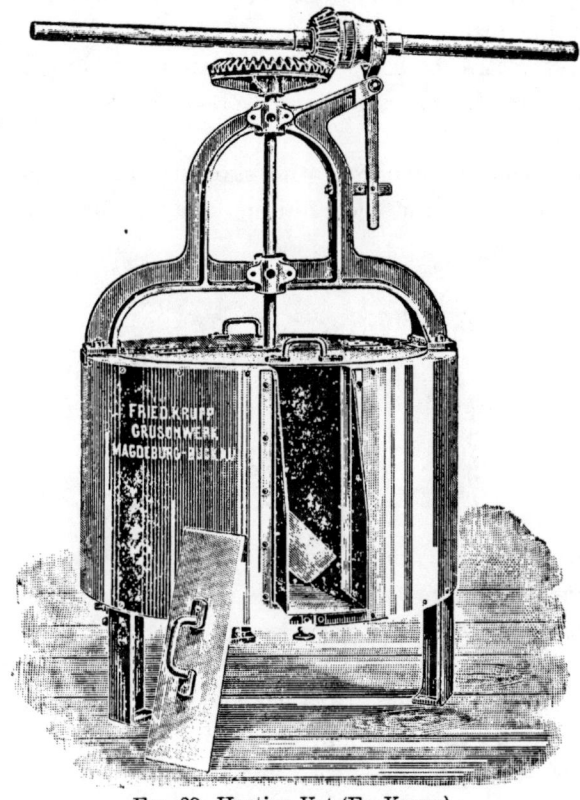

FIG. 29. Heating Vat (Fr. Krupp).

WEDGE PRESSES.

Wedge presses (Fig. 30) consist of a prism-shaped box, the walls of which are formed of strong cast-iron plates, and specially strengthened to resist powerful pressure. In either side of the box perforated press plates g and h are arranged, and, the meal being placed between them in a bag, the wedges are inserted. Distinction is made in ordinary wedges between the driving wedge *c* and the loose or "spring" wedge *b*. The loose wedge is first placed in the position it occupies in the drawing, where it is held by a cord, and then the driving wedge *c* is inserted and driven home by the head of a stamping machine, the compression of the meal between the press plates thereon ensuing, forcing out the oil, which flows through openings below the press plates into a collecting runnel.

The wedge is struck by the stamp head so long as oil continues to run, and the press may be left for a very long

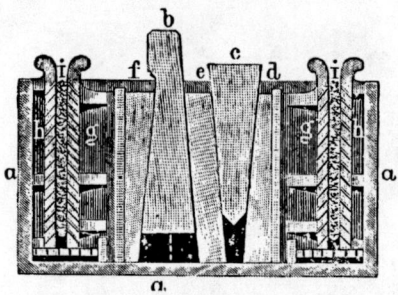

FIG. 30. Wedge Press.

time without the pressure decreasing. To empty and refill the press the wedge *b* has merely to be driven in by a few blows, and the pressure is completely relieved. All the old-fashioned oil mills were fitted with stamps for comminuting the seeds, and the wedge presses were set up by the side of the stamps, so that the latter could be used for driving home the wedges, as described.

HYDRAULIC PRESSES.

These presses are of great importance in factory work on account of the high pressure they give with a small consumption of power, besides being easy to attend to.

They are based on the principle of the regular transmission of pressure by liquids in closed chambers, and consist of two separate parts, the press proper and the pump.

The former is composed of the press plate, terminating below in a piston which moves in the cylinder in the enclosed base of the machine; the head; and the (generally four) pillars connecting the latter with the base. On the lower portion of the press is also situated the stopcock forming the connection between the respective cylinders of press and pump.

The press pump is of the plunger type, with two pistons of different diameters, the larger of which stops automatically at about twenty inches of pressure, whilst the smaller one continues working until the desired pressure is obtained. The minimum pressure varies for each pump, and the automatic opening of a safety valve prevents the maximum being exceeded. The pressure from the pump is evenly transmitted through the liquid—water, glycerin, or a mixture of both—and connecting valve to the liquid in the cylinder containing the press piston, exerting on the latter the same effect per unit of surface as on the same unit of the pump piston. Directly the desired pressure is reached, the stopcock is closed, so that the pressure on the press cylinder may not be reduced by any leakage in the pump.

To empty the press a second tap is opened in the intermediate valve, and the liquid returns to the pump chest without passing through the cylinder. This procedure protects the valve in the press pump on the one hand, and on the other allows the same liquid to be used again and again, without any need of renewal except of the small quantity lost by leakage.

Hydraulic presses are employed of either vertical or horizontal form, the first being the most extensively used. For pressing oil it is usual to arrange a number of trough-shaped

press plates, one above another, so that the bottom part of
each trough presses the seed meal in the trough immediately
below and forces out the oil, which is collected in a common
channel.   In warm pressing provision is made for the circulation of steam around each plate, by means of movable
pipes for admitting the steam and removing the condensed
water.   Where several presses are contained in the one
room, a single pump will serve for producing the pressure,

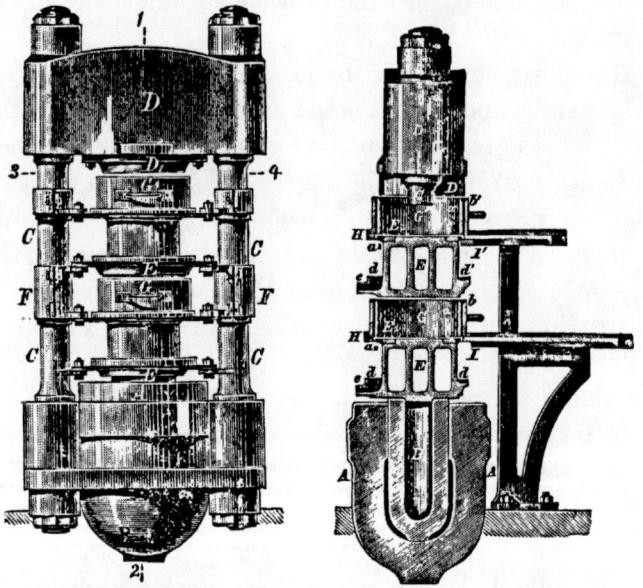

FIG. 31. Hydraulic Pan Press   FIG. 32. Hydraulic Pan Press
(Front View).   (Side View and Section).

but where they are separated in different rooms, accumulators may be used with advantage.

PAN PRESSES.

One of these presses is shown in Figs. 31 and 32, in front
and side views and section.   The hydraulic press, consisting
of the press cylinder A and piston B, is fixed between two

columns, on which the troughs E slide by means of rings. The troughs carry solid iron plates, and are surrounded below by channels *dd* for collecting the expressed oil.

The pans G, containing the seed meal, are jacketed, the inner walls being perforated at the top by a row of holes running all round. These pans are filled with the meal, over which a horsehair cloth is laid, and when the press is set in work the troughs E are forced into the pans G, the oil flows out through the said holes and collects in the channels

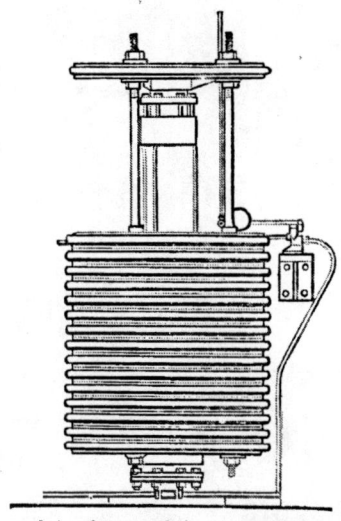

FIG. 33. Accumulator for supplying several Hydraulic Presses.

dd. When the operation is finished the pressure is discontinued, whereupon the different parts of the machine assume the positions indicated in the drawing. The pans G are removed on to the table, and replaced by others filled with meal, so that the time the press is standing idle is reduced to a minimum.

The employment of accumulators presents particular advantages for the regular working of hydraulic presses, and they are very frequently used for this purpose.

5

Some of these accumulators are depicted in Figs. 33 and
34, that in the former being an English model, and those in

Fig. 34. Accumulators (Fr. Krupp).

Fig. 34 representing a type of combined accumulators, one
for high and the other for low pressure, manufactured by Fr.

Krupp of Magdeburg-Buckau. The high-pressure accumulator has a steel piston, that of the other being of chilled cast iron, and both are fitted with iron cases to carry the load, as well as with automatic safety valves.

The oil press made by Lobrée of Driffield is a so-called pan press with four platforms, and makes a tongue-shaped cake. It is of great strength, being constructed of cast and wrought iron, and has a press plunger of 14 inches diameter, easily detachable for repairs without taking the press to pieces. It is tested to 300 tons pressure, but only worked up to 130 tons, which is equivalent to some 154 atmospheres on the cake. The plates for carrying the seed are of strong sheet iron, grooved inside and surrounded by a rim of felt to enclose the meal; fitted with handles on the longer sides and fastened together by leather straps, like hinges, from the opposite ends. In this manner the tearable press cloths are dispensed with, the meal can be easily filled and the pressed cakes as easily removed, whilst the oil has free outlet. The cakes are very firm, with sharp edges. The pump serves six presses at a time; one of the plungers is $2\frac{3}{8}$ inches in diameter, the other $3\frac{1}{8}$ inches. At the outset both of them work together, closing the press quickly, but subsequently the valve of the larger plunger opens and the whole of the work is assumed by the smaller one, until the opening of the valve shows that the limit of working pressure has been attained.

CAKE MOULDING MACHINES.

The moulding presses for oil fruits serve to compress the loose ground material into the smallest volume possible without forcing out the oil. For this work steam suffices to produce the requisite pressure. By means of this process of moulding the oil presses can be charged with a maximum amount of material, whereby their efficiency is raised to its highest limit.   The object of moulding is therefore to econo- mise time and power, which would be wasted if the material were compressed by the hydraulic press alone.

The moulding presses are worked as follows :—

The milled seed is fed into the hopper either by hand or, if warmed, from the outlet of the heating pan.   The feed box is then drawn over an opening in the slide, through which the meal falls on to a press cloth spread over an iron table resting on a sliding frame.   The slide is then lifted up, the

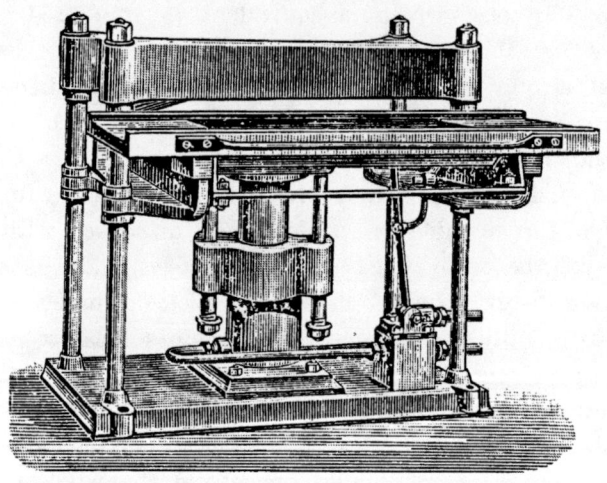

Fig. 35. Cake Moulding Press (Fr. Krupp).

material enveloped in the cloth and pushed, frame and all, on to the pressing table.   Contact is thereby made with the lever of the throttle valve admitting steam to the cylinder; the piston rises and presses the material on the table against the upper plate.   After the pressure has been continued for a few seconds, the steam is released by opening the exhaust pipe and the press table sinks; the slide is again lowered, the iron plate carrying the cake drawn on one side, and the latter transferred to the oil press. By the exercise of a little skill on the part of the attendant in serving the moulding press, the hydraulic press can be charged in a few minutes, so that one moulding press can be made to serve six oil presses.

HYDRAULIC PRESSES FOR COPRAH AND PALM KERNELS.

The press shown in Fig. 36 has a working pressure of about $2\frac{1}{4}$ tons to the square inch. The press cylinder is made of cast steel, and the piston and pressing pan for holding the fruit are both of chilled cast iron, the latter being of square section and grooved at the sides and bottom. The grooves in the side walls are vertical, those at the bottom running towards the discharge pipe. The walls are lined with a steel plate, perforated with fine holes, and keyed by a pair of wedges to the edge of the pan. When the pressure is removed the descent of the pan automatically releases the wedges, which can then be taken out by hand. The press piston forces the pan upwards against the head, and as soon as the operation is finished the piston is released, the head is slid on one side and the cakes taken out of the pan. The press cakes are built up in several layers by the aid of a mould, so that all are of equal size, and a flat or grooved plate is laid between each two. Twelve cakes form the charge, each of which is reduced, in pressing, to a thickness of about four-fifths of an inch. Care must be taken that the meal is spread evenly in the press, to ensure equalisation of pressure and regular sized cakes. The whole operation of filling, pressing and emptying the press takes from thirty-five to forty minutes, which allows, when the workmen are fairly quick, of thirty-three pressings per day of twenty-two hours, the work being continuous. The capacity of the press is about $2\frac{1}{2}$ cwt. per hour or $2\frac{3}{4}$ tons per twenty-two hours' day.

A hydraulic oil press, making round cakes, is given in Fig. 37.   This works in a similar manner to the one just de-

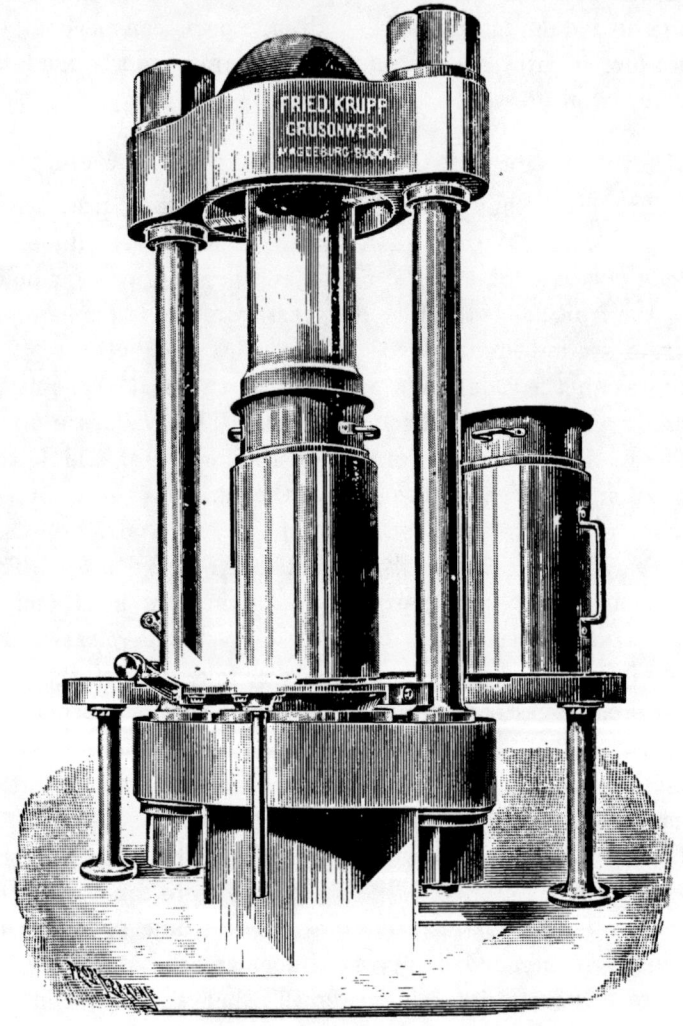

FIG. 36. Hydraulic Press for Coprah and Palm Kernels.

scribed, and has the advantage over the box presses in that the operation of releasing the wedges and·frame is dispensed with. The press may also be worked at a more rapid rate, since whilst one charge is being pressed another strainer is

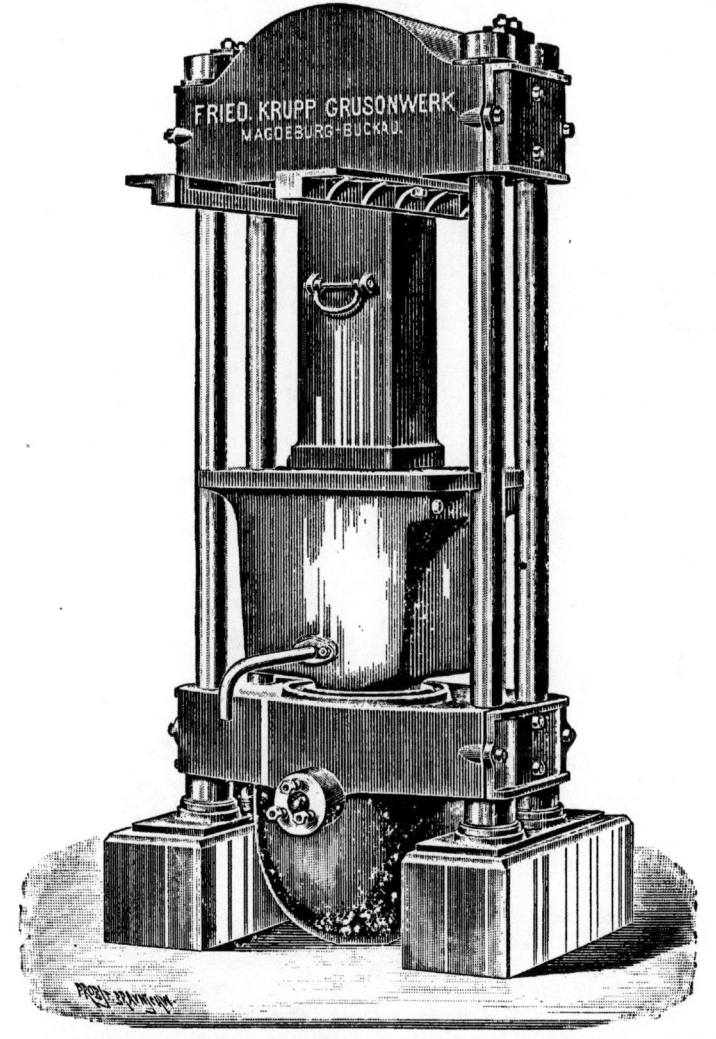

FIG. 37. Hydraulic Press for Round Cakes (Fr. Krupp).

being filled with meal. The press head is fixed, the strainer being removed on to a table or platform for filling and discharging. This vessel is a cylinder of wrought steel,

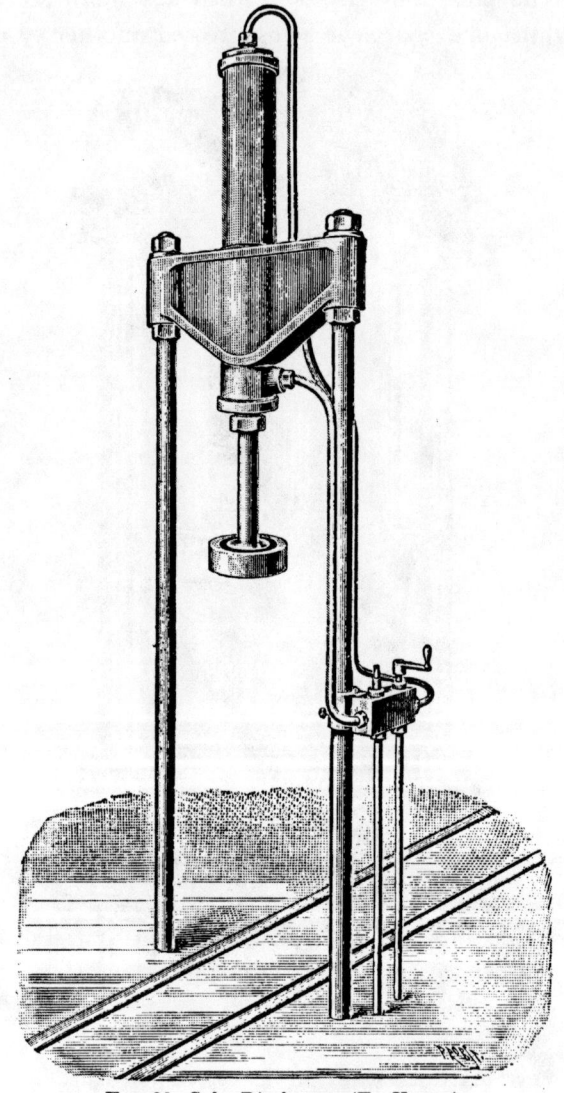

FIG. 38. Cake Discharger (Fr. Krupp).

perforated with bored conical apertures of about $\frac{1}{50}$ of an inch in diameter. The strainer is surrounded by a jacket which prevents the oil from spurting about. In small presses the cakes are discharged by hand, but for large presses, the strainers of which are movable, a discharger (Fig. 38) is used.

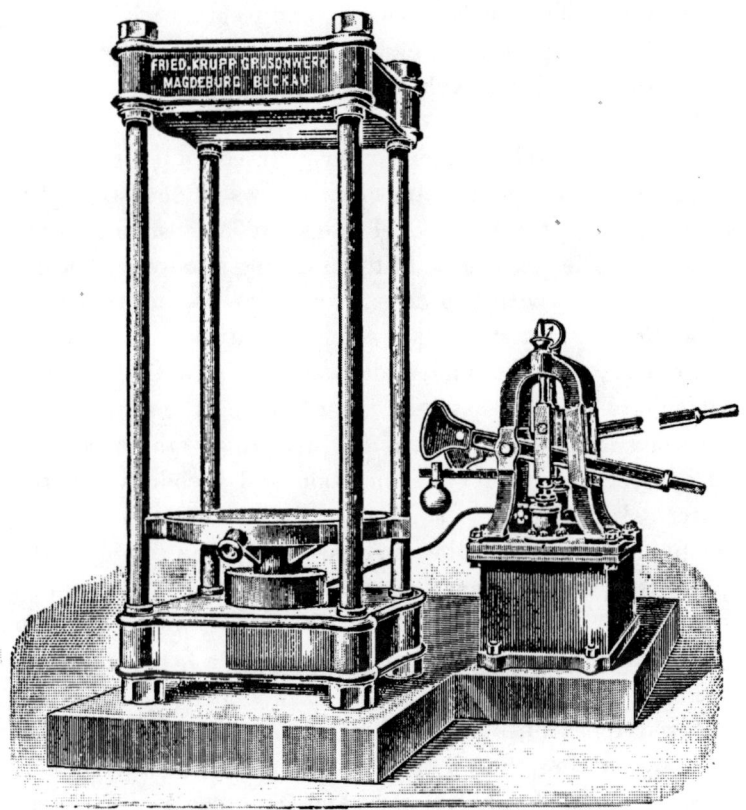

FIG. 39. Preliminary Press for Oil Fruits (Fr. Krupp).

The ram is raised and lowered by hydraulic pressure, regulated by a simple alternate valve.

For the first pressing of juicy fruits, such as olives, etc., the press shown in Fig. 39 is used. The fruit is packed in mat baskets and laid on the table of the press, and the oil collects in a channel in the table, whence it flows into the receiving vessel.

The new presses manufactured by Brinck & Hübner, Mannheim, possess the following decided advantages over those of ordinary construction :—

1. Easier and quicker to serve, and yield more oil.

2. No expensive press cloths are required.

3. Produce fine, evenly pressed cakes which do not need to be trimmed.

4. Very durable without expensive wearing parts.

These presses are arranged as follows : Four, six, eight, or ten wrought iron or steel rings are erected one above another in the press, each of them having a movable bottom of steel pierced with fine holes, and between every two rings a cast iron or cast steel plate is laid, the upper side of which is grooved, but the under side smooth. To these plates, which are inserted between the columns of the press, are attached iron rails in which the press rings are suspended, and serve as guides for the insertion and withdrawal of the latter. In addition to this, each plate is surrounded by a channel for catching the expressed oil. The filling of the press is a simple operation. On the perforated bottom of each ring is laid a cover of plaited horsehair, wool or felt, on which the meal is spread and covered with a horsehair cloth. When the rings are all filled pressure is applied, forcing the grooved upper surface of each plate into the ring above, and thereby causing the oil to flow out through the horsehair cloth, the perforated steel plate and the grooves of the press plate, into the oil channel.

If the regular flow of the oil downwards from the whole surface of the cake is ensured, then the oil, having only to pass through the thin layer of meal, runs away quickly and without difficulty, leaving behind a very evenly pressed cake of regular outline ; on which account the edges of the cake, containing, as they do, no more oil than the central portions, do not need to be trimmed. In presses for making specially large cakes, the rings are too heavy to lift out. Consequently

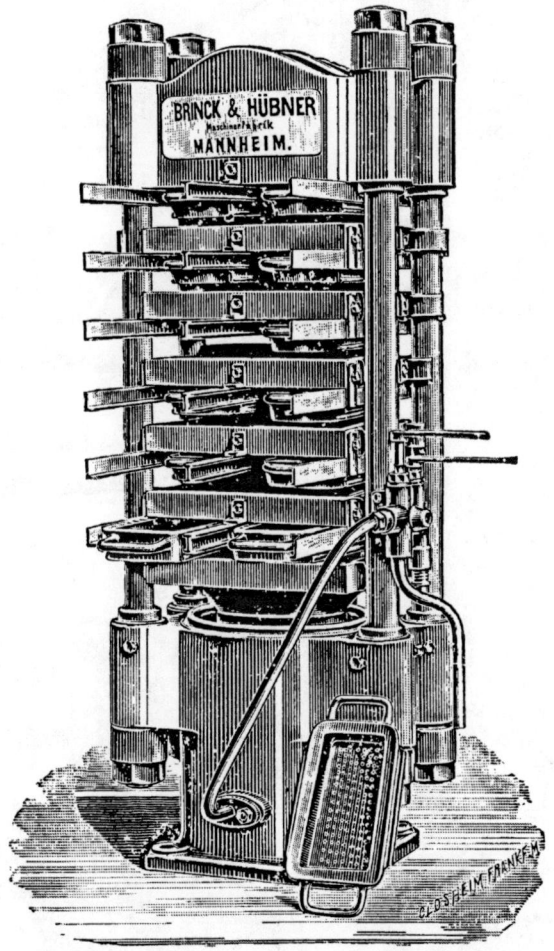

Fig. 40. Hydraulic Box Press (Brinck & Hübner).

these presses (Figs. 41 and 42) are fitted with a double set of slides and extra rings, so that as soon as the press has been emptied by sliding the rings out, another set of full

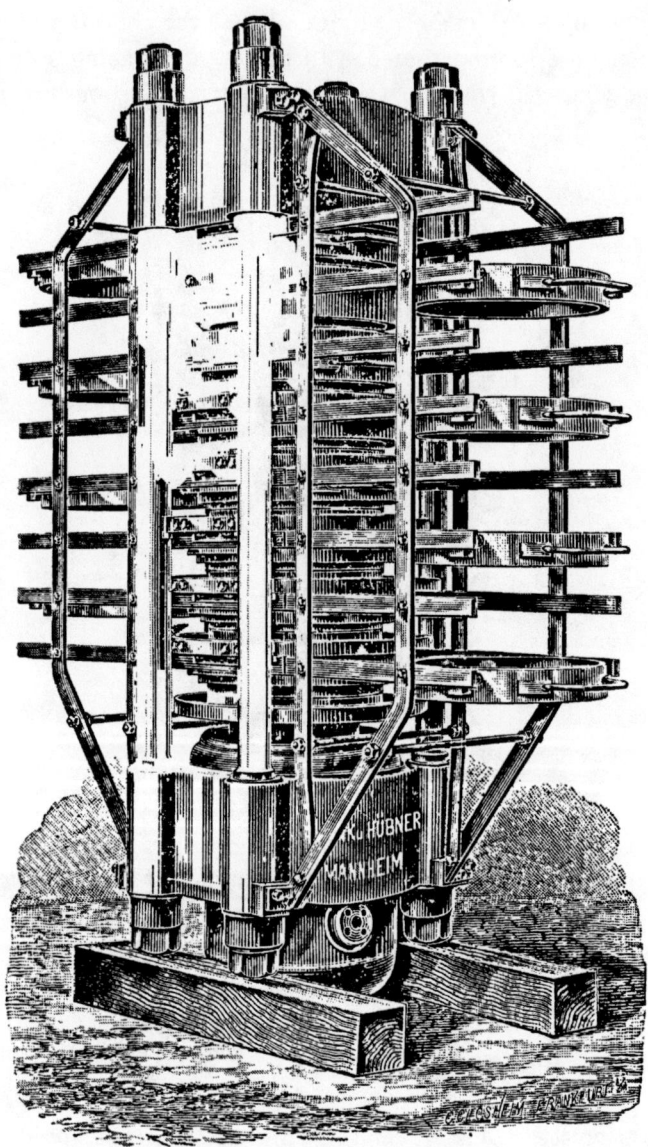

FIG. 41. Hydraulic Ring Press.

rings is pushed in place from the other side, thus rendering the work continuous.

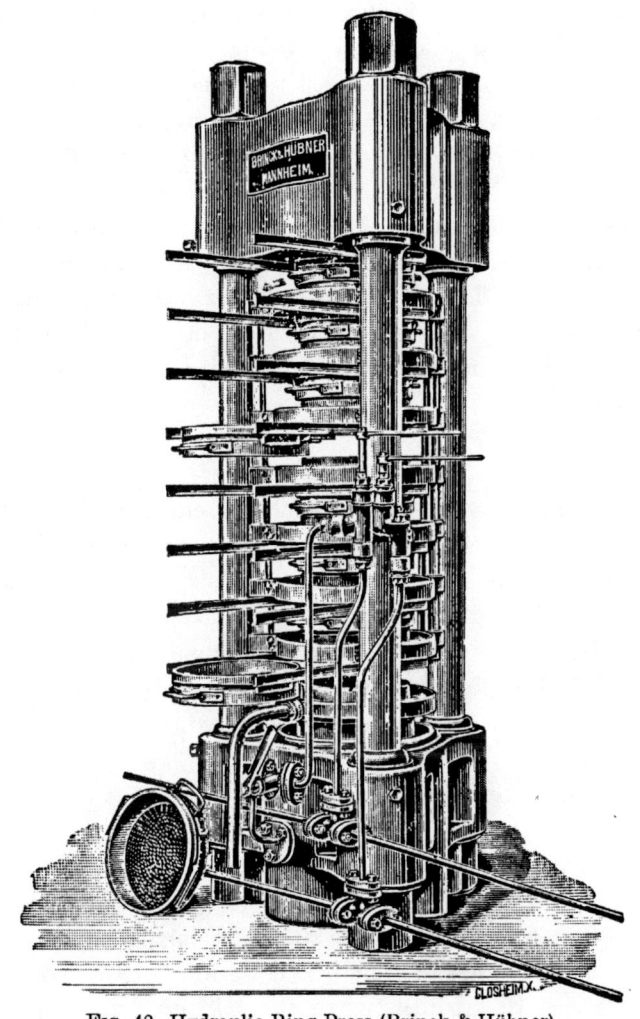

FIG. 42. Hydraulic Ring Press (Brinck & Hübner).

Square and trapezoidal cakes can also be produced in these presses, by substituting press boxes of suitable form in

place of the rings. Steam or hot water heating arrangements
are provided with all these presses, so that each individual
plate can be warmed, and as each cake rests between two hot
plates the warmth is evenly distributed, thus producing results unattainable by any other system of pressing. In order
that the rings may be charged with meal to their fullest
capacity, a filling machine is supplied, by means of which
eight rings can be filled with compressed seed per minute,
the quantity of seed in each being 20 per cent. more than can
be packed in by hand. Heating kettles are also supplied
along with these presses, on occasion, one of which will serve
fifteen presses. They are, however, only used in large works.
The presses are constructed to work at 300 atmospheres pressure and over, and the cylinder, columns and bosses are of
cast steel.

HORIZONTAL PRESSES.

In Figs. 43 and 44 the arrangement of a large four
cylinder horizontal hydraulic press is displayed, Fig. 44
showing the side view (the right-hand side being in section),
and Fig. 43 the ground plan. By attaching suitable supply
pipes all the rams can be actuated by one pump, and provision is also made whereby the rams can be drawn back into
the cylinders by the aid of the pump when the pressure is
removed.

The arrangement of the pressing chamber is revealed in
the right-hand portion of the drawing. The press bags,
which take the form of a flattened prism, are suspended
freely, each between a pair of iron plates, and the expressed
oil is drained from below into the collecting pipe by means of
two inclined planes of iron. The working of the presses is
so arranged that whilst two of them, in diagonally opposite
positions, are pressing, the other two are being refilled, and
only two men are required to a set, each man attending to

the two presses at his own end of the machine. While the ram of the one press is being forced forward, that of the other is being drawn back ; the workman takes out the bags containing the pressed residue and replaces them with bags filled with meal.

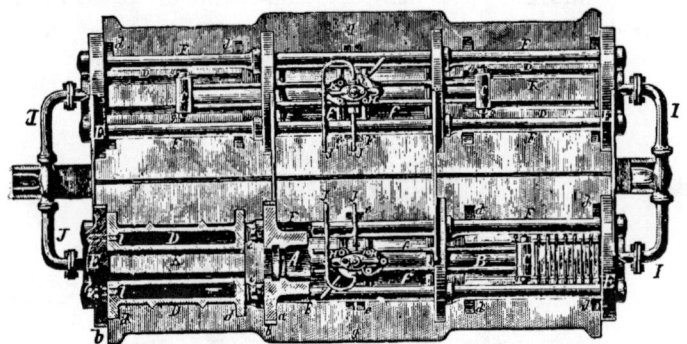

FIG. 43. Horizontal Four Cylinder Press (Ground Plan).

FIG. 44. Horizontal Four Cylinder Press.

OLIVE OIL PRESS WITHOUT SETTING.

This press, manufactured by Rose, Downs & Thompson, of Hull, with attached pump, is intended to replace screw presses for various purposes, and serves for expressing olive oil. The pump and press together form a compact machine, which does not require any technical knowledge in fixing. The weight of the press suffices to impart sufficient stability to the pump without the need of a special setting. Great

care is bestowed on their construction, the cylinders of the
larger presses being of steel, and the pumps, two in number,
of gun metal.

IMPROVED EXPORT PRESSES.

The above-named firm also makes an oil press in combination with a heating kettle and collecting tank for the

FIG. 45. Hydraulic Press with Movable Box.

expressed oil. It occupies a space of about 16½ feet square,
consumes about 11 lb. of coal per hour for heating the
engine boiler, and can be attended to by one man. Of course
a seed crusher is also required. This apparatus is suitable
for treating linseed, rape, sunflower, gingelly, sesame, mustard, poppy and niger seeds, decorticated and undecorticated
cotton-seed, Chinese peas, castor-oil beans, sin, moha,

curdee, jugne, khooras, ground nuts, coprah, lumbang, palm kernels and olives. When the pressing is finished in one

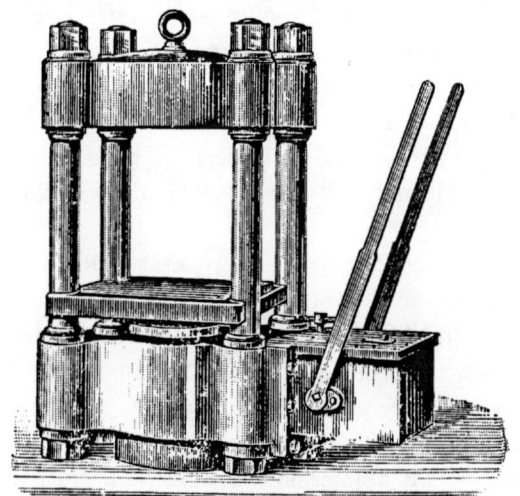

FIG. 46. Hydraulic Press for Oil Fruits.

FIG. 47. Battery of Four Anglo-American Presses on Wrought-iron Case for the Reception of the Oil.

section, the tap merely requires turning round to put the other press into gear. The pump for compressing and with-

6

drawing the liquid in the press cylinder can be kept going without interruption, and the apparatus, if properly handled, is capable of accomplishing a large amount of work. The press chamber can be warmed by steam to prevent the meal from cooling down during the process, and the whole outfit can be worked by steam (or water). The kettles for heating the meal should naturally be set up as near to the presses as possible.

In addition to the pressing apparatus herein figured or described there are of course others, which, however, in the main only differ from each other in external appearance and manner of arranging the combination with the subsidiary appliances (such as pulverising machines, heating pans and the like). The essential points in all presses are that they shall allow of the application of sufficient pressure to force out as much oil from the seed, etc., as possible, being at the same time themselves strong enough to stand this pressure. The selection of a system will depend on the nature of the oil fruit or seed to be treated, and the conduct of operations generally.

INSTALLATION OF OIL AND FAT WORKS.

In the following pages will be described a number of installations for the extraction of oils and fats, which are exported from England mainly to the Colonies, and which are noteworthy by reason of the intelligent arrangement of the various subsidiary machines and the economy of space effected. These installations are particularly adapted for small works.

The "Anglo-American" oil mill displayed in section in Fig. 48 exhibits the ordinary system of arranging an oil-extracting installation, larger establishments being simply a multiplication of this unit, including as many as eight presses or even more. It is capable of treating 15 to

18 cwts. of linseed, or other small oil seeds which only require a single pressing. The pressing room occupies a space of some 12 by 10 yards with a height of 16 to 17 feet, and the machinery requires a motive power of 46 h.p. An installation may consist of any convenient number of such units, each additional one of which will require a further 35 h.p.

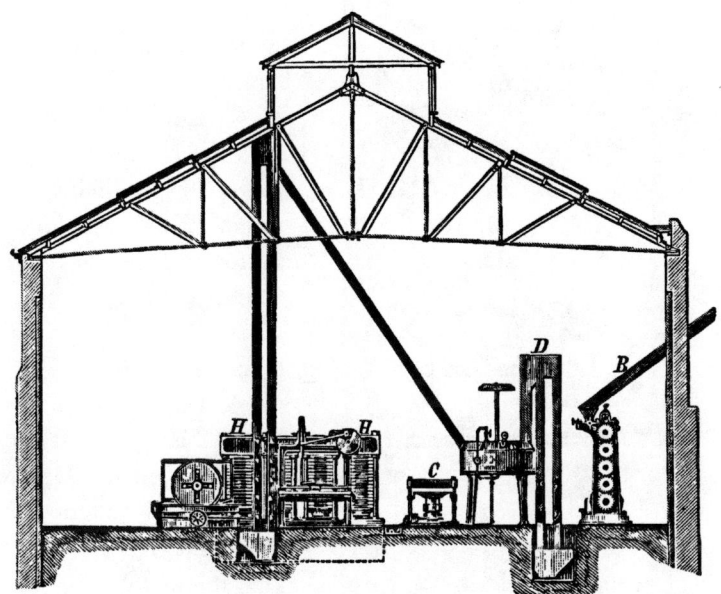

FIG. 48. Section of an Anglo-American Oil Mill.

The whole system of working can be easily understood from the sketch. The seed passes the rollers B, and is thence transferred by the elevator D to the heating pan E. From this apparatus it passes on to the moulding machine C, where it is measured, moulded, and sufficiently compressed to be introduced into the press H. The cakes after leaving the press are trimmed to suitable dimensions in a machine, the trimmings being ground to meal in the edge-runner mill

J and returned to the heater E. The presses stand in a box into which the expressed oil flows, and whence it can be pumped into a storage tank. The advantages of this installation are :—

1. A saving of 20 per cent. of motive power as compared with other systems.

2. Great economy of space.

3. Improved appearance and impression of the cakes, which have under this system a better surface and better fracture than in those where the seed is ground by edge runners.

4. Increased yield of oil. The average residual oil left in the cake is in the old systems $10\frac{1}{2}$ per cent., whereas by this method it is reduced to about 7 per cent., which therefore implies an increased yield of $3\frac{1}{2}$ per cent. of oil.

5. A saving of 50 per cent. in the service of the press room.

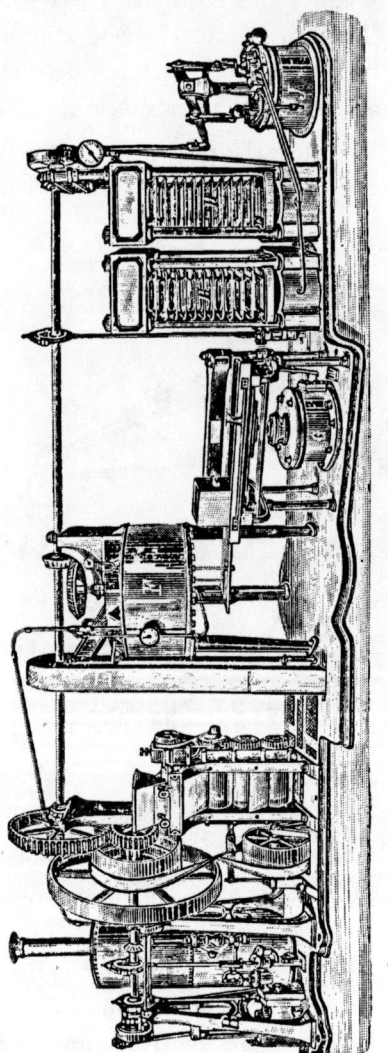

FIG. 49. Colonial Oil Mill (Rose, Downs & Thompson).

6. A saving in press cloths.

7. Reduced weight of machinery per unit of material treated.

8. The system is applicable to all oil seeds and nuts.

9. Horsehair covers are dispensed with.

10. The whole of the machinery being driven by belting, a considerable economy in driving results, as well as a simplification of the apparatus.

THE COLONIAL OIL MILL

of Rose, Downs & Thompson (Fig. 49) is suitable for linseed and other small seeds that only require a single pressing, and is capable of treating 7 to $8\frac{1}{2}$ cwts. per hour. It occupies a space of some $12\frac{1}{2}$ by $5\frac{1}{2}$ yards, weighs about 25 tons, and can be worked by two men.

The mill consists of an iron foundation, on which the following parts are mounted :—

A. Vertical steel boiler, 36 inches in diameter and 96 inches high, in three sections, with a $\frac{1}{3}$ inch jacket and walls $\frac{2}{5}$ inch thick.

B. Vertical steam engine. Diameter of cylinder 8 inches, stroke 12 inches.

C. Mill for grinding the seeds.

A spiral for carrying the seed to the elevator E, which communicates with the heating pan F, provided with mechanical stirrers ; the cake moulding press G attached to F. Next to G stand two hydraulic presses H, worked by the pump J. The cake-trimming machine is set above the moulder.

ANGLO-AMERICAN UNIT OIL MILL.

This combination is adapted for the treatment of linseed and other small seeds only needing a single pressing, and has a capacity of 15 to 19 cwts. per hour. It occupies a space of 12 by 10 yards, and weighs up to 63 tons. Three men are required to work the mill.

The installation consists of the pumps, presses, trimming

machine, edge-runner mill, heating pan, moulder, elevator and roller mill, together with the steam engine to supply the necessary motive power.

In setting up the engine there is no need to attach it to the walls of the buildings by braces, neither does boiler nor engine require any setting or brick chimney shaft. These two machines are of the type extensively employed in India and the Colonies, for tea plantations, gold mines and similar objects. The weight of the heavy machinery, amounting to about 30 tons, is utilised in the support of the intermediate motion, consisting of a single shaft from which the power is transferred to the machinery by pulleys and belting.

The mill rests on a foundation of stone, bricks set in cement, or concrete, and can be enclosed in a building of any convenient light material.

COMBINATION " ECONOMIC " OIL MILL.

This mill is specially designed by Amandus Kahl of Hamburg for pressing seeds in as rational a manner as is possible, consistent with cheapness. The size of the installation corresponds to the requirements of landowners, manufacturers and all who use oil or oilcake or deal therein in the Colonies, India or any other oil-producing country, since, by the erection of a mill of this class, seeds can be ground at the place of production and the products rendered immediately available for use or sale.

The machinery throughout is fitted with the newest improvements, and the entire installation works as rationally and economically as the largest and most perfectly fitted modern mills. It is shown in Fig. 51, and constitutes the simplest and best arrangement hitherto designed, occupying a space of only 6½ by 4 yards, inclusive of the room taken up by the engine and boiler. All the parts of the installation are easy of access, and the whole forms a self-contained mill, independent of fastening or attachment to the walls of any building, etc. The whole of the machinery is driven by wheel gearing, and is mounted, along with the engine, on a massive iron foundation, an arrangement ensuring great stability.

As a result of a special patented arrangement of the roller mill, heating pan, etc., the spirals, elevators, etc., for transporting the seed are dispensed with, thus reducing the cost of the apparatus as well as economising motive power and diminishing the number of wearing parts. Usually the grinding mill is fitted with a wooden feed hopper, but if an elevator is preferred one can be fitted at a small extra cost. Special notice is merited by the system of warming and moistening the seed in the heating pan, effected by an improved method of jacketing the pan and by the use of a steam spray.

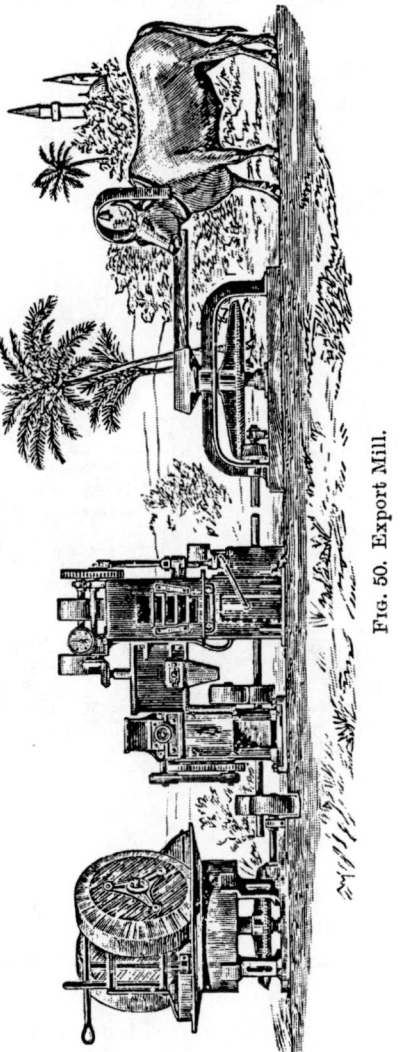

FIG. 50. Export Mill.

The patent pulverising mill for the cake cuttings, which works in conjunction with the trimmer, is highly practical, and grinds the scraps rapidly into a fine meal which can be at once returned to the heater. This does away with the heavy and expensive edge runners previously used, and thereby effects a considerable saving of power. The capacity of the apparatus for linseed or cotton-seeds, which under this system require only one pressing, is 7 to 8

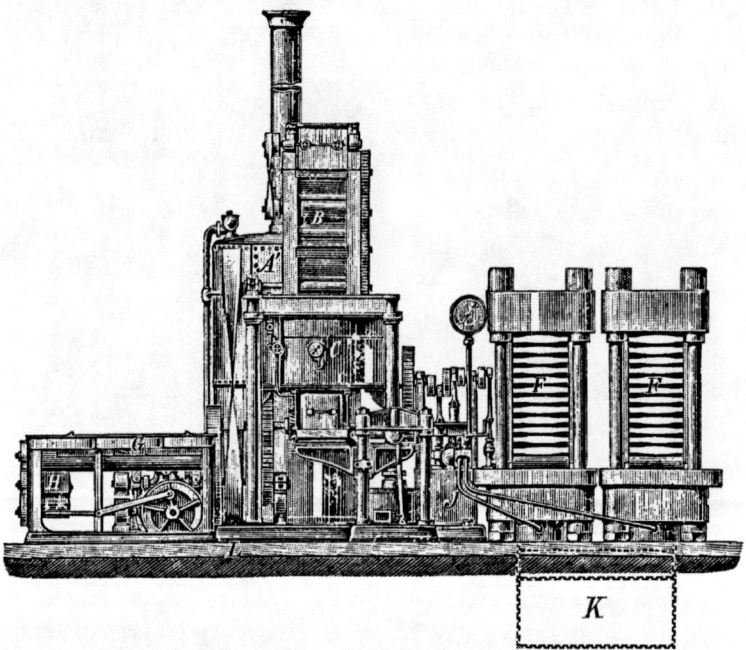

FIG. 51. Combined " Economic " Oil Mill.

tons per hour, according to the thickness of the cakes. In the case of seeds requiring to be pressed twice, the output is reduced by one-third to one-half. Only three men, including fireman, are required for attendance on the machinery in each shift, whereas in other systems of the same capacity twelve and even more are needed per shift.

In the drawing, Fig. 51—

A represents the steam engine with vertical boiler, water heater and feed pump.

B is the roller mill with five superposed chilled cast-iron rollers, 12 inches in diameter and 15 inches in length, with axles of turned steel, wheel gearing and feed hopper.

C. The wrought-iron seed warmer, with steam jacket, insulating layer covered with sheet iron; improved steam spray for moistening the meal; stirrers, pressure gauge and feed and waste-steam pipes.

E. Improved cake moulder with steam press, an automatically closing hopper situated below the heating pan, and two steel cake plates.

FIG. 52. Elevation of Oil Factory Buildings (Knäbel).

F. Two hydraulic presses, each making 14 cakes of $27\frac{1}{2}$ inches long by 11 inches wide and weighing 11 to 13 lb. apiece. The cylinders are of steel, as are also the rams (12 inches in diameter), the four columns and the solid wrought corrugated press plates.

G. Improved cake trimmer with driving gear, six steel knives, spiral and steel scoops.

H. Patent pulverising machine with chilled cast rollers specially grooved for the cake cuttings, with driving gear and feed hopper.

J. A set of hydraulic press pumps, with cast steel pump

chest with rectangular crank axles of Siemens' steel, connecting pipes, safety valve, disconnecting gear and driving gear.

K. Wrought-iron oil tank.

L. Massive cast-iron base plate with iron frame, gunmetal bearings, etc.

Knäbel reports on the installation of an oil factory as follows:—

"The actual factory building is 22 yards long, 13 yards wide, and about 14 yards high, including the storage room

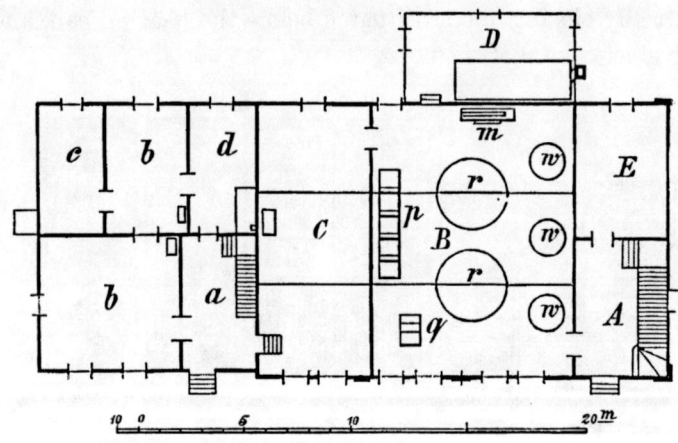

FIG. 53. Ground Plan of an Oil Factory Building (Knäbel).

above the ground floor, strongly built of rough-hewn stone and roofed with slate. The floors of the work rooms are of brick set flatwise in mortar; the beams of the lower storey over the rooms B and C rest on iron girders. The beams over the storage floor are supported by stays and pillars.

"A indicates the entrance hall with steps leading to the upper storage floors, and B shows the position of the oil mill proper. In this room the engine is situated at m, the seed crusher at q; rr are a pair of oil mills, w the heating pans, and p the hydraulic presses. C is the oil refinery, D the boiler house and boilers, for supplying steam to the heating apparatus, etc., as well as to the engine. The latter drives the whole of the machinery, presses, mills, etc., and also pumps the necessary water into the reservoir above the room B, over which room the seed-screening machinery is also situated in a separate chamber. E is the oilcake store.

" The oil store is underground, below the residence of the factory manager, and is lined with brickwork and domed. The manager's dwelling consists of the hall *a*, with staircase leading to the upper storey, the rooms *bb*, the chamber *c* and kitchen *d*. On the top floor is a large gable chamber for the accommodation of some of the permanent staff of workmen.

" In addition to the entrance under the stairs in the hall *a*, the oil store can also be approached from the outside for the transport of casks, etc. The purified oil flows from the refinery through tinned pipes into two large tanks in the oil store. These tanks or reservoirs are lined with bricks set and pointed with hydraulic mortar, and are fitted with wooden lids. From these tanks the oil is filled into barrels for delivery."

A front view of the building is shown in Fig. 52.

"EXTRACTION" METHOD OF OBTAINING OILS AND FATS.

The extraction of oil by means of solvents may be, as has already been stated, effected either completely or partially according as the seed meal is treated by this method alone without previous pressing, or as the cakes from the press are ground down again and subjected to a final extraction by solvents. All the solvents employed are very volatile substances, gifted with the property of rapidly dissolving the fatty constituents of the seed meal, whilst leaving undissolved such bodies as resin, colouring matter, etc., and may be afterwards driven off from the oil or fat by exposure to heat (distillation), with ease and rapidity, without leaving a trace behind, being at the same time readily recoverable. The solvent must also be of such a nature that it will not impart any taste or smell to the residual oil from which it has been separated; in a word, it must leave the oil or fat in a perfectly pure state.

The kinds of apparatus used vary according to the nature and boiling point of the solvent employed—carbon bisulphide, canadol, benzol, benzine, sulphuric ether, carbon tetrachloride. Those allowing the work to be performed continuously, and wherein the loss of solvent is reduced to a minimum, must be regarded as the most perfect.

One of the earliest forms of apparatus was made by Van Haecht of Molenbeck St. Jean, near Brussels. It consists of two upright extraction cylinders, distilling retorts, two condensers with double coils, two reservoirs sunk in the ground to hold the carbon bisulphide, which is prevented from evaporating by means of a supernatant layer of water. The seeds are crushed in a mill and placed in the extraction cylinder, which is then closed tight. Carbon bisulphide is pumped into the cylinder and, when impregnated with oil, drawn out again and distilled in the retort by the heat of a steam coil. The residue in the cylinder after all the oil has been removed is distilled in the same way and recovered by the second condenser.

The engine and boiler are completely isolated by brickwork from the actual factory, in order to obviate the danger of fire, and the connecting pipes are so arranged that the duplicate sets of apparatus can be combined if desired.

DEISS'S EXTRACTING APPARATUS.

This apparatus is displayed in ground plan in Fig. 54, and in section in Fig. 55. The chief parts are: a cistern lined with lead and set in cemented masonry; the extractor

B ; C the condenser ; D the distilling apparatus. After the substance to be treated is inserted in the extractor, where it rests on a perforated false bottom *dd*, a second perforated plate *d'd'* is laid over it and the vessel closed. The carbon bisulphide is pumped up from A by the pump *hh* through the pipe *h* into the extractor, entering below the false bottom. After the solvent has been allowed to exert its action for several hours, the resulting solution of oil is transferred through the pipe *a* to the still D, which is heated by a steam coil. The vaporised carbon bisulphide passes through nine

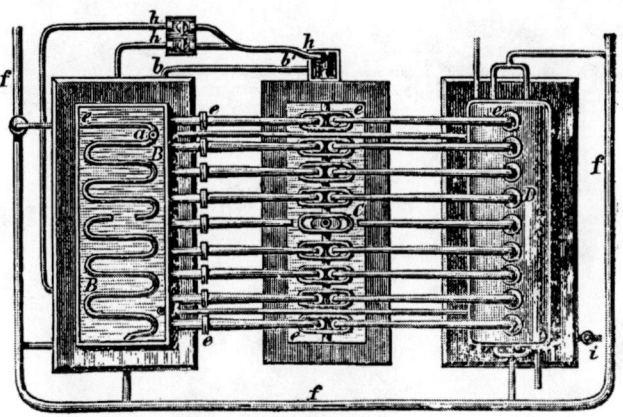

FIG. 54. Deiss's Extractor (Top View).

pipes *e* into the large worm condenser, where it is re-liquefied and returned to the cistern A by way of the pipe *f*.

Carbon bisulphide is forced through the mass in the extractor until all the fat therein is dissolved, whereupon the solvent remaining in B is run back into A, and steam introduced through *b* to *dd*, whereby all the carbon bisulphide present is vaporised and made to pass along with the condensed water into A, where the two liquids separate in the pipe. To make the apparatus continuous, the extractor B should be duplicated.

VOHL'S EXTRACTOR.

This apparatus is designed for use with petroleum spirit of specific gravity 0·650 to 0·700, and with a boiling point of about 60° C., the extraction being effected by the boiling hydrocarbon. It consists (Fig. 56) of a pair of extractors AA, the collecting and distilling vessel B, and condenser C. The extractors, which are tinned inside, are surrounded by jackets *bb* of sheet iron, steam being introduced into the intermediate space through *dd*, and the condensed water run off

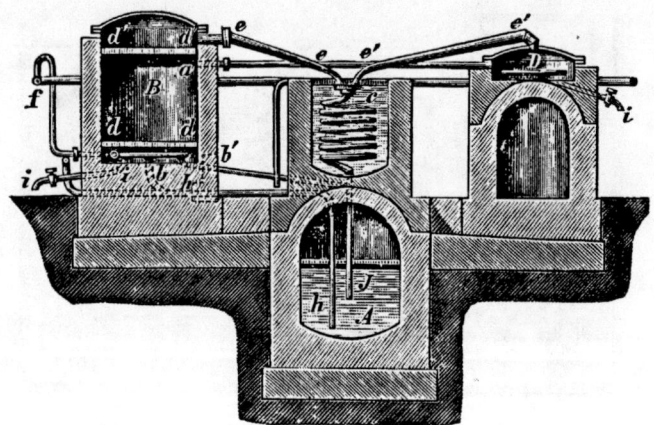

FIG. 55. Deiss's Extractor (Section).

through *ee*. Heating coils *ff* are fitted in the extractors, and are connected with J and C by the tubes *gg* and *ii* respectively. The extractors are filled through the openings *kk*, closed by lids in which debouch the tubes *ll, nn, pp*. The outlets *tt* are closed by lids from which project the tubes *uu*, uniting into the pipe X, terminating in the vessel B. The latter is jacketed, the inner vessel T being of tinned copper and the outer one J of cast iron. Steam is led into the jacket space through Y, and the condensed water drawn off through Z. The tubes X and *g* are set in the copper lid (W) of the vessel Y. The condensing vessel C is composed of a sheet iron cylinder, filled with water through a pipe H, and containing two copper worms which are tinned inside and connected with the extractors. A disc of felt is laid at the bottom of the extractor, and *a* is closed by a wad of leather or felt. The seeds to be deprived of oil are inserted through *k* and covered by another disc of felt, pierced with a hole corresponding to the tube *i*. After screwing on the cover,

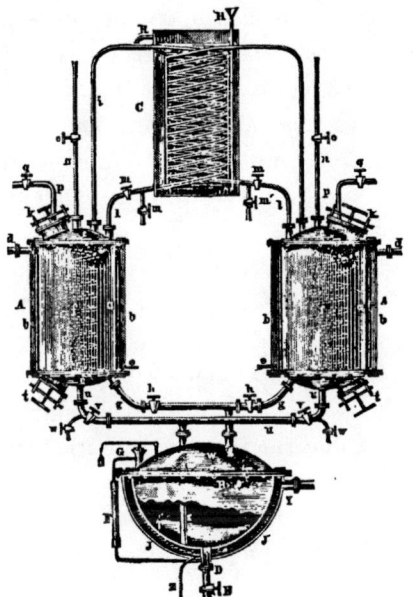

FIG. 56. Vohl's Extractor.

the taps *mm'*, *v* and *h* are opened, *o*, *q*, *w* and E' being shut, and petroleum spirit is run into the extractor from a reservoir above, through *o*. The spirit penetrates the mass of seed, extracts oil therefrom, and flows downward through *u* and X into B. When the latter gets about two-thirds full, the supply of solvent is shut off and steam introduced through Y to bring the contents of B to the boil. The vapours rise through g and condense in f until the contents of A attain the boiling temperature of the solvent, whereupon the vapours rise through i into the condenser, and the liquid, m' being closed, passes through m and l in the interior cylinder of the extractor and returns *via uu*, X.

The operation is continued until the contents of A are freed from oil. This condition is reached when a sample of the liquid, drawn through the tap w and dropped on to paper, vaporises without leaving any fatty mark behind. Thereupon m' is opened and m closed, and steam is allowed to flow into the jacket of the extractor through d. The vapours generated in the extractor force the liquid therein through u and X into B. To prevent B getting too full, the supply of steam is suddenly cut off at a given moment, and the vapours of the solvent allowed to pass into the condenser by opening q and p.

When the distillation is terminated v is closed, q opened, and an exhauster, attached to p, set to work, by means of which the vapours formed in A are withdrawn. The cooling of the tube p indicates that vapour has ceased to form in A, and that all the petroleum spirit is distilled off. Steam is then shut off at d, and the extractor emptied through t. The contents of B are transferred through D and E into a distilling apparatus, wherein the petroleum spirit is distilled off by the introduction of direct steam.

SEIFFERT'S BATTERY OF EXTRACTORS.

This system is composed of four, six or eight cylinders, C_1, C_2, C_3, etc. The cylinders are jacketed for steam heating, and each contains a cylindrical basket of wire netting to hold the material under treatment. When these have been filled, the operation is commenced by introducing petroleum spirit (benzine) from a storage vessel overhead, through S and a

into C_2. As soon as this is filled the liquid passes through a_2, b_2, c_2 into C_3, rises therein and finally enters C_n by way of a_3, b_3, c_3. The benzine, saturated with fat, is conducted *via* d_n and p into a storage vessel, its rate of flow being accelerated by an air-pump exhaust attached to p. When the quantity of liquid collected in the storage vessel is equivalent to the capacity of C_n, d_n is closed, a_n opened, and b_n connected with C_1 by means of b_2 and c_1. The completion of the extraction of the contents of C_2 is indicated by the colourless appearance of the liquid in the glass tube forming part of the circuit of b_2; a_1 and C_2 are then closed, and a_2 and C_3 opened, the

Fig. 57. Seiffert's Battery of Extractors.

result of this step being to disconnect C_2 from the circuit, the liquid taking the course C_3, b_n, C_n. In order to prevent interruption to the flow of liquid through S, the taps a_1, a_2, a_3, a_n are made with two ways, so that they may in one position make connection between S and b, and in the other shut off b, whilst leaving S open. The residual mass after extraction being still impregnated with benzine, the latter has to be recovered, and to this end the benzine is allowed to run off through h, by opening the tap g_2. Opening the tap c_2 in pipe 4 admits compressed air into C_2, the pressure assisting the outflow. As soon as the flow ceases the taps f_2 and f_x

7

are opened, in consequence of which steam enters the jacket space and volatilises the benzine, which passes away through g_2 and h to a worm condenser. When the vapour is blown off, the wire basket containing the residue is lifted out of C, and replaced by one newly filled; C_2 is connected with C_1, and the benzine in C_3 recovered in the manner described above, so that the apparatus works without interruption. If the operation is carried on on a larger scale, a distilling apparatus of sufficient size to treat all the extract delivered from the extractors in a given time will be necessary, to enable the benzine to be recovered as rapidly as possible and used over again. This harmonious co-operation of the extraction and distilling apparatus is very important, as affording the only means of reducing to a minimum the quantity of benzine necessary for the process, and of limiting the renewal of solvent to the amount actually and unavoidably lost by leakage during the work.

The distillation of the fatty solution is exclusively effected, in this and similar systems, by steam stills, one of which is depicted in section in Fig. 58. The still A is in the shape of a low cylinder with a domed top and bottom. The lower portion is jacketed, and steam under pressure admitted through D, circulates through the intermediate space as well as through the coil S, the condensed water running away through the pipe H.

The solution of fat is run by gravitation through E into the still, in which a stirrer is placed and kept in motion during the process of distillation in order that the boiling of the liquid may proceed with regularity. The introduction of the steam is regulated in such a manner that no more vapour is evolved from the still than can be so completely liquefied in the condenser that no smell arising from the solvent can be detected in the still room, otherwise a great waste of solvent will occur, giving rise to the danger of an explosion. When the distillation is completed, a powerful current of air

from a pump is admitted into A, through a perforated ring
of pipe, and continued for several minutes, to remove the
final traces of the less volatile constituents of the solvent,
otherwise they adhere to the fat with great tenacity and can
only be driven off by long-continued heating; whereas by the
method described, their removal is a matter of a few minutes
only. It is advisable to lead the tube R into the cylinder C,
where, by means of a fine spray of water forced through the
rose W, the greater part of the benzine vapour can be condensed and removed (with the admixed water) through J

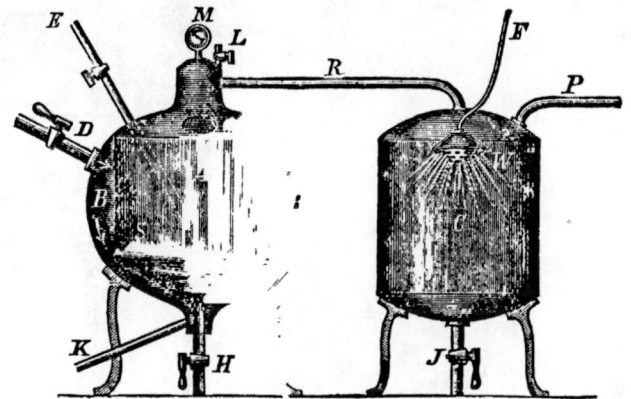

FIG. 58. Benzine Still.

into a separating vessel, the rest of the vapour passing
onward *via p* to the condenser. This arrangement assists in
reducing the percentage of benzine lost in the process.

THE UNIVERSAL EXTRACTOR

of J. G. Lindner & Merz, shown in Fig. 59, is adapted
for the extraction of oil or fat from all fatty materials,
such as the seeds of rape, flax, hemp, ricinus, cotton,
sesame, sunflower, and all other oil seeds, palm kernels,
coprah, ground nuts, beech mast, grape seed, pumpkin seed,
pressed oilcake, olive press residue (Sanza), etc.

In the vessel M, into the bottom of which is fitted a
steam coil *f*, is situated the receptacle L, which is charged
through the manhole *d* with the material to be treated.   The
solvent is then run in from the reservoir V (connected with
the condenser R), and the extract withdrawn by means of
the syphon tube *ggg* into M, as soon as the level of the liquid
exceeds the height of the bend in *g*.   In M the solution is
evaporated, the vapour rising round the walls of L into the

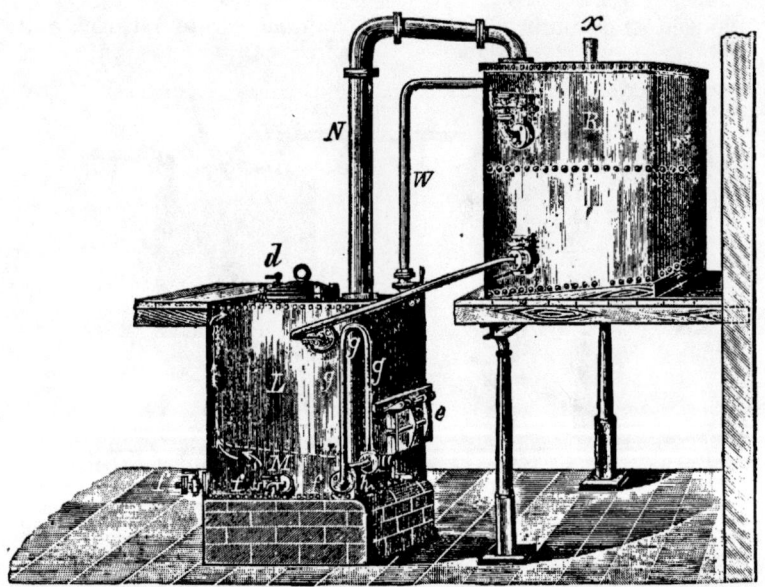

FIG. 59. Lindner & Merz's Universal Extractor.

reversed condenser N, where they are liquefied, the warm
liquid returning to L to be syphoned off again in due course.
    This automatic cycle of operations is only interrupted
when the examination of a sample of the liquid, taken at *h*,
shows that all the extractive matter has been taken up.
The condensing water in N is shut off, and the vapours from
the solution passing from L to M enter the condenser R, to

be collected in the liquid form in the reservoir V. The final portions of the solvent are driven off from the extract, as well as from the residual material, by direct steam. The extract is run off through u, and the extractor L emptied through e.

By means of this apparatus the operation may be performed continuously as well as intermittently. To this end the outflow of the fatty solution is so regulated that the level of the liquid in h is maintained at a constant height by the recovered solvent.

The advantages possessed by this apparatus over others are as follows :—

1. Rapid and complete extraction. By the continual renewal of the solvent liquid and its action at boiling heat, even the last traces of fat are dissolved, and the extraction is so expedited by the uninterrupted circulation and regular heat of the apparatus that three to fours hours suffice for completing the operation.

2. Complete security is afforded against ignition and explosion. In consequence of the judicious arrangement of the apparatus no expansion occurs, notwithstanding that the solvent is at boiling temperature. The danger of explosion, which results from the tension of such easily inflammable vapours, is therefore absent. In view of its absolutely harmless nature, the Merz extractor is allowed by the authorities (in Germany) to be used without the adoption of the precautions for ensuring safety usually prescribed.

3. Minimum quantity of solvent required. The absence of expansion and the provision of an effective method of condensation have reduced the loss of solvent to almost *nil*, nearly the whole amount being recovered. Neither the extracted fat nor the residue exhibits any odour derived from the solvent.

4. Simplicity and economy of working. The apparatus works automatically, and beyond opening the respective

steam and water taps after the extractor is filled, requires no attention ; this, together with the utilisation of the heat from the vaporised solvent, contributes to economical working. The filling and emptying of the apparatus entail no difficulty.

5. Drying. The residual material leaves the extractor in a dry state, and therefore requires no further treatment on this score. The nature of the method prevents the material from becoming wet, and thus, in addition, obviates loss through the extraction of soluble constituents by water or through alteration of any portion of the material thereby. The advantages of a dry residue are particularly important in the case of bones and oil seeds, since, if the latter be left in a wet condition, the valuable food constituents soluble in water will be lost, and cannot be brought back again by any amount of drying.

6. Absence of inconvenience to the surrounding populace. The apparatus being hermetically sealed, it is impossible for any noxious vapour to escape. The effluent water from the condenser is pure.

7. Reduced cost of preparation and economy of space. No subsidiary appliances, such as air pumps or vacuum or superheating apparatus, are required, the extractor being self-contained and delivered in working order, leaving only the connections with the steam and water pipes to be effected. This circumstance, and the high working speed, allow the machine to be made so compact that it takes up but little room, and make the apparatus by far the cheapest extractor in use.

The Excelsior Extractor

made by Wegelin & Hübner of Halle, shown in Fig. 60, is distinguished by simplicity, absolute safety, and great capacity. Its chief advantage consists in the separation of the extractor proper from the vessel in which the extracted fat or oil is collected, a plan that facilitates supervision of the apparatus as a whole, and the individual operations of extraction, distillation and recovery of the solvent proceed more quickly and with a minimum percentage of loss. The apparatus is supplied for hot and cold extraction, is made of wrought iron and copper (the latter may be had tinned), and is equally suitable for any solvent, benzine (petroleum spirit),

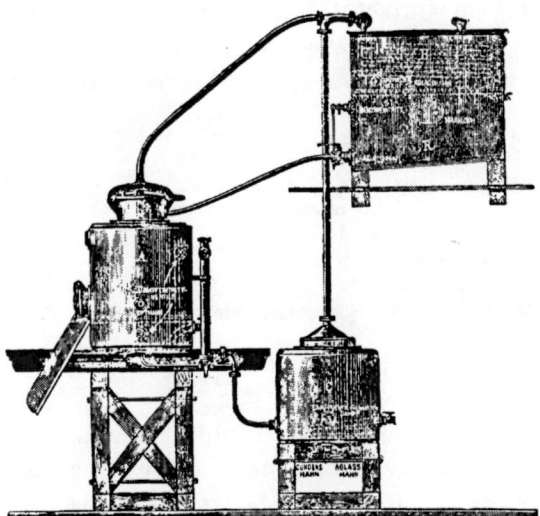

Fig. 60. Wegelin & Hübner's Extractor.

sulphuric ether, carbon bisulphide, alcohol, acetone, etc. If carbon bisulphide is to be used, the specific gravity of this solvent necessitates some modification in the form of the apparatus. For materials extractible without difficulty, for oil seeds (rape, linseed, cotton-seed), and for olive oil residues, castor-oil press cakes and oil press cakes in general, which have to be treated on a large scale, larger machines on this system are made, and are provided with all necessary subsidiary appliances of suitable construction. The oils treated by this apparatus are free from any perceptible taste or smell due to the solvent.

OIL-EXTRACTION INSTALLATIONS.

An installation on the Merz system is sketched in Figs. 61 to 64. The apparatus occupies but the comparatively restricted floor space of about 40 × 65 feet = 2,600 square feet, and the three extractors, each of six cubic metres capacity, can extract the oil from 15 to 18 tons of seed meal, or 25 tons of cake meal, in twenty-four hours.

The working expenses may be reckoned as follows :—

	S.	D.
Steam: 4½ tons of coal at 16s. per ton . . .	72	0
Benzine: Loss 4 cwt. at 10s. per cwt. . . .	40	0
Attendance: 1 fireman (3s.), 1 extractor (4s.), 3 assistants (7s. 3d.) × 2	28	6
Other expenses and wear and tear	11	6
Working expenses per twenty-four hours . . £7	12	0

equal to 5¼d. to 6¼d. per cwt. of seed, or 3¾d. per cwt. of press cake.

Where fine edible oils are not in question, a properly effected extraction by benzine is much to be preferred to pressing, since not only is the yield obtained greater, but the quality is also superior, extracted oil being free from the mucilaginous and protein substances always present in pressed oils, especially those pressed by the hot method. Such substances, however, remain in the residue from the benzine process and increase its nutritive value ; besides, it is eagerly swallowed by cattle, since it exhibits no trace of smell or taste of benzine, but rather resembles new-baked bread in flavour.

Another important point is that extracted meal can be kept for some time without deteriorating, whereas press cakes are liable to spoil by the oil turning rancid, so that they become uneatable, an effect increasing with the percentage of oil present.

The mixed method of preparing oils, largely followed in France (*huilerie mixte*), consisting of a combination of pressing and extraction, is an important one for producers of alimental oils. The seeds are (see page 34) subjected to a cold pressing, and the cakes ground and extracted. The oil obtained by the latter method is much cleaner than by a second pressing, is easily refined, possesses a good flavour (only the fine aroma—the "bouquet"—being wanting), and

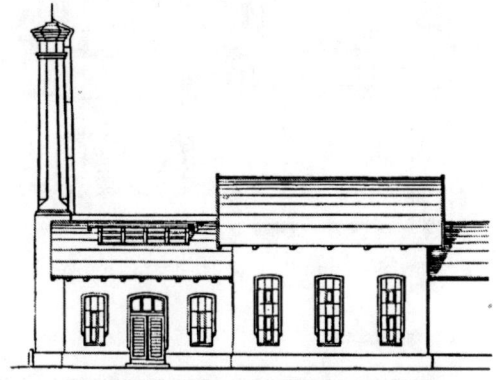

FIG. 61. Façade of Oil-Extracting Works.

when mixed with the pressed oil produces a good alimental oil.

This combined method cannot be too highly recommended, resulting, as it does, in a considerable benefit to the manufacturer. The process was mooted some years ago, but manufacturers (in Germany) hesitated to adopt it, having before their eyes the fear of the more than conservative agriculturists who stick to the one form of oil-cake and demand a certain minimum percentage of oil. (The causes of this stipulation are treated of in the section on Oil-cake.) French and Russian manufacturers, however, led the way, and now sesame, arachis, sunflower, hemp and linseed oils are extensively won by the combination method, the residual meal selling in France at equal prices with press cake.

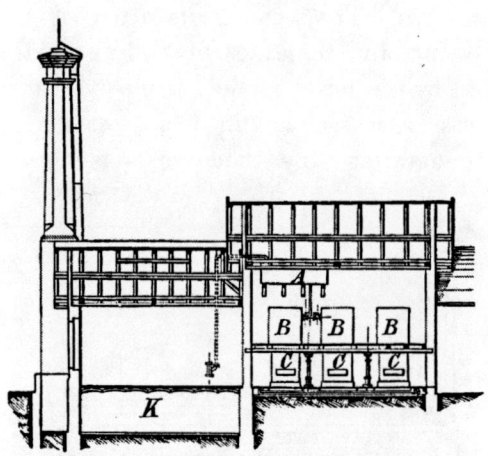

FIG. 62. Sectional View of Oil-Extracting Works.

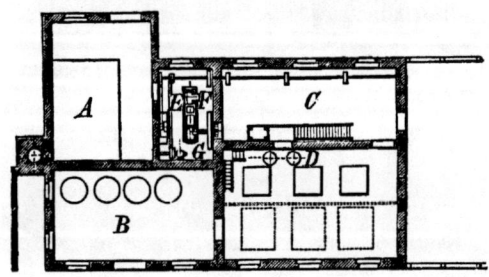

FIG. 63. Ground Plan of Works. A, Boiler House; B, Store and Refinery; C, Grinding Room, Elevator; D, Extraction House.

This operation would be of great value in the olive-oil industry if the pressed fruit were submitted to extraction immediately, instead of following the present practice of boiling up the residue, leaving it to ferment and produce bad oil, and only finally subjecting the "Sanza"—containing 10 to 14 per cent. of oil—to extraction (green sulphur oil), whereas the direct application of the process would result in the production of pale and valuable oil.

PRESS MOULDS.

The moulds in which the oil-cakes are fashioned in the press vary in form from round to square or rectangular; ring presses produce circular cakes, those from other presses being square or in the form of a trapezium. According to Schädler the cakes from the first pressing are round, the trapezoid ones being from the final operation. The dimensions also vary according to the mould, so that, for example, cakes from

the Rhine are 13 inches long.
Berlin   „ 15½ „   „
East Prussia „ 25   „   „
Riga   „ 29½ „   „

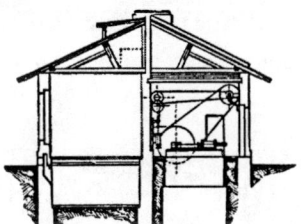

FIG. 64. Cross Section through Extraction House.

The surfaces of the moulds, i.e., the top and bottom, are sometimes flat, but generally corrugated, the upper plate bearing an engraved or cast stamp, as shown in Figs. 65-67, and they may be arranged to make a cake that will readily break up into smaller cakes of trapezoid form (see Fig. 66). The plate in Fig. 65 is fitted with interchangeable stamps, so that the cake can be marked in conformity with the kind of seed used. In course of time the purchasers of oil-cakes have established certain standards, with the result that in one district round cakes only are saleable, whereas in another only the trapezoid cakes are in demand. Certain dimensions are also insisted on by the consumer, and the oil presses and plates have to be constructed to meet these requirements.

The oil-cakes from the first pressing are taken out of the mould—or from between the press plates—to be broken up,

FIG. 65. Cake Plate with Interchangeable Stamp.

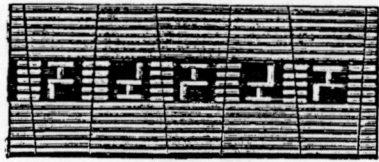

FIG. 66. Divided Plate by which 80 Cakes can be made at a time in one Press.

FIG. 67. Japanese Cake Plate.

ground and pressed for a second, and even, occasionally, a third time to force out the last drops of oil.

MACHINE FOR TRIMMING OIL-CAKES.

The oil-cakes as they come from the press have ragged and irregular edges, which must be trimmed up before the

cakes are saleable. This is effected by a cutting machine
served by two men, one on either side of the table.   To make
the cakes rectangular each side in succession is placed against
a fillet on the table, and cut by the back and forward motion
of a large semicircular knife.   The cuttings are removed
from the machine into a storage chest by means of a feeding
screw.

If it is wished to drive the machine from another

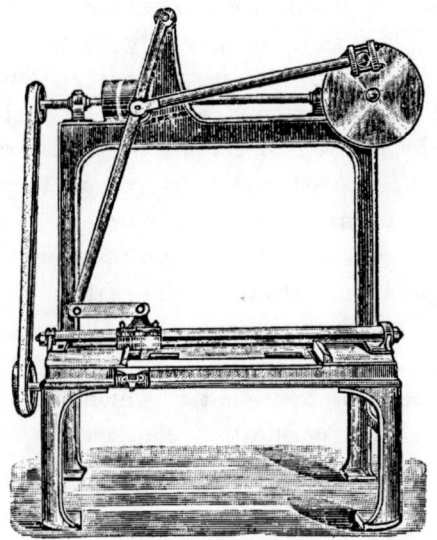

FIG. 68. Machine for Trimming Oil Cakes.

direction than that shown in the drawing, the driving
pulley can be fitted direct on to the crank axle.

In practised hands one trimming machine will square up
and round off the edges of the cakes from twelve hydraulic
presses.

The finished cakes must be thoroughly dried in order to
prevent the development of mould, and they are therefore
placed in a drying room, at sufficient distance apart to allow
free circulation of air around each, whereby they slowly

become quite dry. In this condition, and in this alone, they will keep for any time and with any kind of packing, but the storage rooms must of course be dry, otherwise the cakes will absorb moisture and become mouldy. Care should be taken, in view of the great weight of oil-cakes, that the floor of the storage room is not overloaded.

The oils expressed from the seeds are collected in a suitable manner in iron cisterns, or vessels situated under the presses, but as they naturally contain a number of impurities, especially moisture (water from the seed), albuminoid matter, fragments of vegetable tissue or from the press cloths, etc., they must be transferred into large iron, stone or wooden reservoirs, where they are allowed to remain for a considerable time in order that the impurities may separate out—the heavier ones settling to the bottom and the lighter ones rising to the surface, where they can be skimmed off or removed through taps situated at convenient heights.

The subsequent treatment to which the oil is subjected in the processes of purification, clarification, bleaching, etc., will be discussed in a later section.

CHAPTER VI.

NON-DRYING VEGETABLE OILS.

(Raw material, preparation, properties and uses.)

CASHEW APPLE OIL.

(Acajouöl; huile de noix de Caju.)

Raw material.—The seeds of Anacardium occidentale.

After removing the envelope and washing away the sticky flesh of the fruit, a white, vermiform, edible, oily seed with a mild nutty flavour is left, the lobes of which are plano-convex in shape. The seeds contain 40-50 per cent. of oil.

Method of preparation. — The seeds are ground and pressed.

Properties.—The oil is pale yellow, sweet flavoured and similar to oil of almonds; specific gravity, 0·916.

Uses.—For alimental purposes: in Brazil it has long béen employed as an article of food.

AOUARA OIL.

(Aouaraöl; huile d'Aouaro de la Guayana.)

Raw material.—The seeds of Astrocaryum vulgare, a Guiana palm.

Method of preparation.—The fat occurs in the fruit, just in the same way as palm oil in the palm, and is obtained therefrom in a similar manner, the yield being 22 to 39 per cent.

Properties.—In commerce Aouara oil is grouped with palm oil, although it may be definitely distinguished from the latter by several properties. Both in a fresh state and after prolonged storage, Aouara oil is of a vermilion red colour. Wiesner kept samples from 1869 to 1873 without any alteration in colour resulting, a circumstance which by itself distinguishes this fat from palm oil. The colouring matter seems to coincide with that of the latter fat, and is, similarly, in a state of solution inextractible by water, but removable by the application of heat in the presence of air. The colour is, however, not appreciably altered by the action of acids and alkalis, although destroyed by oxidising agents. Furthermore, the melting point of this fat does not appear to alter so rapidly and decidedly as that of the fat from Elaeis guienensis. At 15° C. the fat is almost completely fluid, and first sets at 4° C. In odour it is agreeable and slightly acid, approximating very nearly to that of the fruit of the locust tree (Gleditschia), and remains unaltered after several years' storage, whereas palm fat very soon loses its odour of violets and assumes an obnoxious rancid smell. The flavour is faint, but slightly acid and aromatic.

When this fat is examined microscopically at 10° C. it presents an almost identical appearance with a preparation of palm fat, even the reddish drops being observed; only the red matrix appears more strongly coloured than in ordinary palm fat, and much richer in crystals than the latter. If the preparation be warmed for a few minutes to about 70° to 80° C. and allowed to cool again slowly, the fatty acids will no longer be found in acicular crystals, but in tabular form or as wide prisms. The red drops will have disappeared, a phenomenon not occurring in palm fat under similar treatment.

Uses.—Same as palm oil.

HIMALAYA APRICOT OIL.

(Aprikosenkernöl: huile d'amandes de l'abricot.)

Raw material.—Seed kernels of the Apricot (Marilla) tree, Armeniaca vulgaris, which contain 40-50 per cent. of oil.

Method of preparation.—Bruising the seed kernels (in the shell), followed by grinding and pressure with or without water and heat. The residue from the press is used for feeding poultry or in the preparation of liqueur.

Properties of the oil.—The pressed oil, clarified by settling, is, when fresh, almost colourless, afterwards turning yellowish and becoming continually darker on prolonged storage; the flavour is mild and agreeable, and the smell recalls that of oil of bitter almonds. The oil easily becomes rancid, has a sp. gr. of 0·915 at 15° C., and sets at –14° C.

Saponification value : 192·9.

Iodine number : 100·00.

Fusing point of the fatty acids : 4·5° C.

Congealing point of the fatty acids : 0° C.

Uses.—For medicinal and cosmetic purposes: same as almond oil.

COTTON-SEED OIL.

(Baumwollsamenöl, cottonöl; huile de Coton.)

Raw material.—The seeds of Gossypium herbaceum L.

The seeds of the cotton plant constitute a bye-product in the cotton industry, and were for a long while regarded as worthless, but in recent times have found employment in the preparation not only of technical but also alimental oils, thereby attaining such value as to be in great demand. Cotton-producing countries — especially North America, Egypt, Algeria and Italy—ship large quantities to European oil manufacturers to be worked up for oil.

The seeds are of a somewhat irregular oval shape, about

8

$\frac{1}{4}$-$\frac{3}{8}$ inch in length and $\frac{1}{6}$-$\frac{1}{5}$ inch greatest width. The stout, rather brittle skin of the seed is, either entirely or at the pointed end, covered with whitish, greenish or yellowish wool. On one side of the seed capsule there runs a sharply defined suture springing out at an angle from the wide end. The capsule, about $\frac{1}{75}$-$\frac{1}{60}$ inch thick, consists of five layers of tissue. The outer layer is composed of irregularly shaped, thick-walled cells, lying perpendicular to the surface and filled with brown material. These cells are 0·018-0·045 millimetre in length, and about 0·017 mm. thick. Then

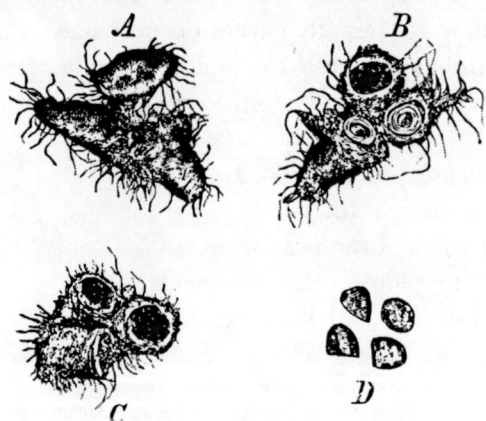

Fig. 69. Cotton Seeds. A, Seed Pod Surrounded by Cotton ; B, After Passing the Decorticator; C, Husk; D, Seeds.

follows a network of rounded cells some 0·016 mm. in diameter, with very thick walls, and a layer of softer long cells, about 0·051 × 0·012 (occasionally) mm., lying parallel to the cells in the external layer. The cell contents are colourless down to the lowest portion, which presents the appearance of a brownish granular mass. This stratum is succeeded by a tissue of several layers, consisting of cells similar in form and arrangement to those described, and only differing therefrom by being completely full of a brown substance. The inside layer of all, lying next to the embryo, consists of greatly flattened, polygonal cells, colourless or brown, and arranged tangentially, their longest diameter being about 0·09 mm.

The embryo exhibits a thick, long rootlet, and a pair of equal, folded cotyledons. The latter consist of a parenchyma of soft, polyhedral cells of various dimensions, often attaining a diameter of 0·045 mm.

In the contents of the cell appear countless small drops of fat and many roundish aleuron granules, 0·0045 to 0·0065 mm. in diameter, which are revealed more distinctly when the section is immersed in fatty oil or oil of turpentine. In the external portions of the radicle appears a ring of glands, and still larger ones are found in the cotyledons, in the section of which they occur in single rows. Their dimensions are so large (0·144 mm. in section) that they are visible to the unassisted eye, appearing as blackish-brown points in the section of the seed. The cellular structure of these glands is most easily examined in sections mounted in oil of turpentine, since, if water is used, the cell walls, consisting probably of gum or mucilage, dissolve, allowing the escape of fine granules of (microscopically) greenish-yellow resinous matter, which manifests very rapid molecular movements in the water.

The maximum yield of oil from the seeds is appraised at 45 per cent. According to the 1880 census, 1,525 persons were employed in the cotton-seed industry in New Orleans alone, their pay amounting to 374,142 dollars, and the value of the produce to 2,742,000 dollars. The total quantity of cotton-seed worked up yearly amounts in the United States to 410,000 tons, or 10 per cent. of the annual crop.

Preparation of the oil.—The seeds are first freed from all dust and dirt by being forced against a screen by means of a blower, so that all the heavy matters fall to the ground. The next step is to clean the seed, which is effected in a machine resembling a cotton gin, only that the teeth engage more intimately in order to remove the adherent cotton. The cleaned seeds are passed into a rotary cylinder containing 24 circular fixed knives and an equal number of cutters, which divide the seed into very small pieces. The hulls are thus separated from the kernels, and form a valued food for cattle. The kernels are pressed between rollers like those in a cane-sugar mill, and the oil runs out. The mass is then put into woollen press bags, laid between horsehair cloths covered with riffled leather to enable the oil to flow more freely, and submitted to hydraulic pressure. The bags are exposed to warm pressing for seventeen minutes, a time sufficient to force out all the oil, which collects in a channel, leaving only the dry kernels behind. These constitute the oil-cake of commerce. The oil is thereafter pumped into a tank, and if destined for sale in the crude state is filled into casks without delay, otherwise it is clarified and filtered or refined for storage.

Grimshaw has elaborated the following table, showing the complete utilisation of the cotton-seed :—

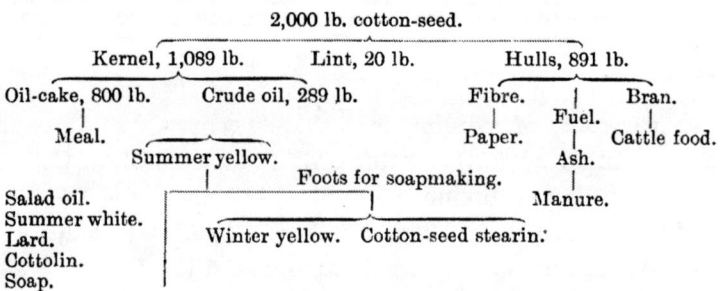

Frequently in the preparation of cotton-seed oil a part of the fat is caused to separate by cooling, and is then put on the market as cotton-seed—or vegetable stearin. A fat of this description, examined by Teuter, possessed at 37·7° C.

(100° F.) a specific gravity of 0·9,115 to 0·912, yielded 95·5 per cent. of insoluble fatty acids, and was completely insoluble in ether and hot absolute alcohol. It melted at 32·2° C. and remained perfectly fluid as a yellow oil, with an odour of fresh cotton-seed oil, congealing only at 1° C. A sample examined by Mayer melted at 39° C.

Properties.—Specific gravity at 15° C., 0·922 to 0·930 (Allen), 0·9,228 (Valenta); at 17° C., 0·923 (Scheibe); at 18° C., crude oil 0·9,224, refined oil 0·9,230, white oil 0·9,288 (Stilurell).

Specific gravity of the fatty acids at 100° C., 0·849 (Archbutt). Cotton-seed oil deposits stearin below 12° C., and becomes solid at 0° to 1° C.

Melting point of the fatty acids, 35·2° C. (Allen); 38° C., setting at 35° C. (Bach); 38·3° C., setting at 35·5° C. (Valenta); 35° C., setting at 30·5° C. (Hübl). According to Bensemann, the substance begins to melt at 39° to 40° C., and liquefies completely at 42° to 43° C.

Hehner number, 95·75 (Bensemann).

Saponification value, 191 to 196·5 (Allen), 195 (Valenta), 191·2 (More).

Saponification value of the fatty acids, 203·9 (Valenta).

Iodine number, 106 (Hübl), 108·7 (More).

Iodine number of the fatty acids, 110·9 to 111·4 (Morawski and Demski).

Crude cotton-seed oil is brown or dark brownish red, the purified oil reddish yellow without special odour or flavour.

Dr. Pribyll remarks that cotton-seed oil is now brought to market in such a highly purified and refined condition as to be absolutely tasteless and inodorous, and can be mixed with other oils without producing the slightest alteration. If stirred up along with caustic potash, the surface layers in contact with the air turn first blue, then violet, the oil then becoming yellow, whilst the potash separates out somewhat darkened in colour.

The refined oil, having been submitted to treatment with alkali, is mostly free from acid ; it is of a straw-yellow colour, and has a nutty taste.

Cotton-seed oil differs from all other oils by the very high melting and setting points of its fatty acids, which, furthermore, behave in a very remarkable manner under the Livache test (capacity for absorbing oxygen), the oil taking up 5·9 per cent. of oxygen in two days, whilst the fatty acids absorb only 0·8 per cent.   The oil itself belongs to the class of slow-drying oils, whereas the fatty acids behave like those from the non-drying oils.

For the recognition of cotton-seed oil and its detection in other oils—particularly in olive oil, for the adulteration of which it is extensively employed—use is made of other properties, described below.

It contains 1·84 per cent. of an unsaponifiable constituent which, according to Rödiger, can be isolated as characteristic yellow crystals.   If the oil be warmed with an alcoholic-ethereal solution of silver nitrate, a dark coloration ensues, according to Becchi, from the reduction of glycerin.   It was implied that this constituted a sure method of detecting cotton-seed oil in olive oil, but it has been shown that this reagent is not absolutely certain, since olive oil may also behave in a similar manner.   The brown colour produced in the elaidin test, and by agitating the oil with an equal volume of nitric acid, of specific gravity 1·37, is characteristic of cotton-seed oil, and it may also be detected by the dark red to brown colour resulting when mixed with concentrated sulphuric acid.

Refining cotton-seed oil.—For this purpose cotton-seed oil is agitated ·for some time (in large mechanical agitators) along with from 7 to 15 per cent. of caustic soda, a current of air forced into the mixture from an air pump being also employed for the same purpose. By this means all admixtures are precipitated, and the acidity of the oil is completely neutralised. The purified oil, about 82 per cent. of the total, is then run off and clarified by settling or filtration. A dark soapy deposit remains behind, and is warmed up in order to allow the contained oil to separate. According to Thalmann, treatment with diluted soda lye removes the colouring matter; the oil is heated by steam until a sample taken from the bulk shows that it is sufficiently bleached; *i.e.*, until the oil separates into three layers, the lowest of which, black in colour, consists of lye and decomposed colouring matter. The central layer has a milky appearance and is composed of saponified oil, whilst the upper one is the bleached cotton-seed oil. Out of 100 parts of crude oil 85 to 88 per cent. are obtained as refined, the loss being due to the saponification of the oily constituents causing the dark colour. In order to prevent the loss of this large proportion of fatty matter, the bleaching lye may be advantageously employed for soapmaking. Longmore of Liverpool prepares a solution of the mucilaginous precipitate by melting it, or by the addition of water, and subsequently adding to the liquor thus produced a sufficient quantity of caustic alkali to effect complete saponification, thereby recovering colouring matter and soap.

The defect exhibited by cotton-seed oil (as compared with olive oil), of setting at higher temperatures than the latter, has been obviated, by means of a secret chemical process, to such an extent that large quantities of the oil so prepared are met with in commerce, and retain their transparency and fluidity at temperatures below 5° C. under freezing point.

BOULTON'S PROCESS FOR REFINING COTTON-SEED OIL.

For the performance of this process a vessel large enough to contain double the amount of oil to be treated, and fitted with an efficient mechanical stirring apparatus, is required. Above the oil vessel are situated others for containing brine and caustic alkali, as well as tubes for the introduction of hot and cold water into the oil pan, which is also steam jacketed,

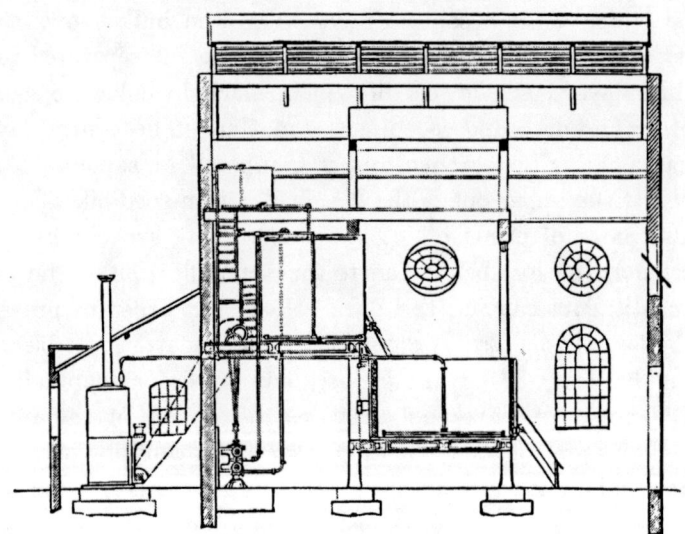

FIG. 70. Cotton-Seed Oil Refinery.

so that the contents may be warmed if necessary. An outlet, closed by a tap, is provided at the bottom of the pan. The crude oil is introduced at 27° C., and, the stirrers being set in motion, a solution of common salt in water (about 10° Tw.) is added, 360 litres being used to each kilogram. Agitation is continued until the oil and brine are intimately mixed, whereupon caustic soda lye (22° Tw.) at 27° C. is run in, with continued stirring. The oil, after treatment in this manner and thorough washing, can be separated from the mechanically suspended water by heating up to 70° C. Provided the process has been properly performed no saponification of the oil takes place, neither is any mucilage formed. Finally the oil may be clarified in the usual manner and is then fit for sale as "olive oil". If intended for market as yellow oil it is still bleached by the ordinary process.

Uses of cotton-seed oil.—Medicinal: for the same purposes as olive oil.

Alimental purposes: as an edible oil, by itself; for adulterating olive oil, or for the preparation of lard substitutes.

Technical purposes: as lubricating oil; for making soap and candles; for painting, burning, etc.

BEN OIL, OR BEHEN OIL.

(Behenöl; huile de Ben.)

Raw material.—The seeds of Moringa pterygosperma Gaertn. (Behen nut, Egyptian acorn), indigenous in the East Indies and also cultivated in tropical America.

Preparation.—By pressing the seed.

Properties.—The Behen oil, known in the East Indies as "Sorinja oil" or "Moringa oil," is either colourless or slightly yellow, inodorous, with a faint sweetish flavour; does not resinify in air nor does it turn rancid, even after prolonged exposure therein. It contains, in addition to olein, palmitin, and stearin, the glyceride of an acid of high melting point named by Völker "Behenic acid," the melting point of which is given as 76° C.

Specific gravity at 15° C., 0·9,120 (Chateau).

Setting point, 0° C. (perfectly solid). Crystals separate out at + 7° C.

BEECH-NUT OIL, OR BEECH OIL.

(Buchenkernöl, Buchelkernöl, Buchenöl; huile de faine.)

Raw material.—Beech nuts, or beech mast, the seeds of the red beech, Fagus sylvatica.   These seeds contain considerable quantities of a fatty oil, which can be obtained therefrom to the extent of some 17 per cent., either by pressing or by extraction with carbon bisulphide. Beech nuts are readily obtainable in large quantities, owing to the extension of the beech plantations in Europe, notwithstanding that the trees do not yield nuts annually, but only after a lapse of four or five years. The fruit is in the form of single nuts, from which the shells are easily separated and which are then treated for the extraction of their oil.   In shape the fruit is like a triangular pyramid with rounded base, the edges being winged towards the apex. The point of attachment at the base of the nut is very prominent, on account of its sharply triangular form and dark colour.   In length the fruit varies from $\frac{7}{16}$ to $\frac{9}{16}$ of an inch, the greatest breadth is about $\frac{1}{3}$ of an inch, and the pointed extremity is closely covered with brown woolly hair.   The outside of the shell is pale brown in colour, very glossy, and with fairly smooth edges; the interior, which is dull brown in colour and without lustre, bearing a number of longitudinal stripes.   Two decided layers are distinguishable in the tissue ($\frac{1}{12}$-inch in diameter) of the shell, the external one consisting of fairly transparent thick-walled cells 0·022 millimetre in diameter, the inner one being composed of brown opaque cells flattened and arranged tangentially.   The epidermis of the seed is brownish black, covered with numerous long unicellular hairs of different diameters, many of them being spiral, and consists of flat polygonal cells, about 0·045 mm. in diameter, brown in colour and opaque. When the seed is dry the epidermis is easily detached.

Method of preparation.—The nuts are opened, the shells discarded, and the kernels pressed or submitted to extraction.

Properties.—Cold pressed beech oil from shelled kernels is an almost colourless, non-drying oil with agreeable odour and taste, and may be used alone as an edible oil. The hot pressed or extracted oil has an acid taste, and is coloured yellow to light brown. According to Chateau, its specific gravity at 15° C. is 0·9,225 (0·920, Souchère), and setting point 17·5° C. It keeps very well, in fact improving with age, and preserves a good flavour after five years' storage; it should keep even twenty years and longer.

According to Benedikt it gives decided colour reactions with several of Chateau's reagents, preferably with zinc chloride, chloride of tin and mercuric nitrate. When saponified by soda lye it produces a somewhat fatty soap, which becomes yellow or greenish in air.

Uses.—For alimental purposes: in the fresh state like olive oil, and as a substitute for lard.

Technical: when produced in large quantities, as a lubricant, for soaps, as burning oil, etc.

CROTON OIL.

(Crotonöl; huile de croton, huile de Tilly.)

Raw material.—The seeds of Croton Tiglium L., indigenous in Bengal, and of Croton Parana Hamilt., from Java. The seeds are about a quarter of an inch in length, $\frac{1}{25}$ to $\frac{1}{20}$ of an inch wide, resembling ricinus seeds in shape, but sloping on both sides, particularly on the back, and therefore almost quadrilateral. The colour is a dirty greyish brown with dark patches, sometimes even black, dull on the outside and without gloss, as though covered with dust. The brittle external shell is lined with a white interior layer, and contains a white solid kernel very rich in oil, which is encompassed by the two albumen lobes of the foliaceous embryo. The flavour is at first mild and oily, quickly becoming sharp and hot. The constituents of the seed are fatty oil, crotonarin, very pungent resin, pungent volatile oil, etc.

Preparation of the oil.—East Indian oil is prepared in Ceylon, Madras, Bombay, and latterly in Buitenzorg (Java), by pressing the seed, preferably after a preliminary process of moderate roasting. In England the latter operation is omitted, the resulting oil being therefore paler. Simple cold pressing is also resorted to in this country, whereas in India the seed cake from the cold pressing is heated on a sandbath to 120°-140° F. and pressed over again.

Properties.—Specific gravity at 15° C., 0·942; older oil, 0·9,550.

Setting point, up to 16° C.

The oil is amber or orange yellow to brown, very thick, of unpleasant flavour, burning the tongue, and forms an effective purgative. It is soluble in 36 parts of absolute alcohol.

In composition it differs so essentially from the other oils that it may be easily distinguished from them by quantitative chemical reactions. In the first place it contains no olein, but stearin, palmitin, myristin and laurin, as well as the glycerides of the oenanthylic acids, caproic acid, valeric acid, butyric acid, tiglic acid, etc. Croton oil yields no elaidin. With concentrated sulphuric acid the oil forms at first a colourless mixture, which quickly becomes darker than the original oil. This affords a means of detecting the presence of extraneous admixtures, the mixture in such case quickly becoming dark, turbid and opaque.

Uses.—Medicinal.

CURCAS, OR PURGING-NUT OIL.

(Curcasöl, Purgirnussöl; huile de Pignon de l'Inde.)

Raw material.—Purging nuts, ground nuts, vomit nuts, the fruit of Curcas purgans. Flavour, almond; subsequently becoming irritating and giving rise to vomiting. The seeds contain 30 to 40 per cent. of oil and 17 per cent. of albumen, together with sugar, starch and casein.

Method of preparation.—Grinding and pressing the hulled seeds.

Properties.—The oil is pale yellow, somewhat lighter than linseed oil, and inodorous; it tastes mild at first, but subsequently irritating, and is strongly purgative, 10 to 12 drops producing the same effect as 30 grams of ricinus oil. It is thinner than the latter, has a specific gravity of 0·915 at 15° C., thickens at 0° C., becomes of a buttery consistency at − 8° C., and sets at − 12° C.

It may readily be distinguished from ricinus oil on account of its low degree of solubility in alcohol. It contains ricinoleic acid and yields capryl alcohol on distillation with caustic potash; it also contains stearic, palmitic, and myristic acids. The isocetic acid found by Bouis in this oil is a mixture of 70 parts of palmitic acid with 30 parts of myristic acid.

Uses.—Medicinal: as a purgative and remedy for cutaneous eruptions.

Technical: as burning oil (burns without smell or smoke), for soapmaking and as a lubricant. Although not a thorough drying oil it undergoes change in the warm, and is used as a paint when boiled with ferric oxide.

CYPERUS OIL (CYPERUS-GRASS OIL).

(Erdmandelöl; huile de souchet comestible.)

Raw material.—The underground seeds growing on the fibrous roots of Cyperus esculentus in Southern Europe, cultivated particularly in Sicily and North America. The brown tubers have a sweet nutty flavour, and are used as food both in the raw state and cooked. They contain up to 20 per cent. of oil.

Method of preparation. — Breaking down the seeds and subjecting them to cold or warm pressure.

Properties.—The oil is of a golden yellow colour, with an agreeable nutty flavour and smell. Its specific gravity at 15° C. is 0·924, and it deposits stearin at below 3° C. According to Hell and Damedoff it consists mainly of the glyceride of oleic acid, with which is associated the glyceride of myristic acid, any other higher fatty acids present being inferior in amount to the last named.

Uses.—For alimental purposes : in Italy and Egypt as best edible oil.

Technical : soapmaking.

GROUND-NUT (EARTH NUT), ARACHIS, OR PEA-NUT OIL.

(Erdnussöl, Arachidöl, Arachisöl, Mandoböl ; huile d'Arachide, huile de pistache de terre.)

Raw material.—Seeds of Arachis hypogaea L. The plant is one of the most important cultivated in tropical countries, being largely grown in South America, the East Indies, China, Japan, and the French West African colonies (Congo, Senegal, etc.), and the seeds, besides being extensively employed as a food stuff, are also exported in enormous quantities to European oil manufacturers, the French colonies in West Africa alone shipping annually over 100,000 tons of ground nuts to Europe, most of which is worked up in Marseilles. Very large amounts of oil are also prepared in England and Germany from ground nuts of East Indian origin (Madras, Calcutta), or obtained from the west coast of Africa.

The blossoms of this herbaceous, creeping, papilionaceous

plant develop in the axes of the leaves; the fruit buds grow
downwards into the earth and develop there into fruit, $\frac{3}{5}$ to
$1\frac{1}{5}$ inches in length, $\frac{2}{5}$ to $\frac{3}{5}$ of an inch in width, and straw
yellow in colour (hulls), which rest, until ripe, about 2 to 3
inches below the surface of the ground.   Usually there are
two seeds—more rarely three—in each capsule, the latter
being constricted once in the one case and twice in the
other.

The seeds are long and generally flattened at the one end,
copper-red to brown in colour as far as the white eye, and
often tinged with violet.   Older seeds are brown; whitish
seeds appear but seldom.   The epidermis of the seed is
easily detachable, resembles parchment, and is traversed by

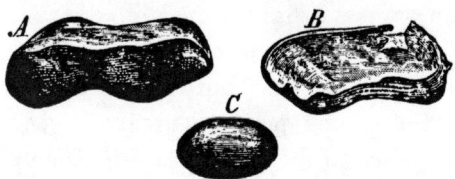

FIG. 71. Ground-nut Seeds.   A, Entire Nut with Capsule; B, Crushed
Capsule; C, Kernel (Nut).

branching veins.   The small thick radicle reposes between
the easily separable cotyledons and bears the acrospire, which
is covered with embryo leaves.   The average weight of the
seed is about 0·2 gram.   The cotyledons have about the
same consistency as a hazel nut; the taste is oily and
reminiscent of that of beans.   The epidermis of the seed
consists of tissue composed of flat, polygonal, porous-walled
cells, to which are attached several interior layers of rounded,
colourless parenchyma cells.   The outer skin is copiously
interspersed with vascular bundles, wherein tracheal fibres
are detectable without difficulty.   The fundamental tissue of
this skin contains iron-blue colouring matters.   The lobes
consist of a parenchyma traversed by soft vascular bundles,

the thin-walled, polyhedral parenchymatous elements being filled with drops of oil, amongst which granules of starch, 0·003 to 0·015 mm. in diameter, and minute agglomerations of albumen are discernible. The parenchyma cells on the inside of the seed lobes measure as much as 0·100 mm., those of the periphery ranging from 0·020 to 0·030 mm.

The amount of fat contained in the seeds varies between 43 and 50 per cent., the albumen amounting to 27-28 per cent., starch and cellulose together to 13 per cent., and sugar and gum to about 7 per cent.

Preparation of the oil. — Comminuting and pressing (extracting) the seeds.

Properties.—The first, cold-pressed oil is colourless, and possesses an agreeable flavour, recalling that of kidney beans. According to Schaedler, a second cold pressing yields an oil commercially known as "butterine oil"; and Benedikt states that the second pressing produces good burning oil. The oil from the third (warm) pressing is employed for the manufacture of soap.

Specific gravity at 15° C., 0·9163, Chateau; 0·719, Souchère; 0·916 to 0·920, Allen; 0·9103, Valenta; at 23° C. the specific gravity is, according to Dietrich, 0·917 to 0·918.

Specific gravity of the fatty acids : According to Archbutt this is, at 180° C., 0·8475; the setting point lies between −3° to 7° C.

Setting point of the fatty acids : 23·8° C. (Hübl).

Hehner number : 95·86 (Bensemann).

Saponification value : 191·3 (Valenta) ; 196·6 (Moore).

Iodine number : 103 (Hübl); 87·3 (Moore); 95 (Erban).

Iodine number of the fatty acids : 95·5 to 96·9 (Morawski and Demski).

Melting point of the fatty acids : 27·7° (Hübl); 27·8 (Allen) ; commencement of fusion 31° to 32°, completion 34° to 35° C. (Bensemann).

According to Benedikt, ground-nut oil consists for the most part of the glycerides of palmitic, hypogaeic and arachic acids. In consequence of the large proportion of hypogaeic acid the elaidin reaction is particularly decisive. The presence of arachic acid facilitates the detection of this oil when mixed with others. One hundred parts of 90 per cent. alcohol dissolve 0·52 of oil.

Ground-nut oil is occasionally adulterated with poppy oil, sesame oil and cotton-seed oil, the presence of which can be detected by determinations of the specific gravity, iodine number, melting points of the fatty acids, and by the furfurol reaction (sesame oil).

Uses.—For alimental purposes : same as olive oil.

Technical : in the adulteration of olive oil, soapmaking, etc.

HAZEL-NUT OIL.

(Hazelnussöl ; huile de noisettes.)

Raw material.—Hazel-nuts, the fruit of Corylus avellana, which contain 40 to 60 per cent. of oil.

Preparation of the oil.—By warm or cold pressing the crushed fruit.

Properties.—Hazel-nut oil is pale yellow, clear, inodorous and of mild agreeable flavour. The specific gravity at 15° C. is 0·928 ; the oil is somewhat thick, being at that temperature 18·14 times, at 7·5° C. 34·2 times, thicker than water ; sets at −17° to −18° C., and contains, in addition to olein, the glycerides of stearic acid, palmitic acid and (very little) arachic acid. Like almond oil it very easily becomes rancid. When exposed to the action of nitric acid, containing a little nitrous acid, it loses its colour at first, afterwards assuming a greenish tinge. Treated with somewhat diluted fuming nitric acid a characteristic evanescent blue coloration occurs, and the mixture sets, after standing for two or three hours,

9

to a yellow mass. Sulphuric acid produces a pale bluish-green tinge, quickly passing into grey, and a mixture of equal parts of sulphuric and nitric acids colours the oil a dirty pale brown. Chloride of zinc causes a greyish-green coloration, but only after prolonged exposure to this reagent.

Uses.—For alimental purposes, when fresh and cold pressed.

Technical: as burning or machine oil, and for soap-making.

WILD-RADISH OIL (HEDGE-MUSTARD OIL).

(Hederichöl, Ackerrettigöl; huile de ravenelle.)

Raw material.—The seeds of Raphanus raphanistrum. The plant thrives so well in sandy soil that crops infested with it often present the appearance of an oil-seed field in full bloom. In 1880 a great deal of this oil was sold in Hungary as rape oil. The seeds are small, resembling those of brassica rapa, and contain 30 to 40 per cent. of oil.

Method of preparation.—Identical with that of rape oil.

Properties.—The oil is of a dark, olive-green colour, with a specific gravity of 0·917 at 15° C., thickening at 2° C. and setting at −8° C. The flavour is mild, but the after-taste irritating and the odour peculiar, recalling that of turnips. Valenta gives the following reaction as characteristic of this oil : " About five grams of the oil under examination are partially saponified with caustic potash and alcohol, assisted by warmth, the soap being thereupon separated by filtration from the unsaponified, golden yellow, almost inodorous and tasteless oil. When wild-radish oil is present in large amount the concentrated filtrate will become decidedly green on the addition of sufficient hydrochloric acid to produce a strongly acid reaction."

Uses.—For technical purposes : same as rape oil.

MILLET-SEED OIL.

(Hirseöl.)

Raw material.—The waste matter resulting when shelled millet seed is polished, containing 18 to 20 per cent. of oil.

Preparation.—Most suitably by extraction.

Properties.—The oil is pale yellow, with a faint, agreeable smell, but produces irritation in the throat soon after it has been swallowed. It dissolves in alcohol in the same way as ricinus oil, and contains a fatty acid (oxyhirseolic acid) isomeric with ricinostearolic acid. This forms at the ordinary temperature a non-setting oil of pale yellow colour and faint odour. By long exposure to air it is bleached, becomes colourless and forms a thick viscid mass with a rancid smell. In alcohol, ether, chloroform, petroleum spirit and benzol it dissolves with facility, and yields, on treatment with alkalis, very soft, soapy compounds, which lather when agitated in a state of aqueous solution, and produce a flocculent precipitate on the addition of salts of magnesia. Hirseolic acid gives no stable compound when treated with nitrous acid (elaidin test).

When millet oil is stored, a crystalline substance, "panicol," is deposited. It melts at 285° C., and when subjected to the action of oxidising agents, yields an acid closely related to gallic acid, but has not yet been thoroughly examined.

CAMELINA (GOLD OF PLEASURE, OR GERMAN SESAME) OIL.

(Leindotteröl, dotteröl, deutsches sesamöl, rapsdotteröl; huile de cameline, huile de sesame d'Allemagne, huile de (camomile corruption).)

Raw material.—The seeds of Myagrum sativa (Camelina sativa), and occasionally of Myagrum dentatum. The small, longish quadrilateral seeds, golden yellow or sometimes red-

brown in colour, contain 25 to 30 per cent. of oil, 18 to 20
of which can be obtained by cold pressing, 23 to 25 per cent.
being obtainable by warm pressing, and up to 28 per cent.
by extraction.

They contain :—

	Seeds. Per cent.	Per cent.	Cake. Per cent.	Per cent.
Organic matter . .	56 to 58		73·13	
Containing protein		25·30		31·40
Ash	6·42		8·85	
Water	7·50		11·15	
Oil	29·50		6·97	
	100·00		100·00	

Preparation.—By ordinary pressure or extraction methods.

Properties.—The cold-pressed oil is somewhat paler than
that obtained by warm pressing; both are golden yellow in
colour, and have a characteristic pungent odour and taste,
the latter being at first bitter, but losing this when stored.
Specific gravity at 15° C., 0·9288.   At this temperature the oil
is 13·1 times, at 7·5° C. 18·3 times, thicker than water; and
at −18° to −19° C. it sets to a soft butter.   Alcohol takes up
rather more than 1 per cent. of the oil.   The oil dries slowly
in the air, and the varnish, prepared by boiling with litharge
or borate of manganese, also dries but slowly.   When
saponified the oil yields a soft soap and is highly suitable
for making this class of soap, particularly in winter time.   If
prepared with a little care it burns without smoke and
with a bright flame.   It consists of glycerides of oleic and
palmitic acids, with a little erucic acid and one of the acids
allied to linolic acid, and has the following elementary
composition :—

Carbon . .	77·12 per cent.
Hydrogen .	11·95 ,,
Oxygen . .	10·93 ,,
	100·00

As a cruciferous oil it answers to the sulphur test. Nitric acid, containing a little nitrous acid, colours both the crude and refined oil brick-red, and fuming nitric acid gives a dirty brown-red coloration. When sulphuric acid is added by drops it colours the oil yellow, exhibiting bluish veins; subsequently the colour changes to orange, and finally a brownish-grey mixture is formed. Sulphuric acid thickens the oil, and a mixture of this acid and nitric acid produces a brownish-red coloration, chloride of zinc causing a greenish tint, whilst nitrate of silver is blackened.

Uses.—Technical: as burning oil and for soapmaking; also, though accidentally, as an adulterant in linseed oil.

LINDEN-WOOD OIL (LIME OIL).
(Lindenholzöl.)

There is no literature on the subject of this oil, but J. G. Wiechmann reports as follows:—

Two samples of linden wood (Tilia Americana), both from the same district (Saginaw, Michigan), came under examination. Both were in the condition of boards, ½ inch thick and 10 inches wide. Sample I. was a sound wood; Sample II. was spotted and manifested an extremely pungent, disagreeable odour, similar to rancid butter. This latter wood had been lying in water for a long time, and had thereby suffered partial decomposition accompanied by the formation of volatile fatty acids. Both specimens were rasped to prepare samples for analysis, and in the course of this treatment the sound wood in No. II. was separated from the decayed portions. Seventy grams of each were treated with pure ether for two hours in a Soxhlet extractor, the ether afterwards distilled off, and the constants of the oils determined, with the following results:—

	Sample I.	Sample II.
Yield of oil in percentages of original wood .	5·23	4·68
Specific gravity at 15° C.	0·938	—
Setting point	10° C.	5° C.
Saponification equivalent	315	—*
Iodine number	111	60
Colour	olive brown	dark brown
Heydenreich reaction	yellow and red brown	yellow and red brown

In the opinion of the author linden-wood oil resembles cotton-seed oil, the constants being similar. Wiechmann considers the high saponification equivalent, as compared with cotton-seed oil, to be due to the presence of resin introduced into the oil during the process of extraction. Finally, an attempt was made to elucidate the nature of the decomposition products in the oil from No. II., whereby Wiechmann came to the subjoined conclusions, *viz.*, that the oil is a glyceride which, most probably as the result of the presence of mucilaginous and albuminoid substances, has undergone partial decomposition. The isolation and examination of the volatile fatty acids showed them to consist of butyric acid and allied compounds.

CHERRY-KERNEL OIL.
(Kirschkernöl.)

Raw material.—Cherry kernels, the seeds of the well-known cherry tree, Prunus cerasus L.

Preparation.—The seed shells are broken and the hard portions removed, the inner kernel being ground and pressed. In Württemberg and the valleys of the Alps the cold-pressed oil is used for alimental purposes, and that from the warm pressing for burning and soapmaking. The seeds contain 25 to 30 per cent. of oil.

Properties.—The oil is golden yellow in colour and of

---

* Could not be determined, the value fluctuating from 152 to 77 in the space of a few hours.

mild pleasant flavour. Specific gravity at 15° C., 0·9184. It thickens at 0° C., becomes cloudy at −16° C., and sets at −19° to −20° C. The fresh oil has an odour of almonds, but quickly loses this and becomes rancid.

Uses.—Medicinal : same as almond oil.

Alimental : the freshly pressed oil is used for cooking, and the same purposes as olive oil.

Technical : as illuminating oil and for soapmaking.

MAIZE (INDIAN CORN) OIL.

(Maisöl ; huile de Maïs.)

Raw material.—The seed of Zea mais, an American grain, also completely acclimatised in Europe. There are numerous varieties, yielding yellow, white, brownish-red, vitreous translucent seeds, which are round or flattened in shape and arranged tightly in rows around a central cone (cob). Their constitution is as follows :—

	Yellow Maize. Per cent.		White Maize. Per cent.	
Organic matter	82·93		80·76	
Containing starch . .		61·95		62·23
„ albuminoids . .		10·71		9·62
Ash	1·32		1·04	
Water	9·50		10·60	
Fatty oil	6·25		7·60	
	100·00		100·00	

Preparation.—Maize oil is not obtained direct by pressing, but as a bye-product, its presence in the grain hindering the technical employment of the latter for breadmaking and in the fermentation of the mash. The oil constitutes, in the comparatively large germ, about 0·01 of the weight of the grain, and is the cause of the peculiar solidity of the bread made from pure maize ; its presence also renders the use of polenta as a food stuff possible without any further addition of fat, and is likewise the cause of the oily layer floating on the "goods" in the mash-tun. The germ contains nearly the whole of the oil in the seed, and in order to make the grain suitable for mashing—it being well adapted for distillery purposes on account of its high content of starch—it is malted and crushed, and degerminised by sifting or riddling. Thanks to the specific lightness of the germ the separation is complete, and 75 per cent. of crushed maize, entirely free from oil, is thus obtained, which is much better suited for breadmaking than the whole meal. The germs are pressed in the usual manner and yield 15 per cent. of pure oil, the residual cake forming a valuable cattle food.

Maize oil cake contains:—

		Per cent.	
Oil	. . . .	4·35	
Organic matter	. . . .	78·85	
Containing albumen	. . .		18·54
Ash	. . . . . .	6·25	
Water	. . . . . .	10·55	
		100·00	

The entire seed yielded only 11 per cent. when extracted with ether, but the carefully cleaned germs gave 22 per cent. of oil.

Properties.—Maize oil is pale to golden yellow in colour; possesses a characteristic agreeable taste and smell; is fairly thick, and has a specific gravity at 15° C. of 0·916. It consists of olein, stearin and palmitin, contains a little volatile oil, and sets at $-10°$ C. to a solid white mass. The percentage of free fatty acids is 0·88, and the total amount of fatty acids 96·87 per cent. associated with unsaponifiable mucilaginous and albuminoid matter, together equal to 1·3 per cent.

The olein content varies between that of olive and cotton-seed oils. The oil resembles freshly ground grain in flavour. If spread out in a very thin layer on paper and exposed to the air, no skin is noticeable at the end of three weeks. At 15° C. it is 19·2 times, at 7·5° C. 25·8 times, thicker than water.

Nitric acid colours maize oil only slightly reddish yellow, the fuming acid producing a dark brown coloration after a time; the oil is thereby caused to set to a yellow soft mass in twenty-four to thirty-five hours. Sulphuric acid causes a highly characteristic dark green coloration, lasting for a few minutes. The colour change effected by mixed sulphuric and nitric acids is merely a reddish-yellow tinge. Caustic soda and potash quickly produce a white soap, whilst ammonia gives a fluid, creamy emulsion. The primary action of zinc chloride is to change the colour to dark yellow, which passes into yellowish green on standing.

When mixed with sulphuric acid (thermal test), the temperature of the oil rises 50° C.

Saponification value: 188 to 189.

Saponification value of the fatty acids: 198.

Iodine number: oil, 119, 119·9; fatty acids, 125.

ALMOND OIL.

(Mandelöl; huile d'amandes.)

Raw material.—Sweet and bitter almonds from the fruit of the almond tree (Amygdalus communis L.). The fruit is enveloped by a tough, parchment-like pericarp, the outside of which is felted, and which, when ripe, splits open along the one side, allowing the stone to drop out. The latter consists of two sclerenchymatous layers, separated by a network of vascular bundles, and the almonds are differentiated into thick- and thin-shelled kinds according to the thickness and density of the envelope, the latter kind being known as soft almonds. The interior tissue of the shell is always dense and glossy. In arrangement the fruit of the almond is double-seeded, but usually only one seed develops, and this is of bi-convex, flattened, and pointed oval form. When there are two seeds developed in the same shell they are both plano-convex and much more flattened than is the case with the single almonds. The almond seed is without albumen, consisting merely of two lobes, radicle, and integument. Bitter almonds contain amygdalin and emulsin, these bodies being, according to Thomé's researches, separated (*i.e.*, in different cells), the amygdalin in those of the parenchyma, whilst the emulsin is located in the soft vascular elements—a circumstance to which is due, according to the above-named investigator, the phenomenon that bitter almonds, when the tissues are broken in the process of comminution, evolve first hydrocyanic acid and then oil of bitter almonds. The sweet almonds—undistinguishable externally from the others—taste sweet, oily and mucilaginous ; the bitter variety having a strongly bitter flavour, and, when broken, the characteristic odour of bitter-almond oil. Sweet almonds contain over 50 per cent. of fatty oil, 6 per cent. of grape sugar, 3 per cent. of gum, 24 per cent. of albuminoid bodies with cellulose, a little acetic acid and colouring matters. In bitter almonds there also occur, as mentioned above, amygdalin and emulsin, but the proportion of oil is lower, falling to about 30 per cent. The amygdalin, of which some 8·5 to 9 per cent. is apparently present, is a neutral, rather bitter, crystalline body, exhibiting the composition $C_{20}H_{27}N_{18}$, soluble in water and alcohol, but insoluble in ether. The emulsin (synaptase), discovered by Liebig and Wöhler, is an amorphous, nitrogenous body, soluble in water, but insoluble in alcohol. When brought into contact with amygdalin and water the former is split up into oil of bitter almonds and hydrocyanic acid.

Preparation of the oil.—The inferior varieties of almonds, coming in large quantities from Northern Africa (Morocco, Tripoli, Algiers), are alone used. The oil is prepared from both sweet and bitter almonds, the former yielding on an average about 45 per cent., and the latter 36 per cent. The residual cake from bitter almonds is utilised for the preparation of the oil of bitter almonds.

As a preliminary step to the preparation of oil, the whole or shelled almonds are ground, and then pressed in the usual manner.

Properties.—Specific gravity at 15° C.: 0·917 to 0·920 (Chateau, Allen), 0·9186 (Valenta); at 12° C.: from bitter and sweet almonds, 0·9154 (Mills and Akitt).

Behaviour on cooling: becomes cloudy and milky at − 20° C. and sets at − 25° C.

Melting point of the fatty acids: 14° C.; setting point: 5° (Hübl).

Hehner number: 96·2 (West-Knight).

Saponification value: 195·4 (Valenta), 187·9 (Moore).

Iodine number: 90·4 (Hübl).

Adulterants: Almond oil is mainly adulterated with poppy oil, sesame, nut, peach and apricot kernel oils. According to Schaedler these may be detected by the flavour.

Additions of poppy, nut or sesame oil increase the specific gravity.

A special characteristic of almond oil is the low melting and setting point of the fatty acids. Nut oil and poppy oil raise the iodine number considerably; sesame oil to a smaller extent.

Bieber, who asserts that most of the almond oil of commerce is peach-kernel oil, detects the usual adulterants by means of a mixture of equal parts by weight of concentrated sulphuric acid, fuming nitric acid and water, one part of this reagent being mixed with five of oil.

Pure almond oil gives a yellowish white liniment, turning later to a reddish tint.

Peach-kernel oil becomes at once a peach-blossom colour, then dark orange.

Sesame oil turns pale yellowish red, and then a dirty orange red.

Poppy and nut oils make a somewhat whiter liniment than almond oil. According to Haag, Bieber's statement requires correction, in that fresh nut oil gives an orange yellow liniment instead of white. By means of this reaction the presence of 5 per cent. of peach oil or sesame oil should be detectable. In order to distinguish between them, nitric acid of 1·40 specific gravity is added, whereby almond oil produces a pale yellow liniment, peach oil a red, and sesame oil a dirty greenish yellow mixture, turning to red. Poppy and nut oils give a white liniment.

According to the Pharm. germanica II. pure almond oil— when well shaken up with a mixture of two parts water and three of fuming nitric acid, in the proportion of five parts of oil to one of acid—should give a white mixture (never brown or red), which separates in a few seconds into a stiff white mass and a colourless liquid. Kremel confirms the immediate detection by this test of sesame, arachis, olive kernel and apricot oils through the yellow (orange) coloration they produce. He furthermore found that the oil from bitter almonds took much longer to set than that from the sweet variety.

Uses.—Medicinal and cosmetic.

NIGER SEED (NIAM) OIL.
(Nigeröl; huile de Niam.)

Raw material.—Niger seed, from Guizotia oleifera, an Abyssinian oil plant, cultivated on a large scale in Abyssinia and India, especially in Mysore; also to some extent in Germany and the West Indies. The seeds, or more correctly fruit, are black, lustrous and cylindrical, terminating in a bent apex, of rounded periphery with one side somewhat flattened. They are about ⅛ to ¼ inch long

and $\frac{1}{12}$ to $\frac{1}{8}$ inch diameter in the widest part; the shell is thin and like pasteboard, and constitutes about one-fifth of the weight of the entire fruit. The kernels contain 40 to 50 per cent. of oil.

Preparation.—By grinding the seed, and hot or cold pressure. In the latter case the yield of oil is 25 to 30 per cent., 12 to 15 per cent. being afterwards obtained by warming and re-pressing the cake.

Properties.—Colour yellow, resembling Provence (olive) oil, with a peculiar nutty taste and smell. The specific gravity is 0·9263 at 12° C., 0·9242 at 15° C. and 0·924 at 20° C. At 7·5° C. the oil is 22·5 times, at 15° C. 16 times, more viscous than water. It thickens at 8° C., and forms at 10° C. a translucent solid white mass; dissolves in ether in the proportion of two parts ether to five parts oil, and in alcohol in the proportion of two parts alcohol to ten of oil.

The drying properties are very slight, merely a tough sticky mass being formed on exposure in very thin layers to air, and the varnish obtained by boiling with lead oxides is poor. (According to one (English) source the oil is "frequently" used as a substitute for linseed oil.) Niger oil is composed of glycerides of oleic, palmitic and myristic acids, and of a glyceride of an acid belonging to the linseed-oil group.

Nitric acid colours the oil golden yellow; fuming nitric acid first reddish yellow, turning later into brown red, the oil thereupon congealing. Sulphuric acid (specific gravity, 1·7) gives a greyish green; stronger acid a greenish colour, developing into brown. Nitric and sulphuric acids, mixed in equal volumes, colour the oil a dirty brownish yellow at first, which darkens progressively until, after a quarter to half an hour, it has become a dirty blackish brown, ultimately passing, after several hours, into red brown, this reaction being characteristic. Nitrate of silver is only reduced to a small extent; caustic potash or ammonia gives a white liniment, and soda produces a hard soap.

Uses.—Alimental: in India the oil is used as food by the poorer classes.

Technical: as burning oil, also as a lubricant and for soapmaking.

OLIVE OIL (SALAD OR SWEET OIL).
(Olivenöl; huile d'olives.)

Raw material.—Olives, the fruit of Olea europaea L.

The true home of the olive tree has never been definitely ascertained, but it is known that it grows wild in Western Asia. However, olive trees, regarded as wild, have been discovered growing in Europe far away from any olive plantations, this being particularly the case in Andalusia and Greece. Owing to the impossibility of determining from the appearance of the trees themselves whether they are wild or have degenerated, the difficulty of a direct solution of the question of origin is increased in proportion with the antiquity and extent of their culture. Grisebach insists, and with reason, that the protracted development of the olive tree points to an origin in countries where the winter is short and mild and the dry season long, and finds these conditions best fulfilled in the regions occupied by the olive in Syria and the sandy coast of Anatolia, considering therefrom that the true home of this important plant is to be looked for in those districts. The olive is cultivated in the Mediterranean countries, Spain, Portugal, Southern France, Italy, Istria, Dalmatia, Greece and the coast of Morocco, as well as in the Crimea and Palestine. Olive plantations have also existed in America for several centuries, particularly in Peru, where extensive olive groves are found, even in the sterile lands in the regions near the coast, and also in many districts of Mexico.

Two chief varieties of the olive tree are distinguished, the wild thorny kind (Olea europaea var. sylvestris L. = Olea Oleaster Link et Hoffmnsg.), and the cultivated thornless olive (Olea europaea culta L. = Olea sativa Link et Hoffmnsg.). The latter alone yields olives suitable for oil pressing. No less than forty-three sub-varieties of this kind are known, differing not merely in habitat and in the form of the leaves and blossoms, but also in the size and chemical characteristics of the fruit. The most widely cultivated varieties are Olea eur. var. pignola, grown already in former centuries in Genoa and Provence, and yielding the best oil; and the Olea eur. var. hispanica, chiefly grown in Spain, yielding a fruit of somewhat disagreeable odour, but producing the greatest quantity of oil of any variety known.

The olive, when fully ripe, is dark violet to black in colour and 1 to $1\frac{3}{4}$ inch in length; the oily kernel is embedded in the fruit, the flesh of which is soft when ripe, the parenchyma cells being filled with a watery fluid containing in suspension drops of oil (bubbles according to Herz) and fine granules, sometimes agglomerated but individually small. The fruit substance is enclosed in a skin consisting of strongly walled cells filled with violet colouring matter.

In order that a good edible oil may be obtained, the olives should be gathered in December, when the fruit is fully ripe; very often, however, they are gathered before ripening has commenced. The oil from ripe olives is yellow and sweet, unripe fruit yields a greenish, mostly rather bitter oil, whilst if the fruit be over-ripe or stored when ripe, the oil will be yellow to colourless, with an acid flavour, and is frequently malodorous.

The olives intended for the finest alimental oil are picked by hand, a method pursued, for example, at Aix and Grasse in Provence.

Where technical or burning oil is to be produced, the fruit is dislodged by shaking the tree or beating with poles.

Preparation.—The oil is obtained by pressing the fruit, from which the kernels have been removed. Inferior qualities are also prepared by pressing the kernels, by a warm second pressing of the fruit, or by throwing the latter into heaps to ferment and then applying pressure. When the kernels are pressed separately they yield olive kernel oil. By treating the press residues with hot water, a further quantity of oil can be obtained, the fruit not being even then exhausted but still capable of yielding oil. For this purpose the residue is stored in deep cisterns, half full of water, and known in France as " enfer," wherein after some months an oil of low quality, but good enough for factory purposes, collects on the surface of the water, accompanied by a very offensive smell. On this account the oil is called in France "huile d'enfer".

A number of varieties of olive oils are met with in commerce, their quality depending on various circumstances, such as the different composition and stage of ripeness of the olives, the mode of gathering, extent of pressing, etc., etc. Fully one-fifth of the olive oil obtained in Italy comes from Sicily, the climate and situation of the island being highly favourable for the cultivation of the olive tree, whilst the natives incline to agriculture and fruit growing exclusively, industrious habits being rare among them.

The olive grows equally well on the hill sides and in the valleys, the fruit from the latter being, however, considered to yield more oil and of better quality than that from the uplands, although it may happen that at higher altitudes fruit of good quality and yield may be grown, provided the trees are well manured and exposed to the sun. The chief in-gathering takes place between the end of September and the end of November, but may occasionally extend up to January. The fruit must be purple red and fully ripe, and the sooner it is crushed after gathering, the paler and clearer will be the resulting oil.

The buildings wherein olive oil is prepared are, like our simplest agricultural steadings, only one storey high and rest on the bare ground, so that there is neither cellar nor attic provided. The fruit is crushed in one room and pressed in the other, there being occasionally a third, serving as a provisional store for the pressed residue. In the first room is a platform about 40 inches high and 10 feet long, built of strong masonry, the upper surface as far as the centre being hollowed, with slightly sloping sides. At the centre a strong vertical wooden axis is erected, to which is affixed, at right angles to the platform, a millstone some 12 inches broad and weighing about 16 cwts.

A strong yoke beam projects from the shaft beyond the edge of the platform, and by this means the millstone is slowly moved around by the aid of a donkey or ox. The freshly gathered olives are emptied into the mill trough and crushed to pulp by the revolving stone, one attendant being constantly engaged at the mill in turning the mass over with the shovel. In this manner about two cwts. can be crushed in half an hour ready for pressing.

The thick pulp of crushed fruit is put into soft flat rush baskets, having only one small aperture in the top, and these are arranged in layers one above another, up to 15, in the press, mouth upwards. Wooden boards are then laid across the pile, and across them comes the strong cross beam of the press, kept in place by guides. To the centre of the cross beam is fixed a strong wooden screw, worked by six to eight men by a lever, at first slowly, then more quickly, and finally screwed home. The oil flows readily and runs through a shoot into a hogshead below, filled to four-fifths of its capacity with water, so that, as the oil runs in, the heavy impurities may be deposited, and the soluble matters taken up by the water, leaving the oil to collect on the surface.

When the press bags have been in the press for five

10

minutes their contents are again passed through the mill, a fresh batch being pressed in the interval. After repeating the operation three times the press residue is piled up to a height of 15 to 16 inches in a dark room, and left for three days, at the end of which time the mass will have become strongly heated, and is then ground and pressed for the fourth and last time. The final residue, amounting to about 70 per cent. of the original fruit, was formerly

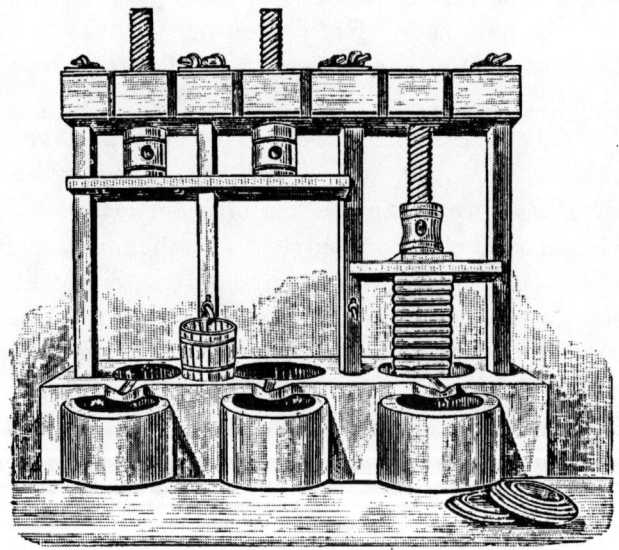

Fig. 72. Olive Oil Press from the Rizza District.

disposed of to the bakers for heating their ovens; nowadays it is sold for the most part to the large oil works, where it is worked over for the fifth time.

Generally about half the total yield comes out in the first pressing, the remaining portion being pretty evenly divided among the three following operations. The perfectly fresh oil is green and cloudy. As soon as a barrel is full, the layer of oil is carefully measured and filled into pipes of turned sheep- or goatskin, for transport to the clarifying and storage room. The most suitable temperature for clarifying the oil is about 15° R. (66° F.), the alternations of day and night exerting no influence on the quality. The oil is emptied from the skins into large earthenware pots, and allowed to remain therein for a week at the temperature mentioned. By the end of the fifth or sixth day the whole of the fine dust-like impurities will be found to have settled down, leaving the oil clear and ready to be transferred into other

FIG. 73. Olive Crusher from the Rizza District.

vessels kept at hand. The oil is then fit for sale, and, as the demand is generally brisk, there is little need of large storage rooms at the oil works.

The Sicilians clean their oil jars with water and vinegar, rubbing them quite dry before use.

Of late years a few oil works have been fitted up with steam power, but the greater part of the Sicilian olive oil is pressed as described above.

The chief difficulty in the preparation of this oil is

occasioned by the association of a hard woody kernel with soft watery pulp in the fruit, a difficulty accentuated by the unsuitability of the olive to bear storage or transport to a distance.   The result is that the olive oil industry is necessarily impressed with the marks of all industries conducted on the small scale, *viz.*, the employment of low mechanical power, and variations in the quality of the produce in successive operations, whereby the retention of a large proportion of oil in the press residue is almost inevitable.

The finest grades of oil :—

Virgin oil (huile de vierge), Provence oil or Aix oil are employed for alimental purposes, the inferior qualities serving for illumination, as lubricants, and for soapmaking. Sundry oils from the press residues are known as "after pressings," "huile d'enfer," Sottochiari, etc.

Tournant oil (Turkey-red oil) is a product obtained from fermented olives, and contains much free acid, on which account it has the property of forming an extremely perfect emulsion when agitated with soda solution. Olive oil is colourless to golden yellow in shade, or occasionally green from the presence of chlorophyll.   The flavour is mild and agreeable.

Properties.—Specific gravity at 15° C.: best oil, 0·9178; Galipoli, 0·9196 (Clarke), 0·914 to 0·917 (Allen) ; virgin oil, 0·9163 ; ordinary, 0·9160 (Paris Laboratory). At 18° C. : yellow green oil, 0·9144 ; pale, 0·9163 ; dark, 0·9199 (Stilurell). At 23° C. : 0·912 to 0·914 (Dietrich).   At 12° C. : 0·9192.   At 15° C. : 0·9177.   At 25° C. : 0·9109.   At 50° C. : 0·8932.   At 94° C. : 0·8625 (Saussure).

Specific gravity of the fatty acids at 103° C. : 0·8429, 0·8444 (Archbutt).

Setting point : the oil begins to cloud at 2° C., depositing 28 per cent. of stearin at − 6° C. (Chateau).

Melting point of the fatty acids: 23·98° to 24·44° C. (Allen), 22° C. (Paris Laboratory).   Fluidity commences at

23° to 24° C. and is complete at 26° to 28° C. (Bensemann). Melting point, 26° C. ; setting point, 21·2° C. (Hübl). Melting point, 26·5° to 28·5° C. ; setting point, not below 22° C. (Bach).

Saponification value : 191·8 (Köttstorfer), 191·7 (Valenta), 191-196 (Allen), 185·2 (Moore).

Hehner number : 95·93 (West-Knight).

Reichert number : 0·3 (Medicus and Scheerer).

Iodine number : 82 (Hübl), 83 (Moore).

Iodine number of the fatty acids : 86·1 (Morawski and Demski).

Olive oil contains 28 per cent. of solid glycerides (palmitin, stearin, and a little arachin), and 72 per cent. of olein ; cholesterin has also been detected.

Many methods of adulterating olive oil are practised, cotton-seed oil, sesame oil and ground-nut oil being used in the alimental oils, and hemp oil, linseed oil, rape oil and mineral oils for technical purposes.

According to Deite, cotton-seed oil is extensively used as an adulterant, and is, moreover, extremely difficult of detection. Rödiger proposes to test for it by saponifying the oil under examination with caustic soda and extracting the dried soap with benzine ; when cotton-seed oil is present golden yellow drops of oil are left on evaporating the extract, that oil containing a small proportion of unsaponifiable oil. This test cannot, however, be relied on if the cotton-seed oil has been well refined, since the oil then contains but little or none of the unsaponifiable oil referred to.

Buckheister proceeds by adding to 10 grammes of the suspected oil 3 grammes of a thoroughly cooled mixture of equal parts of ordinary nitric and sulphuric acids, and well shaking up the mixture. Pure olive oil gives under this test a white liquid with a tinge of yellow ; sesame oil, a grass green ; cotton-seed oil, a somewhat lighter shade. When the two liquids are separated the pure oil is found almost entirely unchanged, whereas cotton-seed oil has become clear brown, and rape oil is more red brown but less deeply coloured. By this means 10 per cent. of cotton-seed oil in olive oil is detectable.   Zechill mixes 5 cc. of the oil under examination with 10 cc. of pure hydrochloric acid of 1·4 specific gravity, agitates and leaves the mixture at rest for five or six minutes ; pure olive oil assumes a faint greenish-brown colour with yellowish reflection ; pure cotton-seed oil, on the other hand, becoming a deep coffee brown, almost black ; whilst a mixture of both exhibits a greenish coloration.   In making comparative experiments by this method it is important to maintain identical conditions throughout, and to make the colour observations at the same regular intervals, since the colour continually deepens.

Schaedler considers that the melting point of the fatty acids forms the most reliable method of detecting adulteration.

According to Bacn the fatty acids of olive oils of different origin melt at 26·5° to 28·5° C., with a setting point of not less than 22° C.   The oils employed in the adulteration of olive oil differ considerably in this respect, the melting and setting points of cotton-seed oil, ground-nut oil and sesame oil being much higher, and those of ricinus oil, rape oil and sunflower oil considerably lower than the fatty acids of olive oil.   For example, the fatty acids of a mixture of :—

		Melting Point.	Setting Point.
Galipoli olive oil + 20 per cent. of sunflower oil .		24·6°	18° C.
Rizza ,, + 20 ,, cotton-seed oil .		31·5°	28° C.
Galipoli ,, + 33 ,, rape oil . .		23·5°	26·5° C.
,, ,, + 50 ,, ,, . .		20·3°	13·5° C.

B. Nickels recommends for the detection of cotton-seed oil in olive oil the determination of the absorption bands by the aid of a small spectroscope.   It should, however, be first ascertained whether the method of preparation and age of the oil have any influence on its optical properties.

Before the introduction of cotton-seed oil, sesame constituted the chief adulterant of olive oil, in fact the greater part
of the edible olive oil sold consisted solely of sesame. This
oil can be detected, according to Baudoin, by agitating 2
grammes of the oil to be tested with 1 gramme of 22° Bé. hydrochloric acid, containing 0·05 to 0·1 gramme of sugar, thoroughly
for a few minutes, and then leaving to subside. The acid
separates out and gradually assumes a rose tinge, the inten-
sity being proportionate to the amount of sesame oil present;
if this exceeds 10 per cent. the oil also assumes the same
coloration.

Poppy oil can be readily detected by the increase in
temperature resulting on the addition of sulphuric acid to
the oil. In the case of pure oil the introduction and mixture
of 10 cc. of sulphuric acid (66° B.) into 50 grammes of the oil
causes a rise in temperature of some 42° C. in three to five
minutes, whereas with poppy oil, under the same conditions,
the temperature rises 86·4° C. Echling's observations tend to
show that this rise in temperature in mixtures of olive and
poppy oils is in exact relation to the amount of poppy oil
present.

For instance :—

10 per cent.		40·5° C.
20 „	of poppy oil gives an average	44·0° C.
50 „	increase of	58·0° C.
80 „		64·0° C.

Curcas oil is revealed by the red-brown coloration manifested during the elaidin test, and ricinus and olive kernel
oils can be extracted by alcohol.

Arachis oil can be detected, according to Souchère, by the
formation of arachic acid crystals ensuing when the solution
of the fatty acids in boiling alcohol is cooled down, the
crystals having a nacreous lustre. If the amount of ground-
nut oil is large, it can be detected without difficulty by the

characteristic flavour of beans possessed by this oil; and furthermore, by the fact that when the temperature descends to 8° C. sandy granules separate out, whereas with pure oil separation only begins at 4° C.

Rape oil may be known by its iodine number, the melting and setting points of the fatty acids, solubility of the same, and by the low saponification value.

Olive, arachis, poppy, and sesame oils are best stored in open lead-lined iron tanks, in rooms from which dust is carefully excluded, and should be sheltered from the sun, the most suitable storage temperature being between 12° and 18° C.

The edible oils from the first cold pressing of ground nuts and sesame should, in particular, not be offered for sale until they have been kept in the above manner for a few weeks. The temporary specific odour manifested by these oils when fresh from the press, and which, when too powerful, is disliked, both in these oils and olive oil for alimental purposes, gradually vanishes as a result of the exposure of a large surface to the air, so that olive and arachis oils become almost equally inodorous. It is found that, during this storage, a slight separation of free fatty acids (up to about 1 per cent.) occurs, causing a faint rancidity, without, however, spoiling the fine flavour of the oil. The storage of fine edible oils in large quantities in closed vessels should be avoided, as kept in this way they evolve a too powerful specific odour. It is much better to leave the storage vessels quite open, as mentioned above, or else to merely cover them with gauze.

Uses of the oil.——Medicinal and cosmetic.

For alimental purposes: for salads, baking and cooking, preserving fish, etc.

Technical: as lubricating oil, either alone or in conjunction with other oils. Also for soapmaking, the manufacture of Turkey-red oil, etc.

TURKEY-RED OIL.

This designation is applied to two entirely distinct oils, employed in alizarin dyeing.

The one, also known as Tournant oil, is a fermented olive oil, and is also prepared from Galipoli oil. It is made from semi-ripe olives, which, for a short time before pressing, have been exposed to the action of water, the oil thereby acquiring a considerable proportion of extractive matter and quickly turning rancid. With solutions of alkali carbonates, it forms an emulsion which exerts a softening action on tissues, and facilitates the absorption of aluminium mordants. The second product, now in general use under the name of Turkey-red oil in alizarin dyeing, is obtained from the reaction of concentrated sulphuric acid on ricinus oil, a process formulated by Müller-Jacobs in 1879.

The treatment consists in running into the oil, slowly and with continued stirring, 20 per cent. of 66° B. sulphuric acid, the operation being performed in a lead-lined iron vessel kept cool by means of ice water. After leaving at rest for two or three hours, the mass is thinned down with water and further diluted by stirring in a thin stream of lukewarm soda solution (2·8 kilos. of crystallised soda to each kilo. of acid used). The finished product settles out on being left overnight. Lichti employs 20 to 30 per cent. of acid in winter, and 15 to 20 per cent. in summer, without cooling the mixture; on the contrary, in winter he warms it up to room temperature.

Turkey-red oil is not always of constant composition. It forms a thick, pale yellow, syrupy liquid, with a specific gravity of 1·023, and is miscible in all proportions with water. From the action of sulphuric acid on ricinus oil result two bodies, one soluble and the other insoluble in water. According to Benedikt and Ulzer the former is an ethylsuphuric acid, ricinoleosulphuric acid, $C_{18}H_{33}O_2$, OSO_3H, the insoluble portion consisting of a mixture of free fatty acids and unsaponifiable oils. Juillard, on the other hand, considers Turkey-red oil as of more complex constitution, containing the sulphuric ester of ricinoleic acid, several poly-ricinoleic acids, and tri-ricinolein, together with the decomposition products of the same, ricinoleic acid predominating. Glycerin is not completely separated by this reaction, one moiety remaining in the oil and increasing its solubility and capacity of emulsification. When boiled with alkalis, Turkey-red oil is split up into ricinoleic acid and ricinoleosulphuric acid. On the other hand water or acid produces pentaricinoleic acid, tri-ricinoleic acid $HO.C_{17}H_{32}.CO_2.CO_2.C_{17}H_{32}CO_2HO$, and di-ricinoleic acid $HO.C_{17}H_{32}CO_2C_{17}H_{32}CO_2HCO_2$. The first stage of the reaction of sulphuric acid on ricinus oil at low temperatures is the production of tri-ricinoleosulphuric acid. Thereafter ensues saponification, in which water chiefly participates, mono-ricinoleosulphuric acid and ricinoleic acid being formed, together with poly-acids.

According to Scheurer-Kestner, the acid product of the reaction does not consist of a solution of fatty acids in sulphurised fatty acids and water, but rather of a hydrate containing ten molecules of water and one molecule of fat.

Turkey-red oil contains two constituents separable by treatment with ether. The insoluble oil is lighter than water, saponifies with difficulty, has an acid reaction, and dissolves in alkalis without decomposition. The soluble oil is heavier than water, in which it dissolves to a clear solution, and contains 8·8 per cent. of SO_3. After being salted out with Glauber salt, it contains 30 to 40 per cent. of water, a portion of which it parts with when heated to 75° C.

Another preparation, also resulting from the action of sulphuric acid on fat, has proved an efficient substitute for Turkey-red oil. Schmidt and Tönges obtained by acting on fatty acids or fats with concentrated sulphuric acid, sulphurised fatty acids or their glycerides respectively. When heated to 105°-120° C. the oxy-fatty acid glycerides, or, relatively, oxy-fatty acids, are formed, and may be converted into di-oxy-fatty acids by a second treatment with sulphuric acid and warming the resulting sulphuric ester.

ARTIFICIAL OLIVE OIL.

(Ol. Oliv. commune.)

This oil is largely used in Russia for pharmaceutical purposes; its constitution is somewhat as follows:—

Cocoanut oil	.	. 150 parts.
Ricinus oil	.	. 150 „
Rape oil .	.	. 150 „
Olive oil .	.	. 50 „
Mineral oil	.	. 500 „

Colour is imparted by means of chlorophyll (green) or palmophyll (yellow), and perfume by butyric ether which reproduces the flavour and odour of olive oil. The chief use of the preparation is, however, for burning in the small cooking and house lamps which are kept burning day and night in even the poorest Russian houses. The addition of cocoanut oil has the object of approximating the setting point to that of olive oil, in addition to which it helps the oil to burn better.

The mineral oil used has a specific gravity of 0·865 to 0·800, and should be perfectly water-white and free from acid.

BRAZIL-NUT OIL.

(Paranussöl, Jurianussöl, Juriaöl; huile de noix de Brésil, huile de Castinheiro.)

Raw material.—The nuts of Bertholetia excelsa, obtained from Brazil.

Preparation.—The nuts damaged during the process of ripening are crushed, ground and pressed.

Properties.—The oil is pale yellow in colour, without taste or smell, has a specific gravity of 0·9185 at 15° C., becomes cloudy at 2° C., and sets at −1° C. to a semi-solid white mass. It very easily becomes rancid, consists of stearin, palmitin and olein, dissolves readily in boiling alcohol and in ether, and is easily saponified. Nitric acid (containing nitrous acid) of specific gravity 1·30 does not produce any coloration of the oil, but causes it to set in about half an hour. A mixture in equal parts of nitric and sulphuric acids and water gives a brownish-yellow colour reaction. One drop of concentrated sulphuric acid colours twenty drops of the oil red, at the outset, turning to brownish red, and also thickens the oil. Chloride of zinc likewise gives a rose-red colour reaction.

Uses.—Alimental : in South America the freshly pressed oil is used as food.

Technical : as burning oil and for soapmaking.

Peach Oil.

(Pfirsichkernöl ; huile d'Amandes de la Pêche.)

Raw material.—Seed kernels of the peach tree (Prunus persica). These—when the external, hard shell, enveloped by the flesh of the fruit, is opened—are almond shaped and covered by a rough brown skin. The lobes are plano-convex and contain 32 to 35 per cent. of fatty oil. In flavour the seeds resemble bitter almonds, being very bitter, and contain emulsin and amygdalin.

Preparation.—The hard shells are broken and the kernels crushed, ground and pressed, without the assistance of water, which must be avoided. The residue is employed for the preparation of a liqueur.

Properties.—The oil is very fluid, light yellow in colour, clear, and resembles almond oil in flavour and smell ; thickens at − 9° to - 10° C. and sets at − 18° C. The specific gravity at 15° C. is 0·915, and 0·916 at 20° C. In addition to olein the oil contains a rather larger amount of stearin and palmitin. Treated with nitric acid it behaves like almond oil, but colours red at first, changing later to dirty brown. Sulphuric acid colours almond oil olive brown, but the colour reaction with peach-kernel oil is pure brown. Concentrated sulphuric or nitric acid gives at once a peach-blossom coloration.

Uses.—Medicinal and cosmetic purposes ; same as almond oil.

RADISH-SEED OIL.

(Rettigöl, Chinesisches Rettigöl ; huile de raidforts.)

Raw material.—The seeds of Raphanus sativus, pale reddish brown in colour, spheroid in shape, small, $\frac{1}{12}$ to $\frac{1}{8}$ inch in diameter, and weighing seven to eight milligrammes, with a very mild, bitter-sweet, oily taste, without smell. They contain 45 to 50 per cent. of oil.

Preparation.—Pressing or extracting the crushed seeds.

Properties.—Radish oil is greenish yellow in colour, of very mild flavour, almost inodorous, with a specific gravity of 0·7195 at 15° C., at which temperature it is 15·8 times (at 7·5° C. 22·2 times) thicker than water ; it thickens at 10° C. and solidifies at – 17·5° C. Its constituents are stearic, brassic and oleic acids, and when treated with caustic soda or potash it forms a yellowish soap. Nitric acid (containing a little nitrous acid) of specific gravity 1·20 gives no colour reaction, but fuming nitric acid causes a red coloration with green zone. Sulphuric acid of specific gravity 1·72 causes a brown coloration, persisting for a fairly long time. Zinc chloride produces no effect at first, but subsequently gives rise to a faint greenish grey tint.

Uses.—Alimental, when fresh.

Technical : as burning oil. It burns away quickly with a smoky flame. The Chinese make lamp black from this oil for " Indian ink ".

Horse-Chestnut Oil (Horse-Nut Oil).

(Rosskastanienöl; huile de marron de l'Inde, huile de fécule.)

Raw material.—The well-known fruit of the horse-chestnut tree, Aesculus hippocastanum.

Preparation.—The fruit and shell are crushed, and boiled in water containing sulphuric acid, whereby starch sugar is formed up to a certain extent, the supernatant oil being skimmed off.

Properties.—The oil is greenish brown in colour, and has a peculiar turnipy flavour, leaving a bitter after-taste in the mouth. Specific gravity, 0·927 at 15° C. Solidifying point, 1·25° C.

Uses.—Medicinal: external application for gout, rheumatism, and neuralgia.

Technical: for soapmaking and as burning oil.

(Colza Coles Seed) or Rape Oil (Rubsen Oil).

(Kohlsaatöl, Colzaöl, Rapsöl, Repsöl, Rüböl, Rübsenöl; huile de Colza, huile de Navette, huile de rabette.)

Raw material.—The seeds of Brassica napus L.; Brassica campestris D.C.; Brassica rapa L.

The rape plant, Brassica napus L., and a few allied plants yield seeds which have long been utilised for the production of oil, and at present form one of the most important raw materials for this branch of industry in Europe. The varieties of Brassica are cultivated as oil plants in almost every European country, with the exception of Greece. In France Brassica campestris is grown to a very considerable extent. The English oil crushers derive large supplies of rape seed from the East Indies, particularly from Calcutta, Madras, Bombay, Guzerat, and Ferozepore. It is not at present known from what plant the Indian rape originated.

The seeds of the Brassica appear to the naked eye as small ground grains, with a dark, almost smooth, integument, in which are visible a pale chalaza and citron yellow germ, with two well-defined cotyledons and a radicle about $\frac{1}{25}$ inch in length. It is not very easy to distinguish between the seeds of these three plants by mere superficial examination. The seeds of Brassica napus are, it is true, mostly blue black, those of Brassica campestris red brown, and those of Brassica rapa a dull brown, whilst the seeds of Brassica campestris are larger than the other two, which are usually only about $\frac{1}{12}$ inch in diameter. A more detailed examination, however, will show that, in consequence of the many variations occurring, the above indications cannot be altogether relied on.

J. Schröder endeavoured to determine the characteristic points of difference between the commercial varieties of Brassica seeds, and succeeded in differentiating the seeds of Brassica oleracea from the others morphologically, but failed to find any guide for distinguishing between the remaining three kinds, either macro- or microscopically. Wiesner agrees with Schröder, having also been unable to find any characteristic points of difference between colza, rape, and rubsen seed. One observation of Schröder's is, however, noteworthy, viz., that the seeds of these latter differ in absolute weight to such an extent as to afford a probable means of differentiation. For example :—

1000 seeds of Brassica napus (hyemalis) weigh 4·538 to 4·786 grammes ; average, 4·667 grammes.

1000 seeds of Brassica campestris weigh 1·869 to 1·917 grammes ; average, 1·901 grammes.

1000 seeds of Brassica rapa (biennis) weigh 2·055 to 2·241 grammes ; average, 2·142 grammes.

Whether this characteristic will afford the desired information will have to be ascertained by extensive weighings of as many kinds of rape, colza and rubsen seed as possible, Schröder's hypothesis being based on the examination of only one sample of each.

The integument of the seed of these three kinds can be made to exhibit its structure very clearly by mounting in oil. The exterior layer of tissue consists of polygonal flattened cells, averaging 0·0132 mm. in length. Adjoining the germ is a layer of cells formed of radially grouped yellow elements, averaging 0·046 mm. in longest diameter, and containing granular matter. The cotyledons are covered with an epithelium of delicate flattened cells adjoining the fundamental parenchymatous tissue, the outer layer of which is composed of small cells of 0·021 mm. average width and 0·070 mm. average length and arranged radially, the inner substance consisting of round thick cells about 0·05 mm. in diameter. The cells of the parenchyma are all filled with globular aleuron granules of varying diameter up to 0·0168 mm. The substance of the lobes is traversed by well-defined branched collections of vascular bundles composed of cambial cells.

Rape and rubsen seed yield 30 to 35 per cent. of oil, colza up to 40 per cent.

Preparation.—Breaking down and crushing the seeds, followed by pressing or extraction.

Properties.—Rape oil is generally brownish yellow to brown yellow, almost inodorous when fresh, and with a mild flavour, so that when cold pressed it is used for alimental purposes in many districts. When old and rancid, it has a particularly disagreeable taste and smell. The crude oil from the press contains mucilaginous and albuminoid substances which have to be removed by a process of refining. The refined oil is yellowish and of unpleasant flavour and smell.

Specific gravity at 15° C.: 0·9102 to 0·9175 (Schaedler), 0·914 to 0·917 (Allen); colza oil, 0·9142; rape oil, 0·9151 (Souchère).

Specific gravity at 18° C.: rape oil, white, 0·9144; dark yellow, 0·9168 (Stilurell); at 23° C., 0·910 (Dietrich).

Specific gravity of the fatty acids at 100° C.: colza oil, 0·864; rape oil, 0·8439 (Archbutt).

Setting point, −2° to −10° C.

Melting point of the fatty acids, 20·1° C. (Hübl), 18·33° C. (Allen); commencement of fluidity, 18° to 19° C.; completion, 21° to 22° C. (Bensemann); setting point, 12° C. (Hübl).

Hehner number: 95·1° C. (Bensemann), 95° (Diessel and Kressner).

Saponification value: 178·7 (Köttstorfer), 177 (Valenta).

Reichert number: 0·25 (Reichert), 0·3 to 0·4 (Medicus and Scheerer).

Iodine number: 100 (Hübl), 103·6 (Moore).

Iodine number of the fatty acids: 96·3 to 99·02 (Morawski and Demski).

According to Jüngst, 100 parts of alcohol dissolve 0·534 parts of rape oil. The unsaponifiable matter amounts to 1 per cent., and the low saponification value is due to the content of brassic acid. The globular masses of fat deposited by rape oil at the ordinary temperature were found by Halenke and Mösslinger to have a melting point of 38° C. and a saponification value of 161·70, the fatty acids isolated therefrom melting at 34° C. and exhibiting a saponification value of 160·05. The deposits therefore consist of the nearly pure glyceride of brassic acid. Rape oil consists of the glycerides of stearic, brassic (erucic), and an oleic acid, which, according to Websky and Darby, differs from ordinary oleic acid by not yielding sebacic acid on distillation.

Thalmann reports as follows on the various rape oils, his remarks referring, however, only to refined oil.

Colza oil. This oil, of which the seeds yield 30 per cent., is, in the fresh state, of a brownish yellow colour, almost completely tasteless and inodorous, but quickly manifests,

11

after a short exposure to air, a very disagreeable after-taste, due to incipient rancidity. The specific gravity at 15° C. is 0·9130, and the oil is one of the most viscous of the vegetable oils. It remains liquid down to nearly – 4° C., but at that temperature begins to deposit white granules, and sets at – 7·5° C. to a yellow buttery mass.

Winter rubsen oil. The seeds yield about 33 per cent. of oil of a specific gravity of 0·9128 at 15° C. and less viscous than the colza oil. As regards setting at low temperatures it is about equal to the latter, but is inferior to it for lighting purposes.

Summer rape oil has a specific gravity of 0·9139 at 15° C. and sets at a much lower temperature than the other rape oils, the deposition of granules commencing at – 8° C. and solidification ensuing at – 10° C. In colour this oil is rather darker than the others.

Winter rape oil is brownish yellow, passing into green. Specific gravity at 15° C. 0·9157, and 0·9184 at 10° C. Stearin is deposited below – 1° C. and the oil sets at – 2° to – 3° C. to a whitish yellow mass. The refined oil is pale pure yellow in colour, with a specific gravity of 0·9132. According to popular opinion rape oil is "fatter" than turnip oil, but this expression refers only to the consistency.

Cabbage oil, from Japan, has a dark brown colour and unpleasant smell. The specific gravity is 0·914; setting point, – 2° C.

"Rüll" oil is a variety of rape oil produced in Austria, olive brown in colour, with a specific gravity of 0·9248, and saponification value, 186. This oil contains sulphur and is used for adulterating rape oil.

Sometimes rape oil is falsified by means of mineral oils and resin oil. Occasionally, also, more through oversight on the part of the oil crusher than by design, linseed oil occurs therein.

The rape oils from Eastern Asia are of less importance, exhibiting scarcely any advantages over the European article. A pale variety, prepared from Brassica campestris, is employed as an edible oil as well as for burning; for moistening tobacco leaves in order to prevent their breaking in consequence of too rapid drying, and also for the manufacture of Indian ink. A darker coloured oil is prepared, in China particularly, from Brassica sinensis, and used for the same purposes.

The oil from the seeds of Camelia Japonica, the well-known ornamental plant grown in our winter gardens, resembles olive oil in colour and consistency, and is used in Japan, especially by watchmakers, on account of its property of remaining fluid in the cold. It is also mixed with Japanese wax, and is employed as a pomade, scented with almond oil or ethereal oils.

A similar oil is prepared in China in very large quantities from the seeds of Camelia oleifera. The seeds are reduced by stamping to a coarse powder, which is boiled and pressed. The oil is extremely fluid, pale, free from unpleasant taste or smell, and might, if prepared by cold pressing, probably compete with almond oil.

The closely allied Tea oil, from China, has a specific gravity of 0·917, deposits a merely insignificant sediment at 13°, and consists mainly of olein. This oil has the undoubted advantage over the olive oil of commerce of being practically free from acid.

The purity of the cruciferous oils (rape oil, radish oil) may best be decided by the aid of the saponification value, care being taken to ascertain that no mineral oil or resin oil is present. Rape oil may be detected in other oils by the sulphur test.

Additions of linseed oil, hemp oil, and poppy oil are betrayed in rape oil by the increased iodine number. This factor varies for pure rape between 97 and 105 (Hübl), the figures for refined oil being generally two or three units below that for crude oil.

Chrome may be detected by the ether reaction and by phosphoric acid.

Uses.—Rape oil is used technically as a lubricant and illuminating oil, as an adulterant of higher priced lubricating oils, and in soapmaking, etc.

MUSTARD (SEED) OIL.

(Senföl, fettes Senföl; huile de moutarde.)

Raw material.—Mustard seed (mustard grains) from Sinapis nigra L. and Sinapis alba L.

Sinapis nigra is a cruciferous plant, found all over Europe, also in Asia Minor, and cultivated in many European countries, North America and India. The seeds are met with in association with those of Sinapis alba, the latter plant being indigenous to the warmer portions of Europe. Sinapis juncea Mayer (Zarepta mustard) grows wild in Southern Asia and North-eastern Africa, and is cultivated in South-east Russia.

Black mustard is readily distinguishable from the other two varieties by its external appearance. The seeds are spherical or ellipsoid, of fairly regular dimensions, their diameter being about $\frac{1}{25}$ of an inch and the average weight one milligramme. Their colour is dark brown of various shades, and, if examined by the aid of a lens, the surface is found to be covered with warty excrescences, with here and there exfoliations of the external tissue. White mustard seed is much larger, spherical, about $\frac{1}{12}$ to $\frac{1}{10}$ inch in diameter and weighing on an average 5 milligrammes. The colour is yellow, and the surface, when highly magnified, exhibits somewhat the same conformation as the black seeds. The exfoliations are also perceptible but not so decided.

The seeds of Sinapis juncea resemble those of black mustard, but average $\frac{1}{20}$ to $\frac{1}{14}$ of an inch in diameter and 2·1 milligrammes in weight.

Mustard seed consists entirely of an integumental cover and a germ exhibiting a well-defined radicle. The skin is composed of four layers of cells, the outer being distinguished by the size of the elements and the distensive capacity of the cells walls, and the second layer by the stoutness of the walls. The outer skin is colourless, but the cells of the second and third layers contain pigmentary matter in their interior. The embryo is composed of delicate polyhedral cells containing fat globules and aggregations of albuminoid matter (aleuron) apparently impregnated with fatty oil.

An emulsion prepared from white mustard seed tastes bitter, but is inodorous, and yields no perceptible volatile oil when distilled. On the other hand the emulsion from the seeds of Sinapis nigra or Sinapis juncea has an intensely bitter flavour, a circumstance sufficient in itself to indicate a difference in the chemical composition of white, as compared with black and Zarepta mustard.

White mustard contains the thiocyanic synapin discovered by Henry and Garot and more exhaustively examined by Babo and Hirschbrunn. This body, which is soluble in water and spirits of wine, but insoluble in ether, turpentine and carbon bisulphide, is crystalline, and produces, like potassium rhodanate, a red coloration with ferric salts. There are also present, in addition to some 30 per cent. of fat, a large proportion of an albuminoid known as myrosin, a little gum, and the usual plant constituents.

The chief substances present in black and Zarepta mustard are myronate of potash, more than 30 per cent. of fatty oil, gum, and traces or small quantities of myrosin. By the action of this body on myronate of potash, the latter is split up into sugar, potassium sulphate and oil of mustard (allyl thiocyanate).   The amount of myrosin in both kinds of mustard is frequently so minute that only traces of mustard oil are found or can be formed therein.   The richness of white mustard in myrosin indicates the advisability of mixing the white and black varieties together if strong mustard is desired.

· *Preparation of the fatty oil.*—Shelling, grinding and pressing the seeds.

In England the ground shelled seed is pressed, and yields a good burning oil, and a little oil may also be obtained by pressing the shells.   In Zarepta the ground meal is also pressed to extract the fatty oil, and in India the mustard plant is chiefly cultivated for the production of oil.   Formerly the English mustard makers obtained large quantities of seed from the East Indies, but at present home-grown seed predominates, the white mustard from Cambridge and the black from Yorkshire being the best.

Properties.—Oil of white mustard is golden yellow with a pungent odour, that from black mustard being brownish yellow with mild flavour and smelling of the mustard (according to Benedikt).   According to Wiesner the fatty oil of mustard is tasteless and inodorous, and contains the following fatty acids : stearolic and erucic acids.   Darby states that the fatty oil of mustard seed contains an acid allied to ordinary oleic acid but differing therefrom.

Specific gravity at 15° C. : 0·9183 (Clarke), 0·9136 (Souchère), 0·914 to 0·920 (Allen) ; black mustard oil, 0·9170 ; white mustard oil, 0·9146 (Chateau).

Black mustard oil sets at −17·5° C., and the white at −15·26° C.

Iodine number : 96·0 (Moore).

Uses.—Alimental purposes : same as olive and other fat oils.

Technical : as burning oil.

SESAME OIL (GINGELLY OR JINJILLI OIL), BENNÉ OIL, TIL OR TEEL OIL.

(Sesamöl; huile de sésame.)

Raw material.—The seeds of Sesamum indicum L. and Sesamum orientale L. Commercial sesame is the seed of both these plants, the latter differing from the former only in the coarser dentation of the leaves and the brownish violet to black coloration of the seeds, and being regarded merely as a variety.

The plant is considered to be a native of Southern and Eastern Asia. In India, for example, and the hill districts of Java, where Sesamum indicum also grows wild, this herbaceous plant has been cultivated from time immemorial. At present both varieties of sesame are, on account of the high percentage of oil in the seed, grown in most tropical and warm countries, such as India, Asia Minor, Greece (Livadia, Bœotia, Messina), Egypt, Algiers, Zanzibar, Natal, the French West African Colonies, Brazil, West Indies, and latterly in the Southern States of North America.

The low price of the raw material and the abundance of oil in the seed cause sesame to be now ranked as one of the most important materials for the production of oil. It is chiefly pressed in France and England, but is also manipulated in Germany and Austria.

The fruit of Sesamum indicum is a rounded quadrangular capsule about $\frac{1}{5}$ of an inch long and $\frac{1}{5}$ of an inch thick, terminating in a short point, the seeds being contained therein in large number and easily liberated when ripe. The seeds themselves are yellow to brownish (Sesamum indicum) or brownish violet to blackish (Sesamum orientale) in colour, of oval form in the principal periphery, and very much flattened laterally. The average length is $\frac{1}{8}$ of an inch, width $\frac{1}{12}$ of an inch, and thickness $\frac{1}{25}$ of an inch, and the weight about 4 milligrammes. From the germ, which is situated at the pointed end and is indicated by a light-coloured protuberance, there extend towards the broad end four fine dark ridges, those on the flattened sides of the seed being more sharply defined. The thin outer integument encloses an oily kernel whereon the cotyledons and radicle are readily discernible. The integument consists of prismatic cells 0·050 to 0·070 mm. long and 0·020 mm. thick, arranged perpendicularly to the surface. Fitting closely to this is the external skin of the seed, a thin flaccid epidermis of indefinite structure. The inner skin immediately surrounding the embryo is formed of three layers of stout cells, and attains a mean thickness of 0·100 mm. Crystalline aggregations, probably consisting of potassium oxalate, occur in the cells of the outer shell. The colouring matter of the dark-seeded variety is contained in the cell membrane of the shell. The cotyledons are covered with an epithelium of cubical cells, and contain three vascular bundles embedded in delicate parenchyma. In the latter tissue occur oil and cloudy masses of albuminoid substances, and Wiesner found all the parenchyma cells of the cotyledons to be packed full of spherical granules of aleuron, 0·005 to 0·010 mm. in diameter. Flückiger found in sesame 4·5 per cent. of water, 6 (yellow) to 8 (black) per cent. of mineral matter, 8 per cent. of gum, and 22 per cent. of albuminoids, the oil amounting to 56·33 per cent. His carefully conducted chemical investigations disproved the hypothesis, frequently put forward, that sesame yields 70 to 90 per cent. of oil. Shinn proved that 48 per cent. of oil can be obtained from the seed by pressure, a very good yield, but which by careful manipulation can be increased to 50 per cent.

Preparation.—By breaking down and pressing or extracting the seeds.

Properties.—The oil is yellow, odourless and agreeably flavoured. It becomes rancid with difficulty, dries but little, and contains a small proportion of a resinous body, extractible by repeated agitation with glacial acetic acid.

Specific gravity at 15° C. : 0·9225 (Souchère), 0·923 to 0·924 (Allen); at 23° C. : 0·919 (Dietrich).

Setting point : −5° C.

Melting point of the fatty acids : 26° C.

Setting point of the fatty acids : 22·3° C. (Hübl). According to Bensemann liquefaction begins at 25°-26° C. and is complete at 29°-30° C.

Hehner number : 95·86 (Bensemann), 95·60 (Dietzell and Kressner).

Saponification index : 190°.

Saponification index of the fatty acids : 193·3 (Valenta).

Reichert number : 0·35 (Medicus and Scheerer).

Iodine number : 106 (Hübl), 102·7 (Moore).

Iodine number of the fatty acids : 108·9 to 111·4 (Morawski and Demski).

A characteristic reaction for sesame oil is that of sugar and hydrochloric acid (furfurol reaction), which gives a red coloration even when only very small proportions of the oil are present; after settling, the aqueous layer resulting from the impregnation of a small lump of sugar by hydrochloric acid and shaking the same up with twice its bulk of oil is coloured red.

Sulphuric acid of 1·72 specific gravity colours the oil at first brown, turning to green when stirred. A mixture of equal parts of concentrated sulphuric acid, nitric acid and water causes a blué-green coloration. According to Flückiger this reaction is rendered more decided by pouring five drops of oil on to five drops of the acid mixture and increasing the surface of contact by inclining the test tube, so that a green intermediate zone is formed. By the immediate addition of five drops of carbon bisulphide, and shaking the mixture, a fine green layer is formed at the top, the colour then being more persistent than is otherwise the case. The iodine number of sesame oil classifies it along with ground-nut oil and cotton-seed oil, but it differs from the latter by the low melting point of the fatty acids, by its behaviour under the Livache test, by the colour reaction with nitrous acid, etc. It may be distinguished from ground-nut oil, with which it is frequently adulterated, by the colour reactions and its much higher specific gravity. For detecting ground-nut oil in sesame the same procedure is adopted as in the case of olive oil, by isolating the arachic acid.

Uses.—Medicinal and cosmetic.

For alimental purposes.

Technical : same as olive oil, of which it forms the most predominant substitute.

SOJA-BEAN OIL.

Raw material.—Chinese oil bean, Sao, Sojabean, the fruit of Doliches Soja L. = Soja japonica, Soja hispida, indigenous to China and Japan. The seeds, which are edible and possess a piquant flavour, contain soja-bean oil, falsely designated "huile de pois," an oil also used for alimental purposes. According to Meissl and Boecker the beans contain :—

10	per cent. of	water.
30	,,	soluble casein.
18	,,	fat.
0·5	,,	albumen.
7	,,	insoluble casein.
2	,,	cholesterin, lecithin, resin, wax.
10	,,	dextrin.

According to Harz the percentage of starch depends on the stage of ripeness, decreasing as that condition progresses, the fully ripe beans containing but little.

Preparation.—Nothing is known on this head, but it is probably obtained by pressing in the ordinary way.

Properties.—There is no information available on this score.

UNGNADIA OIL.

(Ungnadiaöl ; huile d'Ungnadia.)

Raw material.—The seeds of Ungnadia, indigenous to Mexico. The fruit is a broad, flat, three-lobed, triplex, leathery capsule, with flat dehiscent valves and a decided stem. The heart-shaped valves carry the partition walls at their centres, and each segment contains a single rounded seed. The shell of the latter is dark chestnut brown, glossy, brittle, and covered inside with a thin skin. The flavour is agreeably sweet, recalling somewhat that of walnuts or almonds, but the seeds produce nausea and even vomiting. They contain 46 to 50 per cent. of oil, and burn with an illuminating but smoky flame when lighted, like Brazil nuts, walnuts, etc.

Preparation.—Bruising, and pressing or extracting the seeds.

Properties.—The oil has a mild, agreeable, almond flavour, and pale yellow colour, is very fluid, of specific gravity 0·9120 at 15° C., and 0·8540 at 100° C., and sets at − 12° C. to a solid white mass. It is stable in the light and in air, without becoming rancid ; contains no free fatty acid, and consists of the glycerides of oleic acid and (in small amount) palmitic and stearic acids—22 per cent. of palmitin and stearin, and 75 per cent. of olein.

Saponification value : 191 to 192.

Iodine number : 81·5 to 83.

Iodine number of the fatty acids : 86 to 87.

Hehner number : 94·12.

Melting point of the fatty acids : 19° C.

Setting point of the fatty acids : 10° C.

Uses.—For alimental purposes : as an edible, on account of its fine flavour, the action recorded in respect of the seed being entirely absent from the oil.

PLUM-KERNEL OIL.

(Zwetchkenkernöl, pflaumkernöl; huile d'amandes de prune.)

Raw material.—Plum kernels, the inner kernel of the plum (Prunus domestica), which contains 25 to 30 per cent. of oil, some 20 per cent. being extractible.

Preparation.—Crushing, grinding and pressing the seed kernels. The residue is manipulated for the manufacture of brandy.

Properties.—The oil is clear, yellow in colour and possesses an agreeable almond flavour and smell. At 4° C. it thickens, and at −8·75° C. sets to a solid white fat.

Specific gravity at 15° C. : 0·9127.

Uses.—For alimental purposes ; and, technical, same as other fatty oils.

NON-DRYING OILS OF NO COMMERCIAL IMPORTANCE.

Apple-kernel oil from Pyrus malus L.

Lycopodium oil from Licopodium elavatum L.

Paulownia seed (huile de toï) from Paulownia imperialis Sieb. and Zucc.

Pear-kernel oil from Pyrus communis.

Bonduc-nut oil, Fever-nut oil from Caesalpinia Bonducella Roxb.

Jungle-almond oil (Catappaöl ; huile de Badamier, huile d'Amandes sauvages, huile d'Amandes des Indes) from Terminalia Catappa L.

Chebula oil from Terminalia chebula Roxb.

Exile oil from Berbera thevetia L.

Dogwood oil (Hartriegelöl; huile de Cornouiller) from Corniss sanguinea L.

Icoca oil from Chrysobalanus Icoca L.

Indiarubber tree oil (Kautchoucbaumöl; huile de Siringa du Bresil) from Siphonia elastica L.

Dak Kino tree oil, Palas tree oil (Kinobaumöl) from Butea frondosa Roxb.

Korung oil (Korungöl; huile de Korung) from Pongamia glabra Vent.

Lentisk oil from Pistacia lentiscus.

Myrabolam oil (Myrobalanenöl) from Terminalia bellerica Roxb.

Caper-tree oil (Pillenbaumöl) from Cleome viscosa L.

Pinhoë oil (Pinhoenöl, Breeböl) from Jatropha multifida L.

Pistacia-nut oil (Pistazienöl) from Pistacia vera.

Quince-kernel oil (Quittenkernöl) from Pyrus Cydonia.

Sandbox-tree oil from Hara crepitans.

Sapucaja oil (Sapucayaöl; huile des Sapucaya, huile de semences de la marmite de singe) from Lecythis ollaria L.

Spindle-tree oil (Spindelbaumöl; huile de fusoin) from Evonymus europaeus L.

Stinking-bean oil (Stinkbaumöl) from Sterculia foetida.

Tonquin-bean oil (Toncabohnenöl; huile de fève de Tonkin, huile de camaru) from Diptera odorata Willd.

Spurge oil, Purging oil (Wolfsmilchöl, Purgirkernöl; huile d'epurge) from Euphorbia Lathyris L.

CHAPTER VII.

VEGETABLE DRYING OILS.

(Raw Material, Preparation, Properties and Uses.)

BANKUL (KEKUNE, CANDLE-NUT) OIL.

(Bankulöl, Lichtnussöl, Lackbaumöl, Kukinöl ; huile de noix de Bancoul, huile de Bancoul.)

Raw material.—The nuts of Aleurites triloba, Aleurites moluccana, which might be placed on the market in very large quantities from Martinique, Guadeloupe, New Caledonia, Tahiti, Guiana and Reunion, but which do not at present constitute a regular article of commerce. The employment of this material in the oil industry is desirable, not only on account of its low price, but also by reason of the quality of oil it can be made to yield.

According to Wiesner the seeds contain 50 to 60 per cent. of oil. It is stated in a report issued by the French Ministry of Marine, that 100 kilos. of nuts yield on an average 33 kilos. of almonds (kernels), 100 kilos. of the latter producing 66 kilos. of oil; 450 kilos. of nuts are therefore required for the production of 91 kilos. of oil. From information obtained in Tahiti, it appears that the nuts cost about £6 per ton, to which must be added about £3 5s. for freight. The kernels of the bankul nut are sold at £16 per ton, so that since 100 kilos. of almonds yield 66 kilos. of oil, the cost of 100 kilos. of the latter would amount to £2 8s., without counting the cost of extraction, a price that offers no advantage now that linseed stands at a low figure.

Properties.—Cold pressed bankul oil is pale yellow, almost white, but the hot pressed oil is brown in colour and has a repellent smell, the odour of the white oil being agreeable. The oil dries at about the same rate as linseed oil, and, like the latter, may be converted into varnish by oxidation. It also burns extremely well, particularly good results having been obtained at several establishments in Paris.

The author is unaware of any existing analytical records with respect to this oil, and his own investigations have been confined to the applicability of the oil for the manufacture of paints and varnishes, with the following results :—

Small quantities of the brown oil were boiled with lith-arge, minium, lead acetate and manganous borate. The lead varnishes were all very dark coloured ; the oil began to boil at 140° C., and was maintained at that temperature during the short time required for completion by the small volume of oil taken. The smell of the varnish greatly resembled that of the oil, but was rather more unpleasant. The manganese varnish sustained but very little alteration in colour. Examined for drying properties, the varnishes differed somewhat from linseed varnishes of the same strength, drying at least four hours sooner than the latter, and the raw oil also dried quicker than linseed oil. When heated to 325° C., uninflammable vapours were evolved, having a strong odour somewhat resembling that of poppies, but very evil smelling. After losing about 20 per cent. of volatilised fatty acids, a thick tough mass was left, as in the case of linseed oil, but which on account of the dark colour of the oil was almost black. This indicated the presence of a large proportion of vegetable remains in suspension. On repeating these experiments with the pale oil, the varnishes prepared with lead were found to be nearly all darkened, whilst that made with manganous borate was merely of a pale yellow colour. As far as drying properties were concerned, these oils manifested the same superiority over linseed oil, drying quicker by a few hours. On the other hand, when the pale bankul oil was heated to 325° C., it gave the remarkable result that, after losing some 20 per cent. of volatile fatty acids, the residual mass was completely colourless and formed a thick water-white syrup.

With respect to their stability as paint when incorporated with earthy colours and metallic oxides, the whole of the bankul-oil varnishes gave the same result as the varnish colours.

Nevertheless, on account of its higher cost than linseed oil and the comparative rarity of its occurrence in commerce, there is at present no immediate prospect of the extensive employment of bankul oil.

Uses.—Technical : for the same purposes as linseed oil.

HEMPSEED OIL.

(Hanföl ; huile de chanvre, huile de Chênevis.)

Raw material.—Hempseed, the seed of Cannabis sativa. The fruit of the plant is a kind of nut, and comes into the market separated from the sheath-like, laterally sutured capsule. It is oval in shape, about $\frac{1}{8}$ to $\frac{1}{6}$ of an inch long and $\frac{1}{12}$ of an inch wide, somewhat compressed dorsally, simple, bivalvular, containing a single seed. The envelope is thin, hard, green, brown or greenish brown externally, reticulated and smooth, composed of two layers of stony cells separable from each other, the outer one being pale green and the inner brownish green in colour.

The seed is shaped like the fruit from which it is dehiscent, is adherent dorsally, and is covered with a thin green epidermis. The white embyro consists of parenchyma cells containing oil and aleuron granules, and is uncular, the radicle being bent around the inside of the thick cotyledons, with which it coincides in length. When crushed the seeds emit a characteristic odour, they taste mild and oleaginous, and their content of oil amounts to 30 to 35 per cent. The average yield is 25 per cent., or when submitted to extraction 30-32 per cent.

Percentage Composition.		German hempseed. Per cent.	Russian hempseed. Per cent.
Organic matter		54·30	54·95
Containing protein . . .		15·95	15·00
Ash		3·45	4·50
Water		8·65	9·13
Oil		33·60	31·42
		100·00	100·00

Preparation.—Pressing or extracting the crushed seeds.

Properties.—Specific gravity at 15° C. : 0·9255 (Souchère), 0·925 to 0·931 (Allen), 0·9276 (Fontenelle), 0·9270 (Chateau).

Setting point: the oil thickens −15° C. and solidifies at −27·5° C.

Melting point of the fatty acids : 19° C.

Setting point of the fatty acids : 15° C. (Hübl).

Saponification value : 193·1 (Valenta).

Iodine number : 143 (Hübl).

Iodine number of the free fatty acids : 122·2 to 125·2 (Morawski and Demski).

Freshly pressed hempseed oil is greenish yellow, that extracted with Canadol or carbon bisulphide being brownish yellow, and a vivid green when ether has been employed. The green colour of the fresh oil, whether pressed or extracted by ether, disappears after a little while, leaving behind a brownish yellow tinge. Both odour and flavour are those characteristic of hempseed, though mild. At 15° C. the oil is 9·6 times, and at 7·5° C. 11·6 times, more viscous than water. Hempseed oil dissolves in thirty volumes of cold alcohol, and in all proportions in boiling alcohol, and a solution in twelve volumes of that solvent deposits stearin on cooling. One

12

volume of oil requires two of ether to effect solution. The liquid fatty acids in this oil mainly consist of linolic acid, together with small quantities of linolenic, isolinolenic and oleic acids. The following is the elementary composition of the oil :—

		Per cent.
Carbon	.	76·05
Hydrogen	.	11·35
Oxygen	.	12·60
		100·00

In siccative power hempseed oil is inferior to that from linseed. The following are characteristic colour reactions :—

On boiling with caustic soda (1·340 specific gravity) a brownish-yellow solid soap is produced. (Linseed oil gives a yellow fluid soap.)

Sulphuric acid colours hempseed oil (and also linseed oil) an intense green.

A mixture of equal parts water, concentrated sulphuric acid and fuming nitric acid, added to five volumes of the oil, produces a green coloration, turning to black and becoming ultimately red brown, after standing twenty-four hours. Concentrated hydrochloric acid colours the fresh oil grass green, older oil yellow green.

Uses.—For alimental purposes: same as olive oil and fats, when fresh.

Technical: as burning oil for soapmaking, and in the preparation of oil colours and varnishes.

LINSEED OIL.

(Leinöl ; huile de lin.)

Raw material.—Seeds of Linum usitatissimum (Flax). This plant is principally cultivated for the fibre, and it is only in a few countries that it is grown on account of its oleaginous seeds. The countries producing the greatest quantities of flax—*e.g.*, the Russian Baltic provinces, East

Indies, Egypt and North America—also supply the largest amount of linseed. The commercial article is classified according as it is fit for seed or for the manufacture of oil. To the former class belong the well-ripened fresh seeds, still capable of germination; whilst the commoner qualities, whether harvested in an unripe condition or incapable of germinating by reason of prolonged or defective storage, are classed in the second category. The bulk of the oil seed consists of imperfectly ripened seeds obtained as a bye-product of the flax industry, a circumstance due to the fact that in order to obtain a suitable fibre it is necessary to harvest the flax before the seeds have had time to ripen. In this immature condition they are suitable for the oil press, but not fit to use for seed. For technical purposes this class of seed is the only one coming under consideration, since the fresh flax seed is only worked up for oil in small quantities, and in districts where linseed oil is used as an article of food.

Each fruit of the flax plant contains ten seeds of between $\frac{1}{7}$ and $\frac{1}{5}$ of an inch in length, highly polished, oval in circumference, flattened externally, greenish brown to brown in colour, and of an unpleasant, though mild, smell. The germ is situated at the smaller extremity. When examined by the aid of a magnifier the surface no longer appears smooth, but covered with slight depressions. The average weight of the individual seeds is between 0·3 and 0·5 milligramme, the good flax seeds measuring some $\frac{1}{5}$ of an inch in length and weighing over 0·4 milligramme. The seeds that have lost their vitality are also of the same dimensions, and these are preferable for oil pressing to the unripe outshot seeds, which are smaller, lighter, and usually of decidedly greenish colour. The anatomical structure of the seed affords, by the aid of the microscope, a means of discriminating between the ripe and the unripe seeds. Three distinct portions are readily noticeable in linseed—the germ, the albumen and the epidermis. The albumen is closely attached to the epidermis, the greenish-yellow germ with its radicle (about $\frac{1}{25}$ of an inch long) being embedded in the whitish albumen in the interior of the seed. The dense, hard, brittle husk is composed of five strata of tissue, the outer one formed of colourless cells, the external section swelling up greatly under the action of water. Next follows a layer of soft elements, to which is attached a tissue of longitudinal sclerenchymatous cells, imparting density and rigidity to the seed. The fourth layer resembles the second, being composed of soft cells lying closely together, and the fifth or endopleura is formed of polygonal cells, flattened in a direction parallel to the surface and containing brown granular matter. This layer gives to the flax-seed husk its characteristic brown colour. When the seed is ground the tissues of the husk are broken as far as the sclerenchymatous layer and the elements of the endopleura. Portions of the third and fifth strata are always to be found intact in linseed meal, and afford a means of distinguishing this meal, whether loose or pressed, as well as of detecting it when used as an adulterant in flour or other meal. The albumen of the seed is formed of soft polyhedral cells, containing, when the seed is ripe, globules of fat and aleuron granules, and in the unripe state small granules of starch as well. The diameter of these cells is between 0·009 and 0·013 millimetre.

The germ is composed of tissue consisting, for the most part, of cells similar to those constituting the albumen, interspersed with longitudinal stringy groups of elementary organs.

The fresh seeds when immersed in water become enveloped with a vitreous jelly, through the swelling of the epidermal cells walls, the jelly subsequently diffusing through the water if the exposure be prolonged.

Linseed contains some 8 per cent. of water, 33 per cent.

of oil (26 being extractible), 25 per cent. of albuminoid matter, traces of tannin, and yields 4 to 5 per cent. of ash.

Preparation.—Grinding the seeds, followed by pressure or extraction.

Properties.—Specific gravity at 15° C.: 0·9347 (Schübler), 0·9325 (Souchère), 0·930 to 0·935 (Allen); at 18° C.: raw linseed oil, 0·9299, boiled, 0·9411 (Stilurell); at 12° C., 0·939; at 25° C., 0·930; at 50° C., 0·921; at 94° C., 0·881 (Saussure).

Specific gravity of the fatty acids at 100° C.: 0·8599 (Archbutt and Allen).

Setting point: according to Gusserow the oil solidifies at –16° C. after a few days, but according to Chateau it only sets at –27° C.; the melting point is from –16° to –20° C. (Glässner).

Melting point of the fatty acids: 11·12° C. (Allen), 17° C. (Hübl).

Setting point of the fatty acids: 13·3° C. (Hübl).

Saponification value: 189 to 195 (Allen), 195·2 (Moore).

Iodine number: 158 (Hübl), 155·2 (Moore).

Iodine number of the free fatty acids: 155·2 to 155·9 (Morawski and Demski).

Cold-pressed linseed oil is merely tinged with a very faint yellow, but the hot-pressed oil is more or less coloured. That obtained by extraction is also a very pale yellow. In flavour linseed oil differs from the non-drying oils, being characteristically bitter-sweet at first, with an irritating after-taste. The odour is also characteristic, and is not, according to Mulder, solely due to volatile fatty acids, such as butyric, valerianic or caproic acid. Linseed oil dissolves in 16 parts of ether or 40 of alcohol at the ordinary temperature, and in 5 parts of boiling alcohol; it is miscible with turpentine in all proportions. It boils at 230° C., and begins to evolve at 300° C. evil smelling, whitish-grey vapours which ignite spontaneously at 380° to 400° C., the oil burning with a very smoky red flame. When heated for several hours at a temperature near to the igniting point, the oil thickens like syrup, and no longer leaves a greasy mark behind when dropped on paper. The fresh oil is readily saponifiable, and forms with soda a yellow soft soap, from the aqueous solution of which by the action of hydrochloric acid a thin oil or fatty acid can be separated, depositing crystals of stearic and palmitic acids on cooling. On exposure to the air, the oil absorbs oxygen, becoming thick and rancid; in thin layers it dries to a neutral body (linoxyn), insoluble in ether. Train oil, rape oil, hempseed oil, camelina oil and, of late years, resin oil and mineral oils are used to adulterate linseed oil.

The determination of the purity of linseed oil is most readily effected by means of the iodine number, this oil, as the most siccative oil, having a higher iodine number than any other. Hübl found the iodine number of five linseed oils of different origin to be 156, 157, 158, 159 and 160, or an average of 158; Moore, 155·2.

This power of absorbing iodine diminishes but slightly if the oil be kept for a long time; more rapidly if it be boiled to varnish. One oil, fifteen years old, had an iodine number 156, and an oil with the same number when boiled to varnish gave 148, the melting point of the fatty acids concurrently rising to 17·5° C.

Maumené differentiates linseed oil from other oils by saponification with caustic potash. 10 cc. of oil are warmed for an hour with 20 cc. of a solution of caustic potash standardised to neutralise 123 cc. of sulphuric acid of twice the normal strength. The resulting soap is very solid in the warm and also in the cold, and may be separated from the lye by simple draining. The neutralising power of the lye from various samples of saponified linseed oil on $\frac{2}{1}$ normal acid varies greatly, *e.g.*, 72·3 and 105 cc., the original lye neutralising 123 cc. Linseed oil may also be detected by its behaviour towards sulphuric acid, either by measuring the increase of temperature ensuing when mixed together or by observing the reaction occurring on the addition of three drops of the acid to ten of oil. With linseed oil a reddish brown resinous mass results, and where other oils are present the linseed oil is resinified, the flakes of resin floating about in the remaining oil.

In comparing various samples of linseed oil, Maumené found that when 25 grammes of the sample, diluted with olive oil, were mixed with 5 cc. of English sulphuric acid, the temperature of the mixture rose 38° to 66·2° C. The same samples when mixed under similar conditions with a sulphuric acid, previously heated to 320° C. and used immediately after thorough cooling, gave increases of temperature of between 112° and 148° C. The value of a linseed oil depends mainly on its siccative power, the degree of which can be best determined by the Livache method.

Various reactions may be employed for detecting the presence of extraneous oils in linseed oil. For example, an admixture of only 10 per cent. of a non-drying or slightly drying oil (cotton-seed or rape oil, for instance) could be easily detected by the iodine number. Furthermore, rape oil is revealed by the sulphur it contains, and cotton-seed oil by the Rödiger test. According to Crace-Calvert, the presence of hempseed oil may be detected by the action of nitric acid of 1·18 specific gravity, pure linseed oil giving a yellow, whilst that containing hempseed oil gives a dirty green coloration. Linseed oil containing hempseed oil is coloured yellowish green by concentrated hydrochloric acid, pure linseed oil giving a yellow coloration. Train or fish oil is easily detected by the colour reaction, and resin or resin oil by the usual methods.

Uses.—Medicinal, for plasters; alimental, same as olive oil and solid fats; technical, chiefly for making oil colours, varnishes and lacquers, also for soapmaking, etc.

POPPY (SEED) OIL, MAW OIL.

(Mohnöl; huile de pavot somnifière (pavot du pays), huile d'oeliette.)

Raw material.—Seeds of Papaver somniferum L. The poppy is indigenous to the Eastern Mediterranean countries, but has been from ancient times cultivated on a large scale in many parts of Europe, Asia and Africa, and more recently in North America and Australia (New South Wales), partly for opium and partly for its oleaginous seeds. There are two chief varieties of the poppy, Papaver album D.C. and Papaver nigrum D.C., the former producing white, the latter bluish black or grey seeds. The best oil is obtained from the white poppy, and it is the seed of this variety that is used for medicinal purposes; but the black poppy is most extensively grown for oil, being the most profitable. The yield of fatty oil is about the same in both kinds, averaging some 60 per cent.

The flavour and odour of poppy seeds are well known, as is also their form, which, to describe it more closely, is spherical, somewhat flattened and kidney shaped. According to Flückiger, the weight of the air-dry seed averages about 0·5 milligramme. The surface exhibits reticular protuberances.

In each seed may be differentiated shell, embryo and albumen (endosperm). The first-named is about 0·014 millimetre in thickness, and is surrounded by an outer skin covered by a thick cuticle; succeeding and attached to this is a parenchyma of closely congregated cells, with colourless contents in the white variety, but in the brown kind the internal layer of this tissue contains solid brown matter. The germ is relatively large, the lobes and radicle are of equal length, and the curved embryo is composed of soft walled cells, partly parenchymatous and partly of a cambial nature—the former containing numerous oil globules along with large aleuron granules agreeing in form, structure and dimensions with the similar constituents of the endosperm. The latter is a homogeneous tissue filled with small fat globules, along with large aleuron granules, in some of which pale nuclei may be descried.

According to Sacc the seeds of the white poppy contain 54·61 per cent. of fatty oil (poppy oil), 23·26 per cent. of protein bodies, about 12 per cent. of albuminoid matter, nearly 6 per cent. of cellulose and 2 to 3 per cent. of ash, chiefly phosphate of lime. The report that poppy seeds contain morphine has been proved erroneous.

Preparation.—By crushing and pressing or extracting the seeds.

The preparation of poppy oil constitutes an important branch of industry in the North of France; about one-half the output is consumed in the district, the remainder being sent to the South of France, where it is worked up for curd soap. In Germany the chief centres of the industry are Baden, Bavaria and Württemberg.

The poppy heads are opened when they have reached a certain degree of dryness, and their contents emptied on to a plate of sheet iron, then winnowed to remove fragments of the capsule, and afterwards ground to a kind of meal. This is packed in bags made of ticking, and pressed, the oil being caught in tubs, wherein it is left to settle and clarify thoroughly, and is then ready for sale. Two kinds of oil are known in France—the white, edible oil (huile blanche) from the first pressing of best quality seeds, and the red, technical oil (huile rousse) obtained from the second pressing or from inferior seed.

Properties.—The best quality oil is pure white and of

agreeable flavour when fresh, lower qualities being golden yellow, and the second runnings reddish in colour (red poppy oil).

Specific gravity at 15° C. : 0·924 (Souchère), 0·924 to 0·937 (Allen), 0·9262 (Clarke) ; at 18° C. : 0·9245 (Stilurell).

Setting point : −18° C.

Melting point of the fatty acids : 20·5° C.

Setting point of the fatty acids : 16·5° C. (Hübl).

Hehner number : 95·38 (Dietzell and Kressner).

Saponification value : 194·6 (Valenta), 192·8 (Moore).

Iodine number : 136 (Hübl), 134 (Moore).

Poppy oil becomes rancid only with difficulty, and burns badly. It dissolves in 28 parts of cold and 6 parts of boiling alcohol, and is miscible in all proportions with ether. It exhibits none of the effects of opium. When subjected to dry distillation by heating over a gas flame without boiling, poppy oil yields a consistent, oleaginous substance which partly solidifies on cooling, has a faintly acid reaction, but does not give up to water any trace of sebacic acid. If, when distillation ceases, a fresh receiver is provided and the heat increased, the oil begins to boil, gives off acrolein, and an oily distillate comes over, which yields to water a liquid with strongly acid reaction and containing sebacic and acrylic acids. By suspending the distillation when half the oil has passed over, the residue left in the retort forms when cold a thick viscid mass, slightly coloured and possessing many of the properties of the anhydride of linolic acid, but easily melts in the warm.

Uses.—Alimental : like olive oil and fats.

Technical : in the manufacture of soaps, as lamp oil, and as a matrix for colours in oil paint and colourmaking.

WALNUT OIL (NUT OIL).

(Nussöl; huile de noix.)

Raw material.—The well-known fruit of the walnut tree, Juglans regia L.

Preparation of the oil.—The nuts intended for oil should be two or three months old, and contain when fresh a whitish milk, which on being pressed yields a turbid oil, clarifying with difficulty. If stored too long the nuts yield a bad, rancid oil, which is also difficult to clarify. The oil amounts to between 40 and 50 per cent. of the seed. In many instances the seeds are freed from the yellow skin, ground and subjected to cold pressure, which produces 30 to 35 per cent. of oil, and then to warm pressure, giving 10 to 15 per cent. Warm pressing yields up to 45 per cent. of oil.

Properties.—Fresh cold-pressed nut oil is very fluid and almost colourless or pale greenish yellow, but the colour quickly disappears. The smell is agreeable and the flavour nutty, but rancidity quickly sets in, and the oil then acquires purgative properties. Warm-pressed oil is more highly coloured, and has a peculiar sharp taste and smell.

			Warm-pressed Oil.	Cold-pressed Oil.
Specific gravity at	10° C.		0·9300	0·9290
,,	,,	12° C.	0·929	0·9276
,,	,,	15° C.	0·9268	0·9250
,,	,,	20° C.	0·9236	0·9230

At 15° C. the oil is 9·7 times (at 7·5° C., 11·8 times) as viscous as water. It remains fluid at −15° C., and, beginning to thicken at −17° to −18° C., forms at −24° C. a translucent mass, and sets to a solid white mass at −27° to −28° C. One part of oil requires 100 parts of alcohol for its solution; it is, however, more readily soluble in hot alcohol, but deposits crystals of fatty acid on cooling. The oil is composed of the glycerides of linolic, myristic and lauric acids.

Saponification value : 196 to 197.

Iodine number : 142 to 143.

Melting point of the fatty acids : $-20°$ C.

Setting point of the fatty acids : $-16°$ C.

With regard to the iodine number it should be mentioned that this quickly decreases as the oxidation of the oil proceeds.

Nitric acid colours nut oil yellow ; nitrous acid containing nitric acid gives a reddish yellow, and fuming nitric acid a dark red. Sulphuric acid of specific gravity 1·70 produces a brownish coloration, turning to brown. A mixture of sulphuric and nitric acids causes a brownish-yellow colour at first, passing over into brown. Zinc chloride has no effect. Ammonia and caustic potash produce yellowish white liniments, and the oil saponifies with soda lye like linseed oil. Nut oil is chiefly adulterated with bleached linseed oil, the latter being recognisable by the viscid resinous mass it gives under the sulphuric-acid test. Nut oil dries much quicker than linseed oil and does not crack on drying.

Uses.—For alimental purposes : the fresh cold-pressed oil makes a good edible oil.

Technical : for oil colours and printing inks, soapmaking, and also for burning on account of its fine white light.

WOOD OIL (TUNG OIL).

(Oelfirnissbaumöl chinesisches Holzöl, Tungöl ; huile de bois.)

Raw material.—Seeds of Elaeococca s. Aleurites cordate, indigenous to China and Japan.

Preparation.—By cold and warm pressing the seeds.

Properties.—The cold-pressed oil is pale yellow, that from the warm pressing being dark brown. It is thick and of high specific gravity (0·940), but does not set in the cold. This oil, which possesses much stronger drying properties than that from Aleurites triloba, is used in enormous quantities in China and Japan as a natural varnish, especially for painting and preserving woodwork, Chinese vehicles, etc. It must not be confounded with the balsam known as wood oil or gurjun balsam, prepared from Dipterocarpus turbinatus Gaertn., which possesses very different properties, and which it is employed to adulterate.

The examination of the oil by Cloix showed it to consist of two glycerides, ordinary olein and an ordinary glyceride, elaeomargarin, the latter yielding, on saponification, elaeo-margaric or margarolic acid, $C_{16}H_{30}O_3$. This report has, on account of the formula, but little pretension to accuracy, neither (if the drying properties of the oil be recollected) has the assertion that it changes on exposure to the air into a fat melting at $32°$ C. In drying power it is superior to linseed oil, but the warm-pressed oil appears to be endowed with this property in a less degree than that from cold pressing.

When heated with alcoholic potash it saponifies rapidly, and, according to the amount of potash (211 : 1000) required for saponification, would appear to contain a hitherto unknown fatty acid.

Some 200,000 Chinese piculs (1 picul equals 133·33 lb. or 60·479 kilos.) of this oil are annually despatched from Hankow, on the Yang-tse-kiang, to other parts of China, but it has not yet appeared in Europe.

CASTOR OIL (RICINUS OIL).

(Ricinusöl; huile de ricin.)

Raw material.—The seeds of Ricinus communis L.

The ordinary castor-oil plant and a few nearly related and probably subordinate forms of this species (which are, however, classified as separate kinds by many authors) yield seeds now extensively used in many warm countries for the preparation of oil. India is the home of Ricinus communis, and

R. viridis Willd. and R. ruber Rumph.—both of which are cultivated in the East Indies, along with the first-named, as oil plants—also belong to the flora of that country. In addition to these species, there are also cultivated R. americanus, inermis Jacq., lividus Willd., africanus Willd., and probably a few others as well. The largest area under cultivation is in India, but large quantities of ricinus seeds are annually gathered and used for producing oil in several West Indian islands, North America, Algiers, and latterly also in Italy. The ricinus plant was known as an oil plant in ancient Egypt; in the other countries mentioned above the plant only came under cultivation after the seeds found employment for the preparation of oil for industrial purposes. Notwithstanding that a considerable quantity of the oil is used in medicine, this is now altogether insignificant in comparison with the enormous amounts consumed in the manufacture of soap, as burning oil, in the production of Turkey-red oil, leather oil, as a lubricant, and for other industrial purposes.

The seeds of Ricinus communis are between $\frac{1}{2}$ and $\frac{3}{5}$ of an inch in length and about $\frac{1}{4}$ to $\frac{7}{16}$ of an inch wide, those from tropical countries being larger than those of European growth. The individual seeds are oval, a little flattened on one side, a longitudinal ridge being formed on the other by the projecting suture. The suture branches dichotomically towards the upper end, and runs below into the brownish pentagonal eye, which is frequently covered by a light brown caruncle bent upwards towards the suture. The shell of the seed is brown, speckled with grey. The seeds of R. americanus from Martinique correspond with the above description, except that the shell is almost black and the specks, which are few, are of a pale grey colour. Those of R. inermis from India are $\frac{7}{16}$ of an inch long by $\frac{5}{16}$ wide and slightly flattened, the suture projects but little, the germ is small and pale green in colour, and the shell reddish brown, speckled with light brown. The seeds of R. viridis from the Congo are only about $\frac{5}{16}$ of an inch long and barely $\frac{1}{4}$ of an inch in diameter; the sutures do not project, nor is the back flattened. The eye is blackish and almost triangular in circumference; shell greenish brown, plentifully speckled with light grey.

The epidermis of the seed resembles parchment, is composed of flat polygonal cells, and is easily removed when moistened with water. Under this is a thin shell as hard

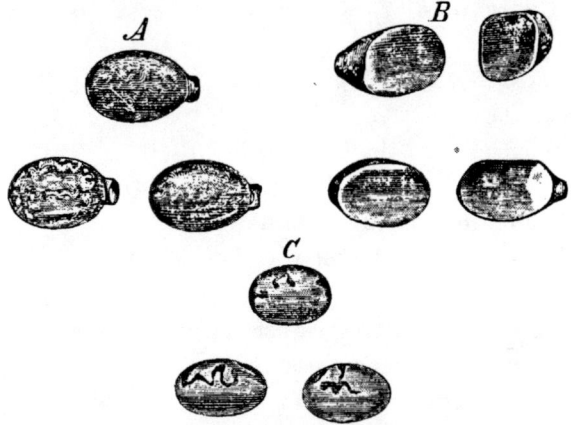

FIG. 74. Castor-Oil Seeds. A, In the Shell; B, Outer Shell; C, Kernels.

as ivory, composed of sclerenchymatous cells, to which is attached the soft endoderm of parenchymatous character, copiously interspersed with vascular bundles.

The germ lies within the seed, and is surrounded by a highly developed albumen. The soft-walled parenchymatous cells of both contain fat globules and large aleuron granules, partly enveloping crystalloid bodies.

The amount of oil in the seeds is estimated at 40 to 45 per cent.

Preparation.—The seeds are powdered and pressed or submitted to extraction.

Properties.—Ricinus oil is very thick and becomes still thicker on exposure to the air, until finally it is transformed into a viscid mass. The flavour is mild, with an irritating after-taste, and the oil possesses the remarkable property of mixing with alcohol in all proportions, and of rotating the plane of polarisation, a property not hitherto observed in any other vegetable oil. It dries scarcely at all in thin layers, or at any rate but slowly.

Specific gravity at 15° C., 0·960 to 0·964 (Allen), 0·9613 to 0·9736 (Valenta) ; at 18° C., 0·9667 (Stilurell) ; at 23° C., 0·964 (Dietrich) ; at 25° C., 0·9575 ; at 94° C., 0·9081 (Saussure).

Behaviour on cooling : sets at −17° to −18° C. ; the American oil at −10° to −12° C.

Melting point of the fatty acids : 13° C.

Setting point of the fatty acids : 3° C. (Hübl).

Iodine number of the oil : 84·4 (Hübl).

Iodine number of the fatty acids : 86·6 to 88·3 (Morawski and Demski).

The glyceride of ricinoleic acid forms the chief constituent of ricinus oil, and it also contains stearin and palmitin. The pure oil is recognisable by its power of mixing in all proportions with absolute alcohol and glacial acetic acid. It also dissolves at 15° C. in two volumes of 90 per cent. or four volumes of 84 per cent. alcohol, but is almost insoluble in paraffin oil, petroleum, and petroleum spirit, 0·5 per cent. of the oil producing turbidity in these solvents at 16° C. At the same time it absorbs its own volume of petroleum spirit and 1½ volumes of paraffin oil or petroleum, the excess of the solvent floating on the surface. These conditions of solubility, differing altogether from those exhibited by other oils, render the detection of ricinus oil in mixtures an easy task. Another characteristic is its low saponification value, which approximates to that of rape oil. Ricinus oil answers to the elaidin reaction. The drastic purgative principle is more plentiful in the emulsion of the seed than in the oil, and it has been ascertained that this property is possessed to a larger extent by extracted oil than by that obtained by pressure, but the chemical nature of the active principle is still unknown.

Ricinus oil may be oxidised by means of a hot air blast, and then acquires the property of mixing with mineral oils. This so-called " soluble " ricinus oil (huile de ricin soluble) is only slightly soluble in alcohol, and belongs to the class of oxidised or " blown " oils.

The presence of ricinus oil in other oils can be detected, according to Draher, in the following manner : Five or six drops of nitric acid are added to a few drops of the oil, and neutralised by sodium carbonate at the conclusion of the reaction. As soon as the smell of nitrous acid has disappeared, the odour of oenanthylic acid becomes manifest if ricinus oil be present, a check experiment being made with some ricinus oil. This oil is seldom adulterated. According to Schaedler, possibly with sesame oil, in which case it does not dissolve perfectly clear in wine spirit, but forms a turbid mixture. The presence of such an admixture may also be detected by the elaidin test, since, whereas pure ricinus oil sets after six or seven hours to a solid mass, adulterated oil will only give a greasy yellow or reddish mass. Furthermore, ricinus oil containing sesame oil gives the blue colour reaction with nitrosulphuric acid.

Refining.—According to Pavesi, the oil is refined as follows : 1000 parts by weight are intimately mixed with 25 parts of well-cleaned bone black and 10 parts of calcined magnesia. The mixture is allowed to stand for three days at 20° to 30° C., being stirred the while, and is then filtered in a suitable manner. The filtered oil is colourless and less liable to thicken than before refining.

13

Uses.—Medicinal : as a purgative.

Technical : as a lubricant, for the manufacture of soap, in dyeing, etc.

SUNFLOWER OIL (TURNESOL OIL).

(Sonnenblumenöl ; huile de tournesol.)

Raw material.—Sunflower kernels, the seeds of Helianthus annuus L.

The sunflower originated in Mexico, but has long been grown as an ornamental plant in European gardens, and is now cultivated on a large scale in South Russia. In its native country it has long been worked up for oil, and attempts were made in the last century to introduce it into Germany and render it industrially valuable as an oil plant, but unsuccessfully. In Russia the kernels are partly used at home for the preparation of oil, and partly exported to other European countries for the same purpose. Russian sunflower oil constitutes a not unimportant article of commerce in Germany.

The fruit of the sunflower is either black, greyish brown or white, but only black seeds (or black with red streaks) are met with in commerce. In the dry state the seeds are long, oval with somewhat sharpened edges, rather depressed or flattened at the broad upper end, about $\frac{2}{5}$ of an inch long, $\frac{3}{16}$ of an inch wide, and $\frac{1}{8}$ of an inch thick. If examined carefully, the seed will be found unsymmetrical. The brittle, woody shell, readily splitting lengthwise, is about 0·5 to 0·6 millimetre thick ; its external, somewhat lustrous surface is either black throughout or streaked with grey, longitudinally on a black ground. The relation of the weight of the shell to that of the seed, both being in an air-dry condition, is about as 53 : 47 ; therefore, as from the dry seeds 15 per cent. of fatty oil is obtained, the shelled seed must contain some

32 per cent. The shell is covered by an integument, consisting of long, flattened cells provided with a clear, externally thickened membrane, and containing brown resinous matter. To this is attached a soft parenchymatous tissue, consisting of one or more rows of cells, and then follows the tissue forming the chief bulk of the shell substance and made up of long, thick-walled parenchyma cells penetrated by numerous porous channels, and interspersed vertically with a tissue, frequently brown in colour, and most resembling medullary tissue in the arrangement, form and position of the cells. The cross section of the integument shows it to be divided into flat leaves at intervals of 0·2 to 0·38 millimetre, the medullary tissue issuing from the points of junction. The tissue of the seed epidermis consists of several layers of conjoined polygonal cells, and is permeated by vascular bundles composed either of cambial elements, or for the most part of tough spiroids. In the seed itself nothing but parenchyma and the epithelium of the cotyledons is visible, the latter differing from the former merely by the flattened shape and light brown colour of the cells, the parenchyma cells being rounded or polyhedral in form. In both sets of tissue the cells contain fat globules and tightly crowded aleuron granules, 0·0036 to 0·0067 millimetre in diameter, in the interior of which, when mounted in oil and highly magnified, are found grains of various sizes.

Preparation.—By shelling the seed, crushing and pressing or extracting the kernels.

Properties.—Specific gravity at 15° C.: 0·9262 (Chateau); 0·924 to 0·926 (Allen).

Melting point of the fatty acids: 23° C.

Setting point: −17° C. (Bach).

Sunflower oil is clear and light yellow, with an agreeable odour and mild flavour, but its properties have not yet been examined.

Uses.—For alimental purposes: like olive oil and other fats.

Technical: for soapmaking, and for paint in place of linseed oil.

Grape Seed Oil.

(Traubenkernöl; huile des pepins des raisins.)

Raw material.—Grape seeds from Vinus vinifera.

The grape seeds intended for the preparation of oil must be freed from the pulpy flesh of the fruit, which is employed for other purposes; and when the latter is to be made into brandy the only method open is to have the seeds picked out by children, since the pulp makes a much finer spirit without the seeds. In all other instances the grape pulp from the press is spread out on a drying floor or kiln and turned every day with a fork. The mass soon withers, so that the stalks can be removed by forking; and when the pulp is a little drier, it can be separated from the seeds by winnowing, any seeds still remaining adherent being easily removed by beating. The seeds are then spread thinly out over a well-ventilated floor and thoroughly dried, this being highly essential to the production of good oil. Reports on the percentage content of oil in grape seeds are conflicting, 12 and even 20 per cent. being obtainable by pressing, according to one authority.

Preparation.—The oil seeds are placed either in an ordinary mill with horizontal stones or in an oil mill with vertical runners, and finely ground, a little lukewarm water being added from time to time to prevent them from sticking to the rollers. The meal, which yields an amount of oil proportionate to the fineness of the grinding, is then placed in a copper kettle, where it gradually receives an addition of one-fourth to one-third of its weight of warm water, the formation of lumps being prevented by stirring. It must also be prevented from scorching, otherwise the oil will have an empyreumatic flavour.

The mass, prepared as above, is laid on ordinary hair cloths, and pressed in an oil press. When the flow of oil ceases, the cakes are repeatedly re-ground and treated as before, whereby a little more oil is won; 10, 12, and up to 20 per cent. of oil being obtained in this manner. The variations in the content of oil appear to be due to the kind of grape used, and the nature of the ground on which the grapes are grown may also have some influence on the result.

Properties.—Grape-seed oil is thick, of a golden-yellow or brownish-yellow colour merging into green, with a faint characteristic odour. The cold-pressed oil is mild in flavour, and forms a good edible oil, but that from warm pressing tastes somewhat tart. The specific gravity at 12° R. (15° C.) is 0·9202. At −9° R. (−11·25° C.) it becomes buttery, and it turns rancid in air, browning and gradually drying. It burns with a bright flame without smoke or smell, and may be refined by sulphuric acid like the other fatty oils.

According to Dr. Wagner, grape seeds from the Unterfranken district, dried at 100° C., contained 11·2 per cent. of fatty oil, and in another experiment 10·8 per cent. A. Fitz found 15 to 18 per cent. of fatty oil, consisting of glycerides of palmitic, stearic and erucic acids, the latter constituting about one-half of the total acids.

Uses.—Alimental: same as olive oil and fats.

Technical: as a lubricant, in soapmaking, and as burning oil.

TECHNICALLY UNIMPORTANT DRYING OILS.

Shial Kaata oil (Argemoneöl; huile de pavot epineux, huile de charbon jaune), from Argemone mexicana.

Belladonna-seed oil, deadly-nightshade oil (Belladonnaöl; huile de Belladonne), from Atropa belladonna.

Camul oil (Camulöl; huile de Polongo), from Mallotus Philippinensis Mull. (Abyssinia, Southern Arabia, India, Malay Archipelago, Philippine Islands, Eastern China, North Australia).

Koëme oil (Castanhasöl; huile de noix d'Inhambane), from Telfairia pedata Hook.

Chironji oil, from Buchanania latifolia W.A.

Colocynth-seed oil, from Cucumis colocynthus.

Koula-nut oil (Coulanussöl; huile de noix de Coula), from Coula edulis (west coast of Africa; an imperfectly drying oil).

Thistle oil (Distelöl; huile de chardon), from Onopordon acanthium L.

Pinaster-seed oil, Red pine-seed oil (Fichtensamenöl; huile de pinastre), from Picea vulgaris Lank.

Garden cress-seed oil, cress-seed oil (Gartenkressensamenöl; huile de cresson alenois), from Lapidium sativum L.

Horn poppy-seed oil (Hornmohnöl, Glauciumöl; huile de pavot cornu), from Glaucium luteum Scop.

Cucumber-seed oil (Gurkenkernöl; huile d'Egusi, huile d'Abobora), from Cucumis sativus L.

Hickory oil (Hickoryöl; huile de Hickory), from Carya alba.

Jy-chee oil, from Euphorbia dracunculoides Lam. (Punjab, Bengal, Madras; a drying varnish oil).

Pine oil, pine-seed oil, Scotch fir-seed oil (Kiefersamenöl, Föhrensamenöl; huile de pin), from Pinus sylvestris L.

Bur oil (Klettenöl; huile de Bardanne), from Arctium Lappa L.

Pumpkin-seed oil, pompion oil, gourd-seed oil (Kurbiskernöl; huile de pepins de citrouille), from Cucurbita pepo L.

Melon-seed oil (Melonenöl; huile de melon), from Cucumis melo L.

Reseda-seed oil, weld-seed oil (Resedasamenöl, Wausamenöl; huile de gaude), from Reseda luteola.

Honesty oil, hesperis oil (Rothrepsöl; huile de julienne), from Hesperis matronalis.

Safflower oil, cardy oil (Saffloröl; huile de carthame, huile de saffre), from Carthamus tinctorius L.

Tobacco-seed oil (Tabaksamenöl; huile de tabac), from Nicotiana tabacum.

Pitch oil, pitch-tree oil, spruce fir-seed oil (Tannensamenöl; huile de sapin), from Abies pectinate D.C.

Cassweed-seed oil (Taschelkrautsamenöl; huile de Thlaspi, huile de cresson), from Thlaspi arvense L.

Watermelon oil (Wassermelonenöl; huile de melon d'eau, huile de Beraf), from Cucurbita citrullus.

Zachun oil (Zachunöl), from Bolonites Roxburghii Planch. (Africa and Senegal).

Stone pine-nut oil (Zirbelnussöl), from Pinus cembra L.

CHAPTER VIII.

SOLID VEGETABLE FATS.

(Raw Material, Preparation, Properties and Uses.)

GALAM BUTTER, NUNGA OIL, ETC.

(Bassiafett, Galambutter, Sheabutter, Schihbutter, Ma-
wahbutter, Illipeöl, Djaveöl, Noungonöl; Beurre de rose de
Chine, huile de Noungon, Illipe, Mahwah.)

Raw material.—Seeds of several varieties of Bassia grown
in India and the west coast of Africa. The fat-producing
species of the Bassia family are not yet sufficiently defined.
Probably Bassia butyracea Roxb. (India, Senegal) yields Shea
butter, and Bassia longifolia L. and Bassia latifolia Roxb.
(India), Illipe oil or Mahwah butter, but the species yielding
the best African Djave fat and Nunga oil has not yet been
identified.

The seeds are large, several centimetres in length, and of
a variety of shapes, covered by a fairly thick shell, in which
the oily kernel is encased. The oliferous tissue of the Bassia
seed (Bassia longifolia) consists of thin-walled cells, measuring some 0·06 millimetres in longest diameter, which
when examined under water appear almost entirely filled
with minute globules of oil. Mounted in oil, each cell is
found to contain numerous double refracting granules and
rods, which, so far as may be determined by their ratio of
solubility, consist of crystallised fatty acids. Colourless
parenchyma cells are interspersed with fairly regular groups
of brown cells of similar nature, containing apparently an

oily liquid wherein aleuron granules, but no crystallised fatty acids, appear. Wiesner observed this in three-year-old seeds, but it is not on that account certain that the same conditions obtain in the fresh seeds used for the preparation of oil.

Preparation.—Pounding the seeds and pressing at moderately warm temperature.

Properties.—All classes of Bassia fats are of the consistency of butter at the ordinary temperature, and are greenish, yellowish (seldom white), or (so it is said) reddish in colour, with an agreeable smell of cocoa when fresh. The fat from Bassia butyracea remains sweet for a fairly long time, but Illipe, Nunga and Djave fats quickly turn rancid, each assuming a characteristic unpleasant odour.

The density of these fats ranges between 0·948 and 0·959 at the ordinary temperature, and the melting point varies from 27° to 43° C. According to the researches of O. Henry, Bassia fat contains stearin; and, according to Pelouze and Boudet, olein. Buff states that palmitic acid is absent, and Thomson and Wood believe that a special fatty acid must be assumed to be present.

Under the microscope Bassia fat appears as a colourless oily mass, enclosing innumerable radial aggregations of crystals along with small isolated crystals. The fat is unusually rich in free fatty acids. The above-named brownish cells also appear, mostly in a highly compressed condition. When the slide is warmed until the fat melts, numerous small, angular, single refractive granules are revealed, and the brown cells appear more clearly defined. On re-cooling the mass, the fatty acids crystallise out in radial groups.

Illipe fat is greenish yellow, becoming white on prolonged storage. It melts between 25° and 29° C., and dissolves with difficulty in alcohol, but readily in ether.

Shea butter is green at first, turning subsequently almost white, and melts at 43° C. It dissolves with difficulty and but imperfectly in alcohol, even at boiling temperature, but completely in ether.

Chorie butter or Pulwara butter is, according to Henkel, obtained in Nepaul from Bassia butyracea, and is said to be white and of high melting point.

Djave fat is greenish yellow in colour, has an agreeable odour of cocoa and melts at 10·2° C.

Nunga oil behaves in a similar manner, but has an unpleasant, smoky smell.

Shea butter is considered the best, and Illipe the lowest quality among the Bassia fats.

Uses.—Alimental: in the fresh state it is used as a food in the countries where it is produced.

Technical: for making soap and candles.

CACAO BUTTER (OIL OF THEOBROMA).
(Cacaobutter; Beurre de Cacao.)

Raw material.—Cacao beans, the seeds of Theobroma cacao L. and of other varieties of Theobroma in Central America, South America, Martinique, etc. The fruit is encased in a dry, tough shell, in shape like a cucumber, and contains some fifty to eighty seeds, arranged in five vertical rows and embedded in a juicy pulp. The seeds are at first fleshy and nearly colourless, but turn golden yellow and reddish to dark brownish red on drying. They are elliptical, both in circumference and cross section, being always more or less flattened; irregularities of shape are not unusual.

Each bean is divisible into shell and kernel (germ). The former consists of a hard, opaque epidermis, with slightly projecting vascular bundles, and a soft translucent inner skin. The epidermis is brittle, and measures about 0·5 millimetre in thickness, its weight amounting to about 12 per cent. of the whole seed. The colourless inner skin is tightly attached to the cotyledons, into the substance of which it is compressed in several places, forming folds of greater or less depth. As a result of this peculiar depression of the skin into the cotyledons, the latter are, as it were, cleft, and may be readily split into angular pieces.

The cacao bean has no albumen ; the seed leaves and the readily distinguishable radicle are attached to the germ. The lobes are dark brown or violet in colour, and are of about the same consistency as almonds. The outer shell of the seed consists of parenchymatous basal tissue, and the soft inner skin of rather flat, polygonal, thin-walled cells from which project appendices named after Mitscherlich. The bulk of the lobes is composed of soft-walled tissue bearing polyhedral or rounded cells. Globules of fat are discernible in old cells, and small granules of aleuron or amylum appear in many. The yield of cacao butter is from 34 to 56 per cent.

Preparation.—The butter is obtained as a bye-product in the manufacture of cocoa from the cacao bean, which is roasted, shelled, ground, and finally pressed.

Properties.—Colour, yellowish white, turning yellow with age; consistency, rather firm; flavour and odour agreeable. The butter contains stearin, palmitin and olein, along with the glyceride of arachic acid.

Specific gravity at 15° C. : fresh, 0·950 to 0·952 ; old, 0·945 to 0·946 (Hager), 0·89 to 0·92 (Chateau), 0·980 to 0·981 (Dietrich). At 100° C. (water at 15° C. = 1), 0·857 (Allen).

Melting point, 33·5° C. ; the temperature rises to 27·3° C. on setting (Rudorff) ; melting point, 29°, setting point, 23° C. (Chateau); melting point, 30° to 33° C. (Herbst), 25° to 26° C., 28° to 29° C. (Bensemann).

Melting point of the fatty acids : commences at 48° to 49° C., and is complete at 51° to 52° C. ; commencement, 49° to 50° C., complete, 52° to 53° C. (Bensemann) ; melting point, 52° C., setting point, 51° C. (Hübl).

Hehner number : 94·59 (Bensemann).

Iodine number: 51·0 (Hübl).

Cacao butter is frequently adulterated with kidney suet (tallow), wax, stearic acid and paraffin. In addition to the usual methods, such as determination of melting point, quantitative chemical reactions, etc., for detecting these falsifications, the following may also be mentioned :—

1. The ether test. Björklund places three grammes of the fat in a tube, pours over them double this quantity of ether, corks the tube, and essays to effect solution by agitation at 18° C. If wax is present a turbidity is produced, which is persistent even on the application of heat. If, however, the liquid remains clear, the test tube is immersed in water at 3° C., and a note made of the time elapsing before the liquid becomes turbid or deposits solid flakes, as well as of the temperature required for their reabsorption by the liquid when removed from the cold-water bath. If the solution, cooled down to 0° C., becomes cloudy in ten to fifteen minutes, and clarifies again at 19° to 20° C., then the cacao butter is pure. For cacao butter containing 5 per cent. of beef tallow these values are, respectively, eight minutes and 22° C., or with 10 per cent. of tallow, seven minutes and 25° C., and so on.

Filsinger modifies the ether test as follows: 2 grammes of the fat are melted in a graduated tube, agitated with 6 cc. of a mixture of 4 parts of ether (specific gravity, 0·725) and 1 part of alcohol (specific gravity, 0·810), and set on one side. Pure oil gives a clear solution.

2. The aniline test. According to Hager, about 1 gramme of cacao butter should be warmed along with 2 to 8 grammes of aniline until dissolved, and then left to stand for an hour if the room temperature is 15° C., or for one and a half to two hours if it is 17° to 20° C. Pure cacao butter will float as a liquid layer on the surface of the aniline.

If, however, tallow, stearic acid, or a little paraffin be present, granules or lumps will appear in the liquid and will adhere to the upper portion of the sides of the vessel if gently agitated. In presence of wax or much paraffin the fatty layer sets, and if there is much stearic acid no separation into layers will occur at all, the whole setting to a crystalline mass.

In the case of pure cacao butter the oil layer sets only after many hours. A parallel experiment should be made with butter of known purity.

Uses.—Medicinal and cosmetic : for ointments, pomades, etc.

Technical : in the manufacture of soap.

CRABWOOD TALLOW.

(Carapafett, Krabholzfett, Andirobaöl ; suif de Carapa.)

Raw material.—The seeds of the crab-tree, Carapa guianensis, in Guiana and Brazil; in the latter country the tree is called Andirobeira.

The seeds, which are about the size of nuts, tetrahedrally flattened, covered with a thin brown shell, and contain about 70 per cent. of fat, are at present employed on a large scale in Guiana and Brazil for the preparation of fat. Carapa Touloucouna (Guinea) yields seeds that contain 65 per cent. of fat, and are utilised for making Touloucouna oil.

Preparation.—The seeds are broken and boiled, whereby the fat separates out as a yellow butter ; the residue is subjected to pressure.

The products vary with the temperature and the extent of pressure applied. From the first pressing a fat, completely solid at +4° C., and melting at 10° C., is obtained. The sample examined by Wiesner was a yellowish mass, light brown in patches, and of the consistency of gruel at 18° C., at which temperature it consisted of an oily matrix with floating islands of harder white matter. The smell is faintly acid and not unpleasantly aromatic, the taste strongly bitter.

According to Cadet this bitter flavour is due to small quantities of strychnine. The bitter substance cannot be removed by agitation with cold water, but prolonged boiling with water takes it away completely.

Under the microscope a colourless, homogeneous, oily matrix is revealed, in which are embedded large numbers of globular masses, composed of fine crystals of fatty acid, in addition to isolated acicular crystals and strongly refractive granules.

Crabwood tallow is completely and readily soluble in ether, but only slightly so in alcohol, and is quickly and completely saponified by alkalis.

Uses.—Technical : in the manufacture of soap and candles.

CHINESE VEGETABLE TALLOW.

(Chinatalg, chinesischer Talg ; suif de la Chine.)

Raw material.—The seeds of Stillingia sebifera, a tree growing wild, and also long cultivated, in China. From the end of the last century it has been extensively cultivated in the north-west of India, the Punjab, the West Indies, and the coast of South Carolina. The seeds are about as large as hazel nuts, black in colour, and are covered with a fairly hard layer of white tallow, the seed albumen also containing fat.

Preparation.—The seeds are gathered in November and December, pounded in stone mortars, and the fairly dry mass exposed to the action of steam for about a quarter of an hour in cylindrical vessels, after which it is subjected to gentle pressure. The congealed mass is warmed over hot embers and filtered through straw.

By strongly pressing the shelled and finely pulverised seeds a liquid oil is obtained, known in China under the name of " Ting-yu ".

Properties.—The properties of the Chinese tallow met with in English commerce are not always the same. The

density varies at medium temperatures between 0·810 and
0·824, and the melting point from 37° to 44·4° C. This fat
is rather hard, leaves but little fatty stain, is white or
greenish white in colour, and has an acid reaction, free acetic
and propionic acids being always present.

According to Thomson and Wood, Chinese tallow consists of palmitin and stearin. It is said to also frequently
contain olein, which is readily comprehensible from the above
description of the manner in which the fat occurs in the
seeds of Stillingia and of the method of preparation. The
stilistearic acid found in this fat by Brack has since turned
out to be palmitic acid.

Uses.—Technical: for making candles and soap.

COCOANUT OIL, COCOANUT BUTTER.

(Cocosnussöl, cocosöl, cocosbutter; huile ou beurre de
coco.)

Raw material.—The inner kernel of the cocoanut, the
seed of Cocos nucifera L., grown in all tropical countries.

The oval, somewhat triangular nuts (stone-fruit) are
about the size of a man's head. The outer envelope is of
tough tissue, beneath which is a thick layer of a brown parenchymatous matrix, containing numerous vascular bundles,
constituting the coir fibre utilised in the textile industry.
Within this again is the hard shell, $\frac{1}{8}$ to $\frac{1}{5}$ of an inch thick,
pierced by three apertures at the base. This shell is used
for turnery work, and encloses the oily kernel of the nut.
The seed itself is a lengthened sphere, light-greyish brown in
colour, and 4 to 5 inches in diameter.

The seed kernels, which before their development consist
almost exclusively of a sweet, liquid, milky albumen—cocoanut milk (forming an important native beverage)—contain
a hard, horny (but fleshy), white, oleaginous albumen—coprah
or copperah—with a nutty flavour, used as food both in the

cooked and raw state, and enclosing a little milky sap in a central cavity. The coprah contains 60 to 70 per cent. of fat.

Preparation.—The kernels are taken out of the shells, boiled for a short time in water, and then broken in mortars and pressed. The resulting milky mass is warmed in large pans and the oil skimmed off from the surface. The residue, known as " Poonak," forms a valuable cattle food.

In Malabar the seeds are cut up by the natives, dried on lath platforms over a coal fire and then on mats in the sun, and finally pressed for oil.

In Tahiti the natives are too indolent to press the seeds, so they are simply crushed and exposed to the sun in perforated troughs. The oil runs into vessels placed underneath, and is sent to market in bamboo tubes holding about a gallon. The most rational arrangements for preparing cocoanut oil in mills are met with in Ceylon and at Coltchin in Malabar, and from these places most of the oil coming to Europe is obtained. Latterly the dried kernels have been shipped to Europe for treatment, the process then adopted being to hot-press the carefully ground material.

Properties.—Specific gravity at 18° C., 0·9250 (Stilurell); at 100° C. (water at 15° C. = 1), 0·863 (Allen).

Melting point : fresh, 22° to 22·5° C.; commercial oil, 24° to 24·5° C.

Setting point, 22° to 23° C.; Brazilian oil mostly 26° to 27° C. (Schaedler); setting point, 19·5° C.; melting point, 23·5° C.; setting point, 15·7° C. (Valenta).

Melting point of the fatty acids, 24·65° C.

Setting point of the fatty acids, 19° C. (Valenta); 20·4° C. (Hübl).

Saponification value, 268·4, 258·3, 257·3; mean, 261·3 (Valenta), 250·3; washed, 246·2 (Moore).

Reichert number, 3·70 (Reichert).

Iodine number of the fat, 8·9 (Hübl).

Iodine number of the fatty acids, 8·39 to 8·79 (Morawski and Demski).

Commercial cocoanut oil is of a fine white colour, with a rather unpleasant smell and a mild characteristic flavour. Under the microscope it appears as a dense network of very long needles. When melted by heat the fatty acids crystallise out of the liquid, cooled to 12° to 15° C., only after a long time. The chief constituent of the fat is cocinin, and small quantities of olein, caproic acid and laurostearic acid are also present. It dissolves in alcohol at the ordinary temperature, and is readily soluble in ether. Cold-pressed oil, which is not met with in commerce, melts below 20° C., sets at 12° to 13° C., the temperature of the fat thereupon rising to 15° C.

Cocoanut oil cannot be saponified by boiling with dilute lyes, but on the other hand saponifies with strong lyes at a moderate temperature (cold saponification). The soaps require a large excess of salt for "salting out," and then form a very solid hard mass. This fat has the highest saponification value of any, and is on that account readily distinguishable from all others, with the exception of palm kernel oil, which stands next to it in this respect. The reason for this peculiarity is accounted for by the large percentage of laurin, myristin, caprin, caprylin and caproin. To the same cause is also ascribable the high Reichert number of the fat.

Uses.—Alimental purposes : in the production of an edible fat.

Technical : in soap and candlemaking.

DIKA FAT, OBA FAT.
(Dikafett, Adika; beurre de Dika.)

Raw material.—The seeds of Mangifera gabonensis (Irivingia Barteri Hook). These are employed not only for the preparation of the fat (which is similar to cacao butter), but

14

also in the production of a chocolate-like mass (Dika bread; chocolat du Gabon) for alimental purposes.

Properties.—Dika fat forms a solid mass of the consistency of cacao butter. At first pure white, it becomes after long keeping somewhat dark yellow in colour externally. According to Wiesner the smell is agreeable, like cocoa, but according to Jackson it is repellent. Old Dika fat kept by Wiesner for six years smelt rather rancid, but not more unpleasant than cacao butter. The flavour is mild and the fat melts at 40° C. Examined under the microscope it is seen to consist of an agglomeration of greatly corroded thick prismatic crystals. Its chemical composition has not apparently been investigated.

According to Deedemans a fat obtained from Mangifera gabonensis Aubry, characterised as Dika, and melting at 30° C., contained laurostearic and myristic acids, but Wiesner asserts that these data are derived from a different fat to the Dika described above. Dika fat is saponifiable, and its hardness renders it highly suitable for candlemaking; it might also be used as a substitute for cacao butter.

BAY OIL, BAY BERRY OIL, LAUREL OIL, EXPRESSED OIL OF BAY.

(Lorbeeröl; huile de laurier.)

Raw material.—Fruit of the Laurel, laurus nobilis; habitat, Southern Europe.

The fruit is about the same size as a small cherry, of round or oval shape, and a lustrous, almost black colour. The thin, brittle integument is covered with fine wrinkles and surrounds a stone as thin as paper, enclosing the loose, light brown, oily-fleshed kernel, which readily divides into two parts. Its odour is strong and peculiarly aromatic, resembling the bitter fatty taste. The kernels contain about

$\frac{5}{10}$ per cent. of volatile oil and 12 per cent. of green fatty oil, together with laurel camphor, a waxy fatty oil (laurostearin), starch, resin, etc.

Preparation.—Crushing and pressing the fruit either in the fresh or dried state.

Properties.—The fat forms a buttery, granular, yellow-green mass, with a strong odour of laurel and a bitter aromatic flavour. It is fluid at 38° R. (47·5° C.), and is completely soluble in ether, whereas alcohol merely extracts the green colouring matter and the ethereal oil.

NUTMEG BUTTER, EXPRESSED OIL OF NUTMEGS, OIL OF MACE.

(Muskatnussöl, muskatbutter ; beurre de muscade, baume de muscade.)

Raw material.—Nutmegs, the seeds of Myristica moschata Thumb.

The tree belongs to the flora of the Indian Archipelago, where it still grows wild, and is also cultivated in those and many other tropical countries. The fruit is about as large as a peach and contains a single seed encased in a carmine coloured integument with numerous fissures. The seed, freed entirely from the hard external shell and superficially from the inner integument, is met with in commerce as nutmeg ; the covering as mace.

Preparation.—The broken nutmegs, or those attacked by insects, are roasted, powdered, and pressed between warm plates.

Uses.—Medicinal and cosmetic.

Properties.—Specific gravity at 15° C. : 0·990 to 0·995.

Melting point : 45° to 51° C. ; 47° to 48° C. The temperature rises on setting to 41·7° or 41·8° C. (Rudorff).

Melting point of the fatty acids : 42·5° C.

Setting point of the fatty acids : 40 °C. (Hübl).

Iodine number : 31 (Hübl).

The commercial Indian oil, known as Banda soap, is met with in two somewhat similar forms.   That from the English colonies is made up in yellowish red, fine-grained, marbled cakes of rectangular form and weighing about 1 lb., which are wrapped in Pisang leaves ; whereas that from the Dutch possessions, though made up in a similar form, is in larger (about 1½ lb.), more coarsely grained, lighter-coloured blocks wrapped in paper.   The oil is of about the consistency of tallow, but more friable ; handles greasy ; is mottled white and yellow, and has a strong smell and flavour of nutmegs.   In hot ether it dissolves completely to a clear solution, but alcohol dissolves only the colouring matter, ethereal oil and liquid oil, of which, along with 40 to 45 per cent. of solid fat, the butter is composed.

Wiesner includes under the group name of Myristica fat both nutmeg butter and two other fats, Otoba and Bicuhiba fat, derived from species of Myristica.   He states that the Banda Islands supply by far the largest quantity of nutmegs in the market, and also send over a large amount of nutmeg butter.   At present this fat is prepared in nearly every country in Europe, but chiefly in Holland, and the Dutch nutmeg butter is esteemed of better quality than that from the Indies in consequence of the frequency with which the latter is adulterated by mineral and vegetable tallow, wax, etc.

Under the microscope nutmeg butter appears to chiefly consist of globular aggregations of acicular crystals of myristin, the granular matter being entirely made up of this substance.   Small globules and small granules, together with entire cells and fragments of tissue from the parenchyma of the seed, are interspersed throughout the mass.   The cells carry the colouring matter and contain starch granules, about 0·02 millimetre in diameter, of regular form, consisting of four to six individual granules.

Otoba fat, also known as American nutmeg butter, is prepared in New Granada from the seeds of Myristica Otoba, in a manner similar to that pursued in the case of the true butter. At first it is tallowy and almost colourless, with merely a faint yellowish tinge, but subsequently becomes granular and assumes a light to dirty brown shade. In the fresh state the odour is pleasant, like nutmeg, but when melted a disagreeable smell is evolved. Microscopically it resembles nutmeg butter, but is poorer in crystalline matter. It melts at 38° C., and, according to Uricochea, contains myristin, olein, and otobite, a substance discovered by this investigator, and occurring as large colourless, tasteless, crystalline prisms, corresponding in composition to the formula $C_{24}H_{26}O_5$, melting at 133° C., and setting into an amorphous condition after being heated to a higher temperature·

Bicuhiba fat is prepared in Brazil from the seeds of Myristica officinalis. It has the same colour and appearance as Indian nutmeg butter, but with a less agreeable odour and sharp acid taste. It behaves like nutmeg butter in presence of solvents and on saponification, and microscopic examination does not reveal any remarkable peculiarities. Its chemical composition has not yet received sufficient attention.

PALM OIL, PALM BUTTER.

(Palmfett, Palmöl ; huile de Palme.)

Raw Material.—The fruit capsule of the palm Elaeis guienensis, plentifully found in Guinea, and latterly extensively cultivated in tropical America, *e.g.*, Brazil (province of Amazona), and the West Indies. Palm oil is also obtained from the fruits of Areca oleiracea and Cocos butyracea, and this oil is likewise produced in the United States, Canary Islands, Madeira, and other places. The fruit of Elaeis guienensis is like a plum in shape, one inch long, of orange

to vermilion red colour, and resembles the olive in consistency.   The individual fruits are so thickly clustered on
the stalk that their mutual pressure causes them to become
polyhedral in shape, and they are so tightly wedged together
that it is a matter of some difficulty to extract one from the
central portion of the bunch.   If, however, the upper fruits
are cut away it is then easy to detach the remainder one by one.

The fat is lodged in the fleshy fruit capsule, in the cells
of which it occurs in lumps.

Preparation.—In the Monbattu country, according to
Schweinfurth, the kernels are removed from the ripe fruit,
and the oil expressed from the flesh, which it resembles in
colour.   The flavour is at first very pleasant, and the oil is
used as food, but it quickly spoils and assumes the gruelly
consistency it subsequently retains, even at the highest
natural temperatures.

The system pursued on the west coast of Africa, south-
ward from Sierra Leone as far as Loango (from which
district the largest quantities of this product are now
obtained), is, according to Sauermann, different from the
foregoing.   The finest oil (which does not come into the
market, being used for home consumption as an edible) is
prepared by boiling the fruit in water, macerating the pulp in
mortars, and boiling up again in water, whereupon the oil
rises to the surface of the liquid.   The method of bleaching
the oil by strong heat (latterly introduced into Europe) is also
understood over there.   In the preparation of the commercial
fat the ripe fruit is kept in heaps until decomposition commences, and the mass is then stamped to a paste in mortars,
warmed, packed into bags, and wrung.   The residual gruel
is then boiled up with water, and the oil collects on the
surface, from which it is removed by skimming.   In this
way the better quality of oil is prepared ; the inferior kinds are
refined on shipboard by boiling in large pans along with water.

Properties.—Fresh palm oil is of the consistency of butter, at medium temperatures, of a bright orange-yellow colour, and with an agreeable odour of violets. On exposure to the air the colour fades continuously, and the smell is no longer pleasant, but turns rancid, especially when the fat has become white. The flavour also is mild when new, and rancid when the fat is old. The melting point of the fresh fat is between 24° and 28° C., but increases with age to 30° to 35° C. Under the microscope the fresh oil exhibits at 20° C. a yellow oleaginous matrix containing small acicular crystals, singly and in groups, and (optically) reddish drops. In old fat the crystals (fatty acid) increase in number, and are massed in large rounded lumps. Even in the semi-rancid state the light yellow oily matrix can be seen by the un-assisted eye to contain whitish portions which are revealed by the microscope as aggregations of crystallised fatty acids. When the fat is melted the fatty acids separate out as small dendritic crystals on cooling. Palmitin (tripalmitin) and olein constitute the chief bulk of palm oil, and free palmitic and oleic acids are also present (their amount increasing as rancidity develops), along with glycerin. There is likewise present an odoriferous substance, probably identical with that found in "violet root," logwood, and in various parts of plants. The colouring matter cannot be extracted by water, being dissolved, not suspended, in the fat. Pelouze and Boudet assume the existence of a ferment in palm oil, its function being to decompose the fat into fatty acids and glycerin. The fat is but slightly soluble in cold alcohol, but readily and completely so in hot alcohol and ether.

Specific gravity at 15° C., 0·945 (Schaedler) ; at 18° C., 0·9040 (Stilurell) ; at 100° C.—referred to water at 16° C.— 0·857 (Allen).

Specific gravity of the fatty acids at 100° C. : 0·8389 (Archbutt).

Melting point : from 27° to 42·5° C., according to the age and origin of the oil.

Melting point of the fatty acids : 47·75° C.

Setting point, 42·5°, 43° C. (Valenta); melting point, 47·8° C.; setting point (average), 44·13°, mostly 44·5° to 45° C., seldom 39° to 41° C. or 44·5° to 46·2° C. (De Schepper and Geitel).

Hehner number : 96·6 (Hehner).

Saponification value : 202·0, 202·5.

Saponification value of the fatty acids : 206·5, 207·3 (Valenta).

Reichert number : 0·5 (Medicus and Scheerer).

Iodine number : 51·5 (Hübl).

The amount of free fatty acids, which even in fresh palm oil approaches 12 per cent., may increase to 100 per cent. in very old oil.

By making use of Chateau's reactions, the following colour changes are observed :—

Zinc chloride gives with the melted fat a deep grey, which becomes a dark grass-green on stirring.

Sulphuric acid colours bluish green.

Mercuric nitrate gives a yellow coloration, turning to pale green, and ultimately pale straw yellow.

Two different kinds of fat are yielded by the fruit of the palm, *viz.*, palm oil (from the outer envelope and flesh) and palm-kernel oil (from the inner kernel of the seed). With regard to the latter, Nördlinger expresses the opinion that its consumption will increase within a short time, especially if the quality be improved, since it is undoubtedly suitable, like cocoanut oil, for edible and pharmaceutical purposes.

Dr. Nördlinger determined the percentage composition of the different palm fruits, and found that the palm kernels richest in fat came from the British possessions at the mouth of the Niger (51·2 per cent.) and the German colonies in the

Togo district (52·1 per cent.), the poorest coming from the British harbour of Winnehah on the Gold Coast, the British possessions on the Sierra Leone littoral (47·5 per cent.), and the Congo State (47·4 per cent.). The Cameroon colonies furnish a medium product containing 49 per cent. of fat.

The setting point of the fatty acids is made use of in determining the value of palm oil, the higher the setting temperature the better the quality. The yield of stearin cannot be reckoned by means of the same tables as are used for tallow, but a separate table has been compiled by Schepper and Geitel for the stearic and oleic acid content of the acids of palm fat.

The table shows the percentage of water, dirt, and neutral fat in a series of palm oils, together with the setting points of the fatty acids obtained.

Variety.	Water.	Dirt.	Neutral Fat. Per cent.	Setting Point of the Fatty Acids. C.
Congo	0·78—0·95	0·35—0·7	16—23	45·90°
Salt ponds	3·5—12·5	0·9—1·7	15—25	26·20°
Addah	4·21	0·35	18	44·15°
Appam	3·60	0·596	25	45·0°
Winnehah	6·73	0·375	20	45·6°
Fernando Po	2·08	0·85	28	45·9°
Brass	3·05	2·00	35·5	45·1°
New Calabar	3·82	0·86	40	45·0°
Niger	3·0	0·7	40—47	45·0°
Accra	2·2—5·3	0·60	53—76	44·0°
Benin	2·03	0·20	59—74	45·0°
Bonny	3·0—6·5	1·20—3·1	44—88·5	44·5°
Great Brassa	2·4—13·1	0·6—3·0	41—70	44·6°
Cameroons	1·8—2·5	0·2—0·7	67—83	44·6°
Cape Labon	3·6—6·5	0·7—1·5	55—69	41·0°
Cape Palmas	9·7	2·70	67	42·1°
Half Jack-Jack	1·9—4·2	0·7—1·24	55—77	39·0—41·3°
Lagos	0·5—1·3	0·3—0·6	58—68	45·0°
Loando	1·5—3·0	1·0—1·9	68—76	44·0°
Old Calabar	1·3—1·6	0·30—0·80	76—83	44·5°
Gold Coast	1·98	0·50	69	41·0°
Sherbo	2·6—7·0	0·3—1·2	60—74	42·0°
Gaboon	2·0—2·8	0·3—0·7	70—93	44·5°

Formerly palm oil was very often adulterated, and not only were additions made to it but entire substitutes were prepared; for example, from wax, tallow and lard, coloured with curcuma and scented with violet root. Such admixtures could be detected by employing acetic ether as a solvent, the pure palm oil alone passing into solution, leaving the others behind. Curcuma would be revealed by the brown coloration ensuing when stirred up with soda lye. At the present price of palm oil these adulterations need not be feared, since they would hardly show any profit.

PALM-KERNEL OIL, PALM-NUT OIL, PALM-SEED OIL.

(Palmkernöl; huile de pepin de Palme.)

Raw material.—Palm kernels, the seed albumen of Elaeis guienensis and a few other palms yielding kernels suitable for oil winning.

Preparation.—On account of the technical difficulties attendant on the process, the pressing is generally performed in Europe, the ordinary mechanical appliances being employed.

Properties.—The oil is white or brown in colour, has an agreeable odour and taste, contains no free fatty acids when fresh, but quickly turns rancid.

Specific gravity at 15° C., 0·952 (Schaedler); at 100° C. (water at 15° C. = 1), 0·886 (Allen).

Melting point of the fat: 25° to 26° C.

Setting point, 20·5° C., old oil; melting point, 27° to 28° C. (Schaedler).

Saponification value: 247·6.

Saponification value of the fatty acids: 265·8 (Valenta).

Iodine number: 13·4 to 13·6.

Iodine number of the fatty acids: crude, 12·07; refined 3·6 to 4·7 (Morawski and Demski).

Uses.—Technical: in soap- and candlemaking, and for solid lubricating materials.

PINEY TALLOW.

(Pineytalg, Vateriafett, Malabartalg, Pflanzentalg; suif de Piney.)

Raw material.—The seeds of the East Indian copal tree, Vateria indica.

Preparation.—Pounding and warm pressing the seeds.

Properties.—The fat is at first yellow, but after prolonged storage it becomes pure white and assumes a granular, or frequently a radial appearance, from the crystallisation of free fatty acids. It is tasteless, and has a faint, pleasant smell. Under the microscope it appears (as a dry preparation) to consist of ill-defined lumps containing here and there small drops of oil; the lumps contain so much air that their form cannot be clearly discerned. If, however, the fat be reduced by olive oil, it is found to consist of a mass of single acicular crystals containing occasional parenchyma cells filled with crystalline needles. When heated to melting point and cooled, the fatty acids crystallise out in fine needles. Babington has examined the physical and chemical properties of this fat, which, according to his researches, has a specific gravity of 0.9260 at $15°$ C. and of 0.8965 at $36.4°$ C. (its melting point). It is saponified by alkalis, and coloured green by chlorine gas; contains about 2 per cent. of a fatty oil extractible by alcohol even in the cold, and possessed of a disagreeable smell. The bulk consists of free fatty acids and fat, solid at ordinary temperatures.

Uses.—Technical: for candlemaking.

VIROLA TALLOW.

(Virolafett, Virolatalg; suif de Virola.)

Raw material.—The seeds of Virola sebifera, from Guiana.

Preparation.—Boiling and pressing the seeds.

Properties.—This fat forms at the ordinary temperature a yellowish, tallowy mass, which when left alone becomes covered with a crystalline incrustation of nacreous lustre. The interior is frequently brownish and interspersed with dots of crystalline aggregations. The smell of the fresh fat recalls that of nutmeg butter, but it quickly becomes rancid. The microscope shows a fatty matrix, enclosing a number of radial fibres of crystalline aggregations (fatty acids), a brown, finely granular mass, and brownish parenchymatous cells, which contain fatty globules and colouring matter along with small aleuron granules.

Virola tallow partially melts at 44° C., and becomes liquid at 50° C. It is completely soluble in alcohol and ether, but only one-half dissolves in aqueous ammonia, and it is but partially saponifiable.

Solid Fats of no Commercial or Industrial Importance.

Alligator pear oil, Avocado oil (Advogatofett, Perseafett ; huile d'Avocatia), from Persea gratisomia Gaertn.

Sierra Leone butter (Afrikanische Pflanzenbutter ; Beurre ou suif de Sierra Leone), from Pentadesma butyracea Don.

Borneo tallow (Borneotalg; suif vegetale de Borneo), from Hopea macrophylla de Vris, H. lanceolata de Vris.

Calaba oil (Calabafett ; huile de Galba, huile de Calaba), from Calophyllum Calaba Br.

Caryocar oil (Caryocaröl ; huile de Piquia), from Rhizobolus amygdalifera Aubl.

Chaulmoogra oil, Gynocard oil (Chaulmugraöl ; huile de Chalmogree, huile de Luiraban), from Gynocardia odorata R. Brown.

Cohune oil (Cohuneöl ; huile de Cohune), from Attalea Cohune Mart.

Comou butter (Comuöl ; huile de Comou), from Oenocarpus Bacaba Mart.

Fulwara butter, Indian butter (Fulwa butter, Phulwara butter, Charea butter; Beurre de Fulware), from Bassia butyracea Roxb.

Gamboge butter (Gambogebutter; suif de Gamboge), from Garcinia pictoria Roxb.

Java almond oil (Java-Mandelöl ; huile de Canaria), from Canarium commune.

Cokum butter, concrete of oil of Mangosteen (Kokum butter, Kokumöl, Goabutter, Brindotalg ; Beurre de Cocum, suif de Goa), from Garcinia indica Chois.

Laurel tallow (Laubeertalg,) from Tetranthera laurifolia Jacq.

Macaja butter (Macajo butter; huile de Macaya), from Cocus aculeata Jacq.

Macassar oil (Macassaröl), from Schleicheria trijuga Willd.

Mafura tallow (Mafuratalg ; suif de Mafura), from Trichilia emetica Vahl.

Mahwa butter, Elupa oil (Mahwabutter, Illipebutter, Bassiaöl; huile d'Illipe, beurre d'Illipe, huile de Mahwa, huile d'Yallah), from Bassia latifolia Roxb., B. longifolia L.

Maloukang butter (Maloukang butter), from Polygala butyracea.

Muriti fat (Muritifett; huile de Muriti), from Mauritia vinifera Mart.

Para butter (Parapalmöl ; huile ou beurre d'Assay), from Euterpe oleacea Mart.

Peka fat (Pekafett), from Rhizobolus butyrosa W.

Rambutan tallow (Rambutantalg), from Nephilium lappaceum L.

Soap-tree oil (Seifenbaumfett; huile de savonnier), from Sapindus emarginatus Roxb.

Souari butter (Souari butter; huile de noix de Sawarri), from Caryocar tomentosum.

Poonseed oil (Tacahamacfett; huile de Taman), from Calophyllum inophyllum L.

Tangkallah fat (Tangkallahfett; beurre de Tangkallah), from Cylicodaphne sebifera Bl.

Tourlourou oil (Turlurufett; huile de Tourlourou), from Manicaria saccifera Gaertn.

Nimb oil, Kohomba oil (Zedraceöl, Margosaöl, Veppamfett; huile de Veppam, huile de Margosa), from Melia azedarach L.

CHAPTER IX.

SEEDS AND FRUITS YIELDING OILS AND FATS—WOOL SOFTENING OILS.

WIESNER in his work on the *Raw Materials of the Vegetable Kingdom* gives the following :—

1. *Mimosae.*

Pentaclethra macrophylla. East coast of Africa. The seeds known as "graines d'Owala" contain about 50 per cent. of a fat akin to olive oil.

2. *Anacardium orientale L.* India.

The Cashews yield some 40 per cent. of an oil, "huile de noix d'Acaju".

3. *Sapindaceae.*

(*a*) Sapindus Pappea Sond. Cap. Cape of Good Hope. Oil is obtained from the seeds by pressure.

(*b*) Sapindus saponaria L. West Indies, South America. Oil is expressed from the seeds in Martinique and Guadeloupe.

(*c*) Sapindus emarginatus Vahl. East Indies. Yields oil seeds.

(*d*) Schleicheria trijuga Willd. India and the Sunda Islands. The seed yields a fatty oil called Macassar oil.

4. *Bombaceae.*

Bombax sp. The seeds are worked up for oil in India.

5. *Sterculiaceae.*

Sterculia foetida L. India. The seeds produce about 60 per cent. of a very fine edible and burning oil.

6. *Camelliaceae.*

(*a*) Camellia japonica L. Japan. Oil-producing seeds.

(*b*) Camellia oleifera Bot. Reg.   China.   Yields oil.

(*c*) Camellia drupifera Lour.   Cochin-China.   Yields oil.

(*d*) Thea oleosa Lour.   Cochin-China.   A burning and edible oil is obtained from the seeds.

7. *Myrtaceae.*

Barringtonia speciosa L.   India.   A burning oil is expressed from the seeds.

8. *Combretaceae.*

Terminalia Catappa L.   India and Java.   Yields an oil preferable, in point of keeping qualities, to olive oil.

9. *Clusiaceae.*

(*a*) Garcinia purpurea Roxb.   The seeds yield fat.

(*b*) Calophyllum Calaba Willd.   West Indies.   The seeds, annually produced in vast quantities in Martinique and Guadeloupe, are suitable for the preparation of oil, and have recently been strongly recommended for this purpose.

(*c*) Calophyllum inophyllum Lam.   East Indies.   See above.

10. *Cucubirtaceae.*

Citrullus sp., Cucumis sp.   The seeds of several of the wild varieties of these two families are gathered in Senegambia and the French East African colonies on account of their richness in fat, and are met with in commerce under the name of " Béraf ".   The oil obtained therefrom may be used as an edible and for soapmaking, the same as olive oil.

11. *Capparodeae.*

Moringa pterygosperma Gaert. (= Moringa oleifera Lam.).   The oily seeds, gathered annually in enormous quantities in Guadeloupe and Martinique, have latterly been recommended for pressing to oil.   The oil (huile de Ben ailé) is highly suitable for perfumery on account of its stability.

12. *Papaveruceae.*

Argemone mexicana L. (= A. spicata Moenih.).   Central America.   Cultivated in India.   The seeds yield oil.

13. *Bignoniaceae.*

Bignonia tomentosa Thumb. Japan. According to Thumberg, the seeds yield oil.

14. *Laurinae.*

Tetranthera Roxburghii Nees. The seeds yield fat.

FRUITS YIELDING OILS AND FATS.

1. *Sapindaceae.*

Peckea butyrosa Aubl. Guiana. The fruit yields a buttery fat.

2. *Compositae.*

(*a*) Polymenia abyssinica L. Abyssinia. Oil is expressed from the fruit.

(*b*) Guizota oleifera D.C. East coast of Africa. The fruit yields oil.

3. *Laurinae.*

(*a*) Laurus glauca Thumb. Japan. Burning oil is obtained from the fruit.

(*b*) Tetranthera laurifolia Jacq. (= Sebifera glutinosa Lour. = Berria chinensis Klein.). Oil is prepared from this fruit in Reunion.

WOOL SOFTENING OILS.

(Wollspicköle, Wollschmelzöle.)

By the above designation are understood compositions for softening sheep's wool in the textile industry. They consist either of neutral oils (olive oil, rape oil, cotton-seed oil, etc.), fatty acids, mixtures of soaps with neutral fats and fatty acids (extract oils, oleic acid from the candlemakers), or of emulsions of oil and water, bone fat (particularly that melted by high pressure steam), or olive sulphur oil. Most wool softeners, especially freshly prepared extract oils, contain variable proportions of water and substances volatile at

15

100° C. (volatile fatty acids and sometimes mineral oils of low boiling point, such as petroleum spirit, etc.), as well as sediment (dirt), and frequently also mineral acids (chiefly sulphuric acid).

The requisite qualifications for a good oil for wool are: easily washable and freedom from drying and "gumming" substances and mineral oil. The drying oils are liable to cause spontaneous ignition of the oiled wool, and resin gives rise to patchy dyeing, in respect of which mineral oil is equally blamed. However, it is only in rare instances that pure mineral oil is employed, the oils most generally used being mixtures of neutral oils and fatty acids with mineral oil, so that the latter is got rid of in washing the cloth, the mixture forming with the soap (containing an excess of soda) employed emulsions, miscible with water and therefore passing away in the effluent.

Dealers, consumers and fire insurance companies stipulate that wool softening oils shall contain at least 85 per cent. of saponifiable fats, and at most 15 per cent. of mineral oil. This rule, however, is not always adhered to.

Formerly pure olive oil was alone used for this purpose, then mixtures containing cheap seed oils were introduced, and finally oleic acid was adopted as being more easily washable, and cheaply produced as a bye-product in the manufacture of stearin. It is true that this acid corrodes the metal carding pins, but this defect is more than counterbalanced by its cheapness and easy manipulation. With the recovery of the fat from the waste liquor, the so-called extract oil—true fulling oil, a mixture of the softening oil and the soap employed—came into use. At first this consisted solely of pure saponifiable oils, but the introduction of the cheap composite oils and the dark colour of the extract oil facilitated adulteration with mineral oil, so that now, unfortunately, mineral oils are generally present up to 20 or 30 per cent., a circumstance unfitting the oil for use in soapmaking, since soap cannot be prepared from such a mixture.

The most suitable oils for wool softening are the so-called "soluble," or, more properly, emulsifiable oils, which facilitate regular manipulation, the fat spreading better over the fibre by reason of the homogeneity of the emulsion; this also induces the spinner to add a larger proportion of water than to non-emulsifiable oil.

The emulsions of oil and water which are sold for wool softening frequently contain as much as 88 per cent. of water. One of them was found on examination to consist of :—

> 12 per cent. olive oil
> 88   ,,   water

and another—

> 33·4 per cent. impure wool fat
> 7·0   ,,   mineral oil
> 1·06   ,,   iron soap
> 58·04   ,,   water

Mestone gives the following formulae :—

OLIVE OIL.

> 30 per cent. olive oil
> 70   ,,   rape oil, with rosemary oil

OLEIN.

> 36 per cent. fatty acids
> 64   ,,   mineral oil

EXTRACT OIL.

> (1) 90 per cent. fatty acids
>   5   ,,   mineral oil
>   5   ,,   water
>
> (2) 65   ,,   fatty acids
>   24   ,,   mineral oil
>   9   ,,   neutral fat
>   2   ,,   water
>
> (3) 30   ,,   fatty acids
>   50   ,,   mineral acids
>   7·5   ,,   resin
>   12   ,,   neutral fat
>   0·5   ,,   water

CHAPTER X.

TREATMENT OF SOLUBLE OILS.

FATTY acids and neutral oils, containing ammonia soap in solution, with or without resin.

Moritz Stransky's method of preparing (by sinolisation) wool softening oils is based on the production of the animal and vegetable fats (used for oiling the wool in the manufacture of shoddy or in spinning) in such a manner that they are no longer capable of taking up oxygen, and therefore cannot become rancid or "turn"; the possibility of spontaneous ignition of the oil or oiled wool and yarn being thereby obviated. In the course of the process the albumen and glycerin are extracted from the vegetable oils and the drying power destroyed, and the fatty acids of the animal fats are neutralised. The oils become soluble in water, whereby they acquire a series of properties of economic value. In a much higher degree is the circumstance worthy of note that the operation of spinning is rendered much safer, in that the danger from fire, always imminent when unsinolised oils are used, is reduced to a minimum.

TREATMENT OF THE OIL AFTER LEAVING THE PRESS.

As we have seen on page 13, the freshly pressed oil contains such a quantity of impurities—portions of the seed-constituents, such as cellular matter, colouring matter, gum, mucilage, albuminoid bodies, etc., that have escaped through the cloths and bags during the operation of pressing—that it appears turbid and dirty, and requires to be left at rest for a long time in order that such portions as are heavier than the oil may subside. Oils prepared by extraction, on the other hand, exhibit these impurities either not at all or in very slight degree, and have usually merely taken up a small quantity of colouring matter which can be altogether or partly destroyed by refining or bleaching.

When freshly pressed oil is left to settle for some time, the impurities containing moisture are the first to be deposited, and their early removal is desirable, since they tend to produce rancidity. The greater portion of the impurities will come down in a comparatively short time, but there still remains in suspension a small quantity which must be got rid of by a suitable filtration (as generally with linseed oil) or treatment ("refining") with chemicals.

Refining is frequently inevitable, although it cannot be denied that the difficulties in the way of subsequent clarification, thereby engendered, are considerable; the risk of loss from the formation of a layer of emulsion between the oil and water (subsequent to the water treatment), from which the oil is only recoverable with difficulty, being also great. Refining, however, constitutes the only known means of quickly rendering the oil ready for use, and preventing the formation of free fatty acids so especially prejudicial to oils for alimental and lubricating purposes.

Prominent among refining processes for oils are :—

1. Sulphuric acid treatment, the quantities recommended by various authorities being somewhat divergent.

2. Treatment with sulphuric acid and zinc oxide or lead oxide.

3. Treatment with caustic lyes, ammonia, carbonates of the alkalis, lime, zinc chloride.

4. Refining with tannin.

5. The Ekenberg process (emulsification).

6. Various new processes, which will be minutely described.

The mechanical and other appliances used in refining, and the subsequent filtration, will be dealt with in a separate section.

The whole of the vegetable oils and some of the fats are coloured, and as this colouring is prejudicial in many of the uses to which they are put, they require to be bleached. Oils for alimental purposes neither require, nor should they be submitted to, bleaching, because this process, whether performed with or without the aid of chemicals, impairs their quality. This notwithstanding, oils destined for the adulteration of edible oils in general, and olive oil in particular, are mostly bleached.

The bleaching of oils intended for technical purposes is, notwithstanding the number of powerful bleaching agents obtainable, attended with difficulties arising from the formation of a layer of emulsion between the oil and the bleaching liquid, whereby considerable loss is incurred.

Among the well-known methods of bleaching may be cited :—

1. Hydrogen peroxide process.
2. Sodium peroxide process.
3. Sodium bichromate and hydrochloric acid method.
4. Potassium permanganate method.
5. Chlorine process.
6. Bleaching with nitric acid and nitrates.
7. Sulphurous acid bleaching.
8. Bleaching by common salt and electricity.
9. Air bleaching.
10. Bleaching by sunlight.
11. Bleaching by absorption.

The inconvenience of bleaching by chemical reagents has already been referred to, but they nevertheless afford the sole means of rapidly attaining the end in view. Air bleaching, as also bleaching by sunlight, induces considerable modifications in some oils, since it necessitates contact with oxygen. Bleaching by light requires, furthermore, a very long time to accomplish, and the absorption process also possesses numerous drawbacks.

REFINING BY SULPHURIC ACID.

The sulphuric acid treatment is the one most commonly pursued for refining fatty oils, particularly rape oils and other technical oils. It was first proposed by Cowen, but subsequent improvements have been introduced, so that there are in existence a number of methods, differing in the details of the reaction of the acid upon the oil and in the effect of the concomitant conditions, the best known processes being those of Thenard, Cogan, Twistleton Hall and Puscher.

Whatever advantages refining by sulphuric acid may possess, it is none the less attended with a variety of inconveniences, which may, it is true, be avoided by the exercise of sufficient care in the conduct of the operation, but are still calculated to detract from its value. If only a small quantity of the acid be added, the decomposing action is restricted to the albuminoid and mucilaginous substances, but if a large amount is employed, the oil easily suffers decomposition by the conversion of the triglyceride into glycerin and fatty acid. This decomposition is accompanied by a reddening of the oil, a coloration which the most powerful bleaching agents are unable to remove. Temperature also exerts considerable effect on the reaction, the red coloration becoming manifest should the temperature be too high.

The removal of the sulphuric acid from the oil plays an important part at the end of the process, since every trace of sulphuric acid must be completely taken out by washing with water.

The purifying action of sulphuric acid on vegetable oils rests on its powerful affinity for water. The oil is deprived of water by the process, and a portion of the impurities is removed from solution, separating out as carbonised flakes.

COGAN'S METHOD.

400 to 500 parts by weight of oil are placed in a vat, and to them is added a mixture of 5 parts of concentrated sulphuric acid with an equal quantity of water, the acid mixture being divided into three portions, one of which is added and

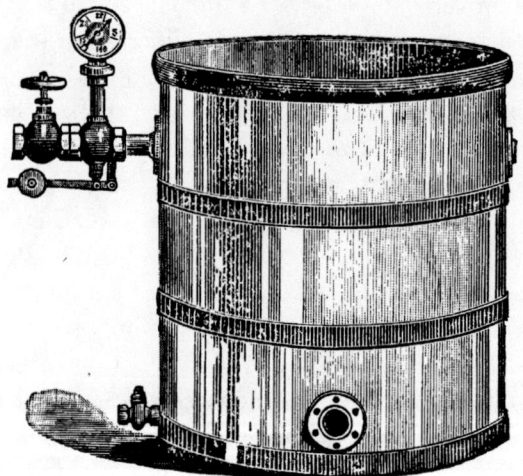

FIG. 75. Jacketed Refining Pan.

stirred in for half an hour, followed by a second portion, kept stirring for one hour. After adding the final portion of acid, agitation is continued for two hours. In the meantime the oil becomes darker and darker, and finally almost black like coal-tar. The temperature of the oil rises considerably, especially when large quantities of extraneous substances are present, and sulphurous acid gas is evolved.

After the oil has remained in contact with the acid for eleven hours, it is transferred to a copper boiling pan, fitted near the bottom with three steam pipes, each of which

terminates in a rose. Steam is admitted until the oil has
attained the boiling temperature of water, whereupon it is
run into a funnel-shaped cooler, fitted with a tap at one
side some 4 inches from the bottom. In this vessel the
oil remains for twelve hours, after which the lower tap is
opened, the acid liquid carefully drawn off, and the tap turned
off again. The upper tap is now opened and the perfectly
clear oil run out, leaving behind 4 inches of very turbid
oil, which remains in the vessel until the next batch of oil is
run in. When the turbid oil has increased to such an extent
that it reaches above the level of the upper tap, it is drawn
off specially and filtered. Cogan's process yields an extremely
well-refined oil, but it is rather expensive, the 500 kilos. of oil
having to be heated for six hours before a temperature of
100° C. is attained. Lead-lined wooden vessels may be substituted for the copper pans, but the leaden plates used must
be soldered together with pure lead, in the same manner as
those employed for lining sulphuric acid chambers; since
were ordinary solder (a mixture of lead and tin) used, it
would be corroded by the acid liquor, and the oil contam-
inated by metallic compounds, whereas pure lead is totally
unaffected by sulphuric acid.

TWISTLETON HALL'S METHOD.

In this patent process the oil is treated with a volatile
hydrocarbon, such as benzoline (benzine) or petroleum ether
or other suitable solvent, in which it is dissolved and then
refined by sulphuric acid. Rape oil and linseed oil in particular are refined in this way by being incorporated with
about their own weight of hydrocarbon and then agitated
along with some 5 per cent. of sulphuric acid (specific gravity,
1·840 to 1·750). The liquid is then separated from the
sludgy sediment, and, after being completely freed from the
acid by washing with water, is filtered through bone black,

the solvent being subsequently driven off by means of direct steam. The process is of particular interest for oil obtained by extraction, the benzine extract being concentrated as far as is necessary, and the removal of the solvent completed after the oil has been refined. The increased efficiency of the sulphuric acid is attributable to the finer state of division rendered possible by the greater fluidity of the liquid, and to the fact that many of the impurities are more or less insoluble in benzine.

PUSCHER'S METHOD.

Puscher facilitates and assists the action of the sulphuric acid by means of alcohol. Equal parts of 96 per cent. alcohol and sulphuric acid of 66° B. are mixed with the oil. As soon as flocculent turbidity commences, the oil is left to settle for twenty-four hours, drawn off from the sediment and washed. This process is said to decolorise the oils to a greater degree than any other, the increased efficiency being ascribed to the formation of ethylsulphuric acid.

THENARD'S PROCESS.

Oil clarified by storage is intimately mixed with 1 or 2 per cent. of 66° B. concentrated sulphuric acid by means of mechanical stirrers, an air blast, or latterly by centrifugal emulsifiers. The acid is most suitably introduced in the form of small drops from a leaden vessel, the oil being already in motion, a condition necessary to prevent the acid settling at the bottom, where it would completely decompose the adjacent oil. The oil vessel consists either of a large wooden tub or a lead-lined iron pan. Within a few minutes after the introduction of the acid, a greenish coloration of the oil may be observed, which gradually passes into black, so that by reflected light the oil looks like tar. If the oil be examined in thin layers by transmitted light, the presence of small black flakes may be observed swimming in a water-white liquid. After prolonged reaction the flakes collect together, and the process may be regarded as complete when a drop of the mixture placed on an opaque surface appears clear.

According to Thenard the oil should be left at rest for several hours to allow the flakes and the unaltered sulphuric acid they envelop to settle, so that the oil may become ready for separation from the deposit.

In practice, however, it is found that by this method the oil acquires a pale reddish tinge, and that it is better to add to the oil, as soon as the acid reaction is completed, some 20 per cent. (by weight) of hot water, the agitation being continued until the water is well mixed with the acid, which it dilutes and renders harmless. The stirrers are then stopped, and the mixture left at rest. At the end of four or five hours three layers will have formed; the upper one of oil, with a somewhat milky appearance from small particles of water in suspension; the central layer of sludge or sediment, resting on the mixture of water and acid constituting the bottom layer. The sediment, which amounts to about 1 or $1\frac{1}{2}$ per cent. of the weight of the oil, and consists of glycerosulphuric acid along with palmito-, stearo- and oleosulphuric acids (the so-called conjugate or Fremy's acids), finds employment in the manufacture of spirit and tinplate; acting in the former case presumably as an instigator of fermentation, and in the latter assisting, by reason of its acid nature, in the production of a clean surface of metal.

In order to free the oil in the washing vessel from the final traces of sulphuric acid, it is washed with 30 to 40 per cent. of water at 60° C. After long settling the acid water separates from the oil, which may then be designated " free from sulphuric acid ". It is, however, advisable to add a small quantity of milk of lime in any case, but the amount must be carefully regulated, otherwise at the high temperature (60° C.) of the operation an emulsion of lime may be formed that will be difficult to get rid of.

Inconvenience frequently arises in the washing process, through the formation of emulsions, which may even occur in acid solutions; the under water, although having a strongly acid reaction, appearing quite milky from the oil in suspension, and it is only after some weeks' storage that the oil (up to 10 or 15 per cent.) separates out. Of course this quantity of oil cannot be allowed to run to waste, so it is advisable to provide collecting reservoirs suitable for all purposes. These dreaded emulsions may be avoided by careful manipulation in drawing off the oil from the refining pan, and by a proper conduct of the operation of refining, their formation being due to the introduction into the oil of the gummy matters in the acid sludge, a property of gums well known and utilised on a large scale in the preparation of artificial emulsions.

Should, however, an emulsion be produced notwithstanding the precautions adopted, the inconvenience may be minimised, if not entirely obviated, by a supplementary washing with water containing Glauber salt, common salt, copper sulphate or other substances to increase the density of the water. In many oil works it is customary to employ these salts constantly as a preventive of emulsions, but the *raison d'être* of their action is seldom known. The increase in the percentage of the ash of the oil, resulting from this treatment, must be regarded as a defect.

The next process the oil has to undergo is that of filtration, to free it from contained water and impart the necessary brilliance. The construction of the filter is described in a separate section. Thenard's method is extensively applied to oils intended for burning, particularly rape oil. When the oils are to be used for lubricating purposes, regard must be had to minimising the percentage of free fatty acids, as well as removing the sulphuric acid. The fatty acids almost always present in oil refined by the Thenard process are most effectively removed by adding a suitable amount of lime, which results in the formation of lime soaps.

BRUNNER'S PROCESS.

Brunner proposes the following process for refining oils (especially rape oil) by sulphuric acid, based on the express condition that the amount of acid must be reduced to a minimum, in order to make the oil acid-free. This reduction in the amount of the reagent increases the duration of the reaction, which must then always be assisted by warmth. The freshly pressed oil is run into a large lead-lined vat fitted with paddles, and containing a steam coil. The oil is rapidly heated to the temperature of boiling water by means of high pressure steam, and the acid is then run in in a thin stream, the paddles being set in rapid motion, and the stirring continued until the whole of the liquid has turned black. As soon as this condition is reached the steam is turned off, but the paddles are kept at work for another half-hour or so.

The dark-coloured liquid is then transferred to another vat, where it is washed with water, the liquid being stirred until all the oil is in. When the oil and water are mixed the stirrers are stopped, and the liquid soon separates into two layers, the oil floating on the surface of the acidified water, which latter is dark coloured from the fine carbonaceous particles it holds in suspension. This washing process is repeated, and, if necessary, performed a third time, the operations in any case succeeding each other without delay. By this abbreviated treatment of the oil with a small proportion of acid and quick separation by washing, the action of the acid is confined to the decomposition of extraneous substances, and, what is important, does not extend to the production of changes resulting in the separation of oleic acid in the oil itself. Usually two washings suffice to entirely free the refined oil from sulphuric acid.

According to Wilke, 1800 parts by weight of oil and 6 parts by weight of English sulphuric acid should be mixed and stirred for two hours. Then are added 14 parts by weight of calcined lime and 6 parts by weight of clay, previously mixed, and 1800 parts by weight of water, the whole being thereupon boiled for three hours with continued stirring. When cold the oil is drawn off, and will be found perfectly purified. It is of the utmost importance that all traces of sulphuric acid should be removed from the oil, on account of the energetic action of this acid on metals. To ascertain whether any sulphuric acid still remains in the oil, a sample should be shaken up with a little barium chloride solution. If the oil remains unaltered it is free from sulphuric acid, but if it becomes opalescent or exhibits a white turbidity, a certain proof is afforded that free sulphuric acid is still present, and in sufficient quantity to exert injurious action. It must, however, be mentioned that the performance of the test in the above simple manner is likely to lead to erroneous conclusions, since the liquid may be rendered turbid without there being any sulphuric acid present; the salts of phosphoric acid in the oil also producing a precipitate with barium chloride. To avoid this error, the barium chloride solution should contain a fourth or fifth part of pure hydrochloric acid, which will prevent the precipitation of the phosphates, and leave only the sulphuric acid precipitate visible.

CHAPTER XI.

THE oil to be treated is first mixed with a minimum quantity of sulphuric acid, then separated therefrom and repeatedly washed until the oil gives no precipitate with barium chloride. In the course of the reaction of sulphuric acid on oil, a compound of sulphuric and oleic acids is formed, which on treatment with a large volume of water is split up again into its constituent acids, so that the refined oil always contains a certain quantity of free oleic acid. To remove this and render the oil perfectly free from acid, use is made of the property of zinc oxide of forming an insoluble compound, zinc oleate, with oleic acid. Zinc oxide is met with in commerce in the form of zinc white at a comparatively low price, and only a small quantity, *viz.*, 1 part by weight, of zinc white is required for the treatment of 100 parts of oil. Intimate mixture of the two substances is ensured by stirring up the zinc white with three or four times its weight of the oil, until they form a thick whitish liquid, which is thereupon stirred into the oil by degrees. After several hours' rest the greater part of the unchanged zinc oxide will have settled down along with the zinc oleate, but as it takes a very long time for the whole to subside, the operation is expedited by filtration. It is also proposed to pass the oil into a vat containing zinc turnings, which after a short time become covered with a white deposit of zinc oleate, whereby the oil is refined. It is, however, difficult to produce a clean surface on the zinc turnings for use over again, and for this reason the zinc white process is preferable. Provided the work has been well done, the oil purified by this means possesses in a high degree all the qualities of good oil. It is very light in colour, and may be almost colourless if the original oil was already pale in colour. It is inert towards metals, and does not readily turn acid, even after prolonged exposure to the air.

The lead oxide process of refining is carried out, in the main, on the lines laid down for the zinc oxide method, but the actual behaviour of the reagent is somewhat different. The resulting lead oleate does not subside so readily as the zinc compound, but remains dissolved in the oil. The latter is, it is true, freed from all traces of free acid, but acquires by reason of the lead oleate a high degree of consistency, which may, when, for example, more lead oxide is used than is absolutely necessary, and when the action is assisted by warmth, even attain that of butter. This change usually occurs if the oil contains about $2\frac{1}{2}$ to 3 per cent. of lead oxide.

REFINING WITH CAUSTIC ALKALIS, AMMONIA, CARBONATES OF THE ALKALIS, LIME.

1. *Caustic Potash method.*—The purification of oils by caustic potash is based on the fact that, when strong potash is brought into contact with oil for only a short space of time, it will completely destroy extraneous matter without specially attacking the oil. The operation is performed by placing the oil in a large pan, heating it up to the temperature of boiling water, and then stirring in 2 to $3\frac{1}{2}$ (at most) per cent. of the strongest caustic potash. In a short time, the agitation having been maintained, the liquid begins to turn very turbid, a frothy head and flocculent scum appearing on the surface, the flocculent matter soon, however, sinking to the bottom and leaving the supernatant oil clear.

As the mucilaginous matters are partly soluble in caustic potash and partly coagulated as a curd resembling egg albumen, they are easily separated from the oil. For this purpose, which is accomplished by filtration, flannel filters are used, the rough side of the cloth being turned towards the oil, which is in this way obtained perfectly clear.

In this method also it becomes a question of using the minimum quantity of the reagent—in this case, caustic potash—since the employment of large amounts involves too great a loss of oil. If more potash is used than is absolutely necessary for the removal of the impurities, then the caustic lye attacks the oil itself, and converts a portion into soap, which will remain dissolved in the layer of liquid below the oil. In the case of refineries which are carried on in connection with soapmaking, or which have opportunities of utilising the once-used lye, the loss in question becomes of little importance.

The minimum quantity of lye cannot be determined with accuracy, since it depends on the degree of impurity present in the oil. For instance, a freshly pressed oil prepared under very high, _e.g._, hydraulic, pressure, will evidently contain a larger quantity of impurities than an oil that has been stored for some time. Therefore a larger amount of alkali will be needed for refining a freshly pressed oil than for older oils that have been stored. The only way to ascertain the minimum amount of lye required by an oil is by accurately testing a small quantity of the oil to be refined, and by practical experience. The advantages of refining by caustic potash lye are not inconsiderable, the process being rapid and unobjectionable, yielding an absolutely acid-free product, every trace of acid having been promptly neutralised by the alkali. If performed in wooden vats heated by steam, or in clean iron pans if steam is scarce, the oil does not acquire any dark coloration; copper pans should, however, be

16

avoided, the metal being attacked by the potash, and a green coloration, due to the solution of copper compounds, imparted to the oil.

The only objection that can be urged against the potash process is that the oil does not lose any of its original colour, but may, on the contrary, if an excess of potash has been employed, even become darker; this may not be noticed in isolated cases, but is nevertheless undesirable.

2. *Caustic Soda method*.—This is chiefly employed for cotton-seed oil, linseed oil, etc., and acts similarly to caustic potash by partially saponifying the fatty acids and forming a paste with the resultant soap and the water, whereby mechanical impurities are enveloped and carried down. A few of the impurities are, however, attacked chemically, such as the resin acids, which are converted into resin soaps. Saponification of the oil must be avoided, the endeavour being to saponify only the fatty acids and resin, leaving the oil unchanged. Moreover, concentrated solutions of soap exert a powerful emulsifying influence on oil, and difficulties arising from this cause have not infrequently to be coped with. The residue is much greater than from the acid treatment, but, as has already been stated, can be utilised in soapmaking.

On the other hand, the freedom from mineral and fatty acids, resulting from the alkali treatment, renders the oil advantageous for lubricating purposes.

(*a*) Bareswille's method. The oil is incorporated with 2 to 3 per cent. of concentrated lye (36° B.), and gradually heated up to 65° to 70° C., whereby a foamy head will be formed, which afterwards becomes flocculent. The coagulum encloses mechanically suspended impurities, and gradually subsides when the oil is left at rest. The supernatant oil is thoroughly washed with hot water to remove any dissolved soap, and the deposited residue, consisting of lye and soap, is utilised for soapmaking.

Care should be taken in carrying out this treatment that the temperature does not exceed 75° C., since otherwise the soap formed would granulate and float on the surface, rendering the purification illusory. The loss in this process may amount to 10 per cent. of the weight of the oil.

(b) Dangivillé prescribes the use of very dilute lye, air being excluded. The Patent Specification states that the oil should be heated to 35° to 40° C. in a vacuum pan with lye of 0·25 to 1·5 per cent. strength, the evaporated water being constantly replaced. After a short time the contents of the pan are transferred to a suitable clarifying vessel. The watery liquid should be equal in volume to the oil.

(c) According to Longuerre, in refining cotton-seed oil with lye, the colouring matter should be recovered by saponifying the residue with strong lye and separating the resulting soap with highly concentrated lye. The sub-lye containing the colouring matter is treated with alum or protochloride of tin, which precipitates the colour as an alum or tin lake.

No practical value is attributed to the processes b and c.

(d) Errard employs only weak lyes of about 12° to 14° B.

By a preliminary determination the most suitable quantity is ascertained, and this amount is added to the oil, agitation being continued until the reaction is complete. After prolonged rest three layers form in the liquid, the oil uppermost, then an emulsion of soap, oil and dirt, and, underneath, the strongly alkaline water. If this separation does not take place, some brine is added to effect a kind of salting out, subsidence being at the same time facilitated by the increase in density imparted to the water. After settling, the clear oil is drawn off and repeatedly washed with water, an operation that must be continued until the effluent water comes away perfectly clear. All the washings are united, and the fatty acids thrown down by means of an acid. If the washing has not been well done, the danger is incurred that the oil may become turbid within a few days, and may, moreover, encrust the wick with a deposit of alkali carbonate, causing it to break off.

3. *Ammonia method.*—For several reasons refining with ammonia is preferable to the lye methods, but the evil of emulsions, difficult to remove, is also encountered. Ammonia attacks organic compounds, and renders them insoluble in oil. The ammonia method is also suitable for application to rancid olive oil as follows: 100 kilos. of oil are intimately mixed with 1 kilo. of water containing $\frac{1}{2}$ kilo. of ammonia in solution, and, after the emulsion is formed, left to stand for a considerable time to allow the precipitated salts to subside. According to De Keyser, better results can be obtained by using concentrated ammonia and leaving the emulsion to settle, with exclusion of air. A subsequent careful washing with hot water is essential to remove the last traces and smell of ammonia. The washings, which are at first turbid, must be collected and left to settle, in order to prevent loss of oil. The method has only met with limited application.

4. *Lime Water method.*—To every 100 parts, by weight, of oil, 24 parts of lime water, $\frac{1}{16}$ part of Seignette salt, and $\frac{1}{16}$ part of zinc sulphate are used.

The lime water is prepared from 12 to 15 parts, by weight, of well-burned lime, and 30 to 36 parts, by weight, of soft water; and, if not intended for immediate use but stored for some time, care must be taken to prevent, as far as possible, access of air.

The finely powdered salts are dissolved in the boiling lime water, and the liquid, still at boiling temperature, stirred into the oil by degrees. The oil is agitated for another half-hour, or a full hour, so as to complete the mixture. The separation and clarification are effected at 15° to 18° C. within twenty-four hours, the operation having to be performed in a specially warmed room when the temperature is lower. The settling vessel is capacious and made of deal, the lid, which is pierced by a hole in the centre, being fastened by a bolt or wedge. A plunger resembling a churn dasher, but bearing several disks with larger perforations, serves to agitate or beat the oil, being raised and lowered by means of a handle fitting into the hole in the vat lid.

After beating and stirring for an hour the impurities floating on the surface are removed by a ladle, and the oil left at rest until the following day.

A tap at about an inch or so above the bottom of the vessel serves to draw off the water from the purified oil, and as soon as the next layer of soapy matter begins to issue the tap is turned half off, and care taken to collect the clear oil separately directly it appears.

The turbid liquid should also be collected separately, since a little oil will separate from it in a few days, or it may be used as it is for cart grease.

After the lime treatment the oil must be washed repeatedly with hot water until perfectly pure and clear.

5. *Zinc Chloride method.*—For refining rape oil zinc chloride is recommended (either used in the dry state or as a highly concentrated solution), behaving like sulphuric acid and effecting a greater or less degree of change in organic substances. It has been ascertained by experiment that zinc chloride dissolves, and in course of time carbonises, the mucilaginous bodies in crude oil, but does not attack the oil itself, provided the correct proportions of oil and reagent are adhered to. In Wagner's experiments rape oil was continuously shaken up with $\frac{1}{2}$ per cent. of a syrupy solution of zinc chloride (specific gravity, 1·85). The oil at first assumed a yellow-brown colour, turning afterwards to dark brown, and at the end of a few days deposited dark

brown flakes at the bottom of the vessel, the oil itself still remaining dark and turbid. On heating, with introduction of steam and addition of hot water, the oil, after standing for a few days, separated clean and pure from the subjacent watery liquid.

6. *Boiling with water.*—A few oils—such as linseed oil, castor oil, etc.—are refined by simple boiling with water. To this end the oil is mixed with 20 per cent. of its bulk of water and the temperature gradually raised to 100° C. The albumen coagulates and throws down mechanical impurities.

REFINING WITH TANNIN.

The oil is strongly warmed in a suitable vessel (wooden vat with steam coil), and a 5 per cent. solution of tannin added and well stirred in. The tannin solution is most easily prepared by extracting fresh tan in water and sieving the brown decoction. When mixed with the oil it forms a milky liquid, which after cooling and long standing separates into an upper layer of clear oil, a central zone containing oil, and a bottom stratum of water. The oil is drawn off, and the intermediate layer of sediment is filtered, since it yields up a certain amount of oil. Tannin coagulates albuminoid bodies, and therefore brings the albumen in the crude oil to a curd, which, by surrounding suspended impurities, also effects a mechanical purification. This explains the difference in the results obtained by the use of tannin solution at various times. Decomposition of resin and removal of dissolved impurities (other than albuminoids) are here out of the question, and for this reason the tannin method is only employed for linseed and cotton-seed oils, its chief use, however, being for fish oils. The colouring matter of the oil also remains unaffected, so that oils refined with tannin are always dark coloured.

CHAPTER XII.

EKENBERG AND ASPINALL'S METHODS OF REFINING OILS.

MARTIN EKENBERG, as the result of experiments made with the centrifugal emulsifier of the "Aktie Bolaget separator" of Stockholm, elaborated a process for the refining of oils, which was tested by Dr. Rudolph Benedikt, and reported on by him as follows:—

"The centrifugal emulsifier affords, as is well known, a means of emulsifying liquids in a most intimate degree, so that it may be advantageously employed for mixing fatty oils, melted fats, tar oils, etc., with sulphuric acid, alkali solutions, and the like, or for washing these oils with water. The resulting emulsions can, in so far as they do not unmix completely when left at rest, be separated by the Laval separator."

Ekenberg's method of refining oils consists in passing them continuously through a system of emulsifiers and separators, and in this manner subjecting them to the action of various reagents as well as performing the necessary washings. The combination of an emulsifier and a separator constitutes an "element" of the system. In cases where the emulsion separates so readily as to render the separator unnecessary, a Florentine receiver is used instead. The number of elements required to form a battery depends on the number of washings to be performed. As a rule the emulsion passes from the emulsifier direct to the separator, the reaction between the liquid or dissolved purifying agent and the impurities to be removed from the oil occurring without delay, by reason of the intimate contact produced.

When, in individual instances, prolonged reaction is necessary, one has merely to add a couple of reservoirs to the
system to receive the mixture alternately. Should, for
example, the mixture have to remain twenty-four hours, each
of the storage vessels must be large enough to hold one day's
production, and whilst the one is being filled the contents of
the other from the previous day are being passed through
the separator. The proportions of the mixtures are regulated either by attaching conical regulators to the supply
taps, or, in large installations, employing pumps of known
capacity. Preliminary heaters and surface coolers are used
for quickly applying or withdrawing heat. The liquids are
transferred from one element to another by means of centrifugal pumps driven direct from the shaft of the emulsifier
or separator, and therefore working in unison with these
machines.

Any desired amount of oxidation by air or deodorisation
with dry steam is effected by Ekenberg in a newly invented
gas emulsifier.

The capacity of a battery with emulsifiers and separators
of the usual size varies with the kind of oil, the method of
refining, and the mixing proportions, from 3000 to 6000 kilos.
per diem; but when fatty oils very rich in acid—up to 25
per cent. of free fatty acids—are to be refined, for which
purpose larger amounts than usual of dilute lyes are required
in the washing, the capacity of the apparatus falls below
these limits.

The plates of the emulsifiers and the drums of the separators are made of acid steel, capable of offering an unusual
amount of resistance to the action of alkalis and concentrated
sulphuric acid. For dilute acids bronze plates are used, the
drums of the separators being dipped in a molten alloy of
lead and antimony. The following examples serve to illus-
trate the Ekenberg method :—

1. *Refining vaseline oil and heavy mineral oils.* — For refining these oils the usual quantities, 8 to 25 per cent., of sulphuric acid are employed, and the oil washed with dilute lye and finally with water.

The oil is run from the tank No. 1 into the emulsifier along with once-used acid from a separator and intimately mixed therewith, the mixture passing into a separator which removes the acid and leads to tank No. 2. The quantity of acid depends on the quality of the oil. This treatment with once-used acid, which had become reduced in the first operation from specific gravity 1·84 to 1·5 or 1·6, is to deprive the oil of contained water.

The oil thus freed from water passes into a third emulsifier, and is there mixed with fresh acid from tank No. 3, the mixture being separated in the second separator, and the acid conducted to the first emulsifier.

In the washing elements the oil is washed with lye. The last tank contains fresh lye, and the fifth one lye that has been used twice. When a second washing with lye appears superfluous, one of the elements is disconnected. Finally, the oil is washed in the fifth emulsifier with warm water from the tank, and is left to settle in a Florentine receiver. The whole of the emulsifiers and separators are driven by a steam engine.

As a result of this treatment the acid resin, instead of separating out in big hard lumps as is otherwise often the case, forms a homogeneous viscous resin solution, which, after standing for some time, sets to a hard mass of acid resin. The acid separators are arranged to empty themselves automatically as soon as they are stopped. They are simple cylindrical separators, whereas the alkali separators are provided with internal plates, which considerably increases reaction.

The separators rapidly separate all thin emulsions of

mineral oils, irrespective of the acid or alkaline character of the washing water. When properly regulated, it is seldom that more than 0·1 per cent. of oil remains in the washings.

The twice-used acid may be diluted with water, and, after the supernatant tar has been skimmed off, employed for, *e.g.*, the manufacture of sulphate of ammonia. The twice-used lye may be partly recovered by the aid of lime.

2. *Refining fatty oils.*—An installation of this class, for refining by sulphuric acid alone in the ordinary manner, consists of only three washing elements. The sulphuric acid is mixed and removed in the first, the second serves for the cold and the third for the warm washing with water.

Rape oil from the press is first freed from water and fragments of the seed by settling, otherwise a larger quantity of sulphuric acid would be required. The oil runs away clear after washing, but becomes turbid after a few hours by the separation of about 0·1 per cent. of water, which can be removed by the separator.

In the case of oil rich in fatty acids, dilute lye is substituted for water in washing after separation of the sulphuric acid.

3. *Removing the acid from very acid fats and fatty oils.*—The preparation of perfectly neutral oil is possible by the Ekenberg system, even from products containing as much as 25 per cent. of free fatty acids. The purified fats may, in many cases, be employed direct for alimental purposes, but in other instances they require to be first freed from bad-flavoured, non-acid constituents.

An installation for treating cocoanut or olive oil is displayed in plan in Fig. 76. It contains six washing elements, three of which are fitted with Florentine receivers in place of separators.

The oil is run from the tank 1 to the element E_1S_1, where it is washed with lye from tank 2.

In E_2S_2 it is washed with water; in E_3S_3 with lye a second time; in E_4S_4 with water again; in E_5 with very

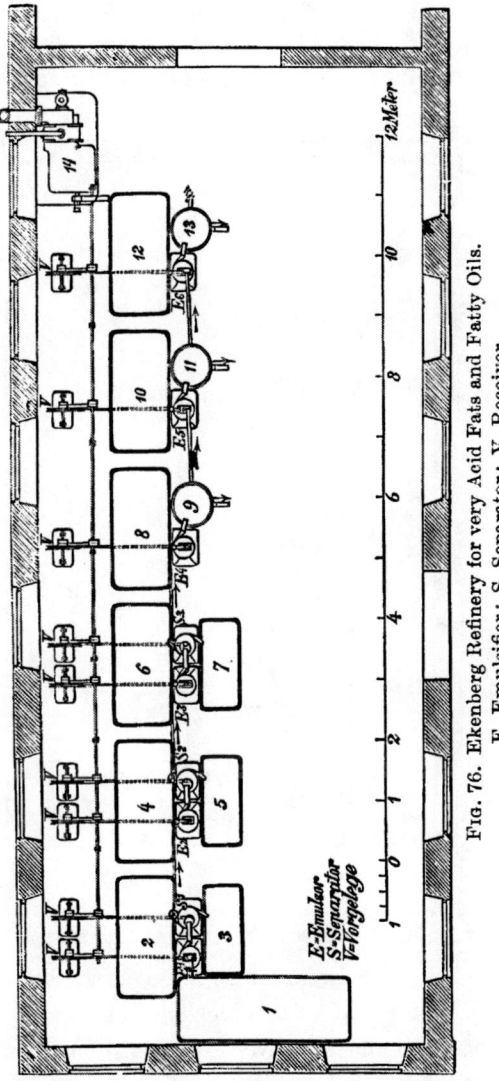

Fig. 76. Ekenberg Refinery for very Acid Fats and Fatty Oils. E, Emulsifier; S, Separator; V, Receiver.

dilute sulphuric or hydrochloric acid; and finally with warm water in E_6. The strength of the lye depends on the quantity of acid to be washed out, and the volumetric ratio between oil and lye, and varies generally from 0·25 to 0·5 per cent. Tanks 2 and 6 contain lye; 4, 8 and 12, water; and 10, acid; whilst 3, 5 and 7 receive the soapy solutions.

Cocoanut oil must of course be melted and treated with

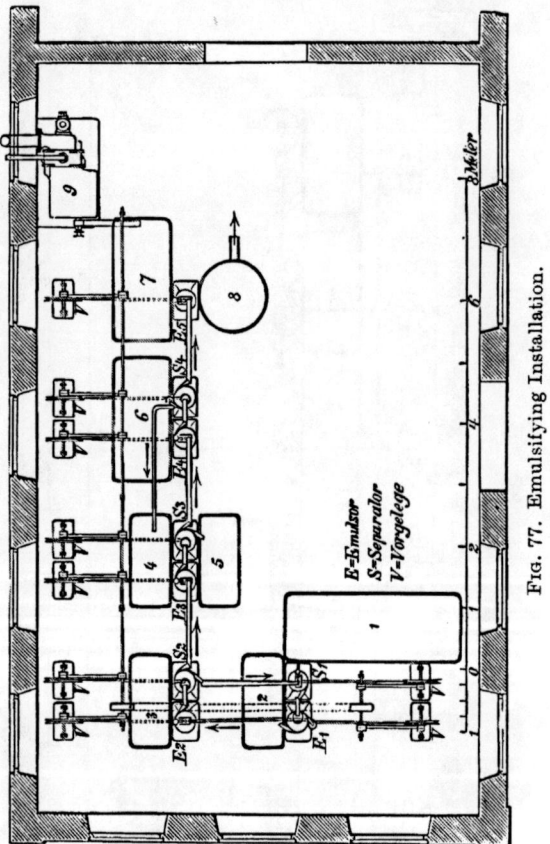

Fig. 77. Emulsifying Installation.

warm lye. The great advantages possessed by the Ekenberg system as compared with older methods will be again referred to; it should, however, be mentioned that frequently difficulties of no little magnitude are encountered.

The centrifugal emulsifier works well in all cases, even

when the plates are arranged at considerable distances apart.

So much cannot, however, be said of the separators, which sometimes fail to dissociate the components of the mixture with a sufficient degree of perfection. The cause of this may be sought in an incorrect adjustment of the apparatus, each separator needing to be specially arranged in accordance with the difference between the specific gravities of the liquids to be separated. The separator drum has the same form as a Florentine bottle mounted on a vertical axis, and though the action of the separator is computed in a different and highly complicated manner, nevertheless the

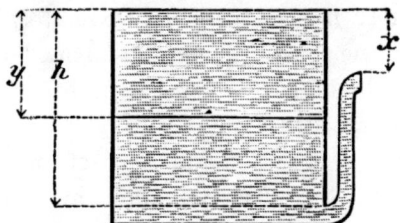

FIG. 78. Florentine Bottle.

example of the Florentine bottle may serve to indicate the importance of a correct adjustment of the separator.

If two liquids of different density and quickly separable from each other be continuously poured into a Florentine bottle together, the heavier will run out through the outflow pipe and the lighter one flow out over the brim. If now h be taken to represent the height of the bottle from the edge to the mouth of the lower pipe, x the distance of the effluent from the edge of the bottle, y the height of the lighter layer of liquid, s its specific gravity, and s^1 the density of the heavier liquid, then

$$s\,y + (h-y)\,s^1 = (h-x)\,s^1$$

$$y = \frac{x\,s^1}{s^1 - s}$$

y is, therefore, the specific gravities being known, dependent on x, and it then becomes a question of adjusting the distance x in such a manner that the separation of the liquids is as complete as possible. x attains its highest value when $y = h$, viz. :—

$$x \; max. = \frac{h \; (s^1 - s)}{s^1}$$

If x be made greater then oil will escape through the pipe along with the heavier liquid. On the other hand, should x be too small the emulsion has not time to separate, and oil mixed with the heavier liquid escapes over the brim.

It is therefore necessary to approximately estimate the value of y from the specific gravities of both liquids in every instance, and subsequently make an empirical adjustment to secure the most efficient action.

The position of the zone of contact in the separator, corresponding to the distance y, is independent of the proportions of the liquids in the mixture.

Nevertheless, even if the adjustment be correct, it may happen that the emulsion is not perfectly separated. In the washing of fatty oils with lye it frequently occurs that large quantities of fat are left in suspension in the watery liquid, and there are even emulsions (designated by Ekenberg as "critical") which, so far from being separated, become more intimately mixed by their passage through the separator. In such cases satisfactory results may generally be obtained by altering the proportions or concentration of the mixture, or by working in the warm. Assistance may sometimes be afforded by the addition of moderate quantities of common salt or Glauber salt, but the washing water should not contain enough salt to salt out the soaps that are to be washed.

For the reason mentioned a washing battery arranged

for one kind of fat cannot be used for another kind without adjustment. Furthermore, when using warm washing liquids the exact degree of warmth necessary for the operation should not be exceeded, since the aroma of many oils would suffer thereby.

For the recovery of the fatty acids and small quantities of emulsified oil carried away in the washings, the latter are acidified, the fat being thereby caused to rise to the surface. The small quantities of oil remaining as an emulsion, after the process of washing by water or dilute acids, may also be recovered by one of the methods prescribed by Ekenberg, and returned to the crude oil or disposed of as second quality fat to the soap boiler.

When an Ekenberg battery is once in proper working order it affords the following advantages, in addition to the possibility of continuous working :—

1. The crude oil may be treated direct as it comes from the press, or may, if considered advantageous, be first emulsified with water, for the removal of cellular matter, etc.

2. In refining with concentrated sulphuric acid, some 40 to 60 per cent. less fat is saponified than by the ordinary method, so that the product is correspondingly less acid.

3. The separator removes the sulphuric acid down to 0·2 per cent., a result otherwise only attainable by several days' standing.

4. The residual acid is completely removed by a single washing or by two at most.

5. When the alkali treatment follows direct on the sulphuric acid treatment, the amount of reagent—provided no free fatty acids are present (mineral oils)—required is reduced to a minimum, only 0·2 per cent. of sulphuric acid having been left.

6. The yield of purified oil is as a rule greater than from the old process, if the operations have been correctly performed.

7. Free fatty acids can be washed out, down to 0·05 to 0·10 per cent.

The apparatus consists chiefly of two flat plates of particular shape, placed opposite each other, with their polished edges engaging one in the other. The lower plate is fastened on a vertical axis which is prolonged above the plate, the upper

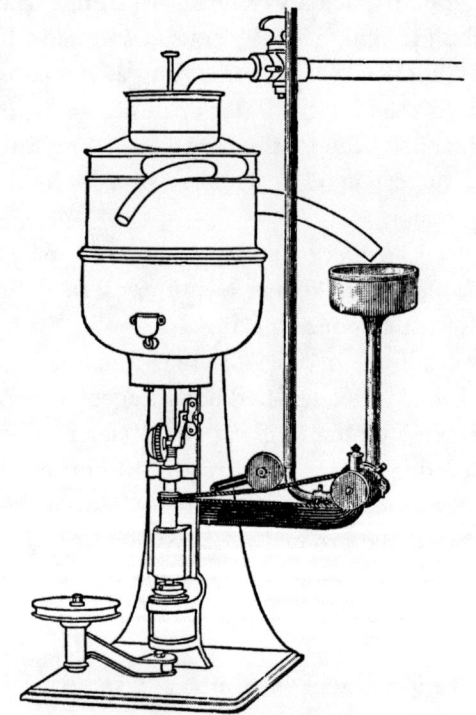

Fig. 79. Emulsifier with Centrifugal Pump (Section).

portion being bored out in the shape of a truncated cone, with the apex at the top. The tube so formed conveys the liquids to be mixed into the apparatus. To this end it is pierced immediately above the lower plate by a couple of apertures, from which the liquids escape into the space between the wide plates. A screw thread is cut on the outside of the tube, and on this the upper plate is laid and fastened by the aid of two nuts. The adjustment of the two plates is effected by means of three micrometer screws in the edge of the upper one, an arrangement admitting of accurate and readily calculable regulation of the distance between them.

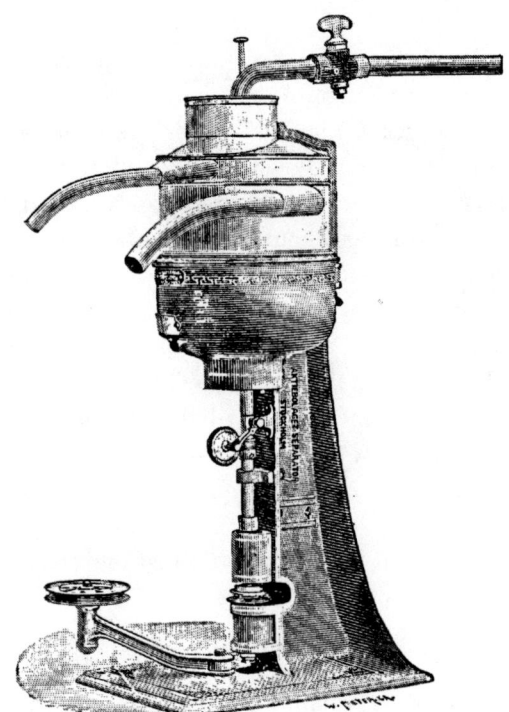

FIG. 80. Emulsifier with Centrifugal Pump (Elevation).

The shaft is driven either by a small turbine, which is particularly suitable for experiments on a small scale, or, for practical working, by a driving cord. A speed of some 7000 revolutions a minute is maintained.

The plates are enclosed in a fixed lead-lined case, which serves to catch the commingled liquids, and to convey them, by means of an outflow pipe, either direct to the separator or into a collecting vessel. On the top of this case an open cylindrical vessel, separated into two divisions by a partition, is fixed, one of the liquids to be mixed being run into each of the compartments. At the bottom of each chamber is an opening, closed by means of a plunger, which allows the liquids to flow into a feed hopper, debouching into the hollow apex of the driving shaft. The delivery of the liquids is regulated by the plungers, and the proportions of the mixture thereby controlled. The adjustment is facilitated by a graduated scale, marked on the stem of each plunger from 0 up to 100, and a constant level of the liquids in the upper vessel is maintained by a float situated in each, this arrangement ensuring a constant rate of outflow.

The materials used in the construction of the apparatus are selected with an eye to the class of work to be performed. For weak acid liquids, acid-resisting bronze, for strongly acid ones, acid steel, and for alkaline liquids, wrought steel is employed. When the plates will be exposed to the action of hydrochloric acid, they are coated with a lead-antimony alloy. For laboratory work, plated apparatus is recommended.

The method of construction must be characterised as good, since but few parts are used, and these are extremely solid and easy to take to pieces, clean and renew. The apparatus runs at the above-named speed of 7000 revolutions a minute, without the slightest noise or vibration, and the danger of "explosion," i.e., the blowing out of the upper portion, is totally prevented. In one experiment the speed was increased to 12,000 turns per minute without any further damage than a spoiled bearing, which was immediately replaced. The apparatus, which was driven by a turbine, braked automatically. A similar case cannot occur in practice, since cord driving gives a definite and not greatly varying speed. Furthermore, the experience of years de-

monstrates the safety of the machine, which is built on
exactly the same lines as the Laval separator, and the speed

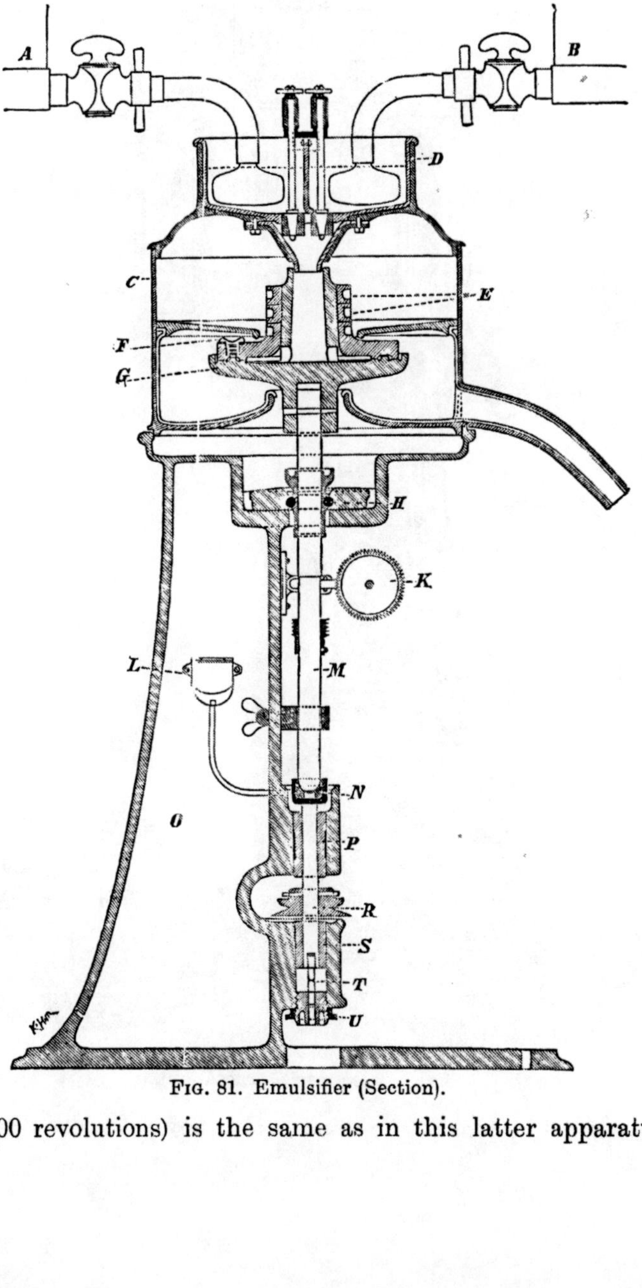

FIG. 81. Emulsifier (Section).

(7000 revolutions) is the same as in this latter apparatus,

with which it has proved perfectly reliable in instances

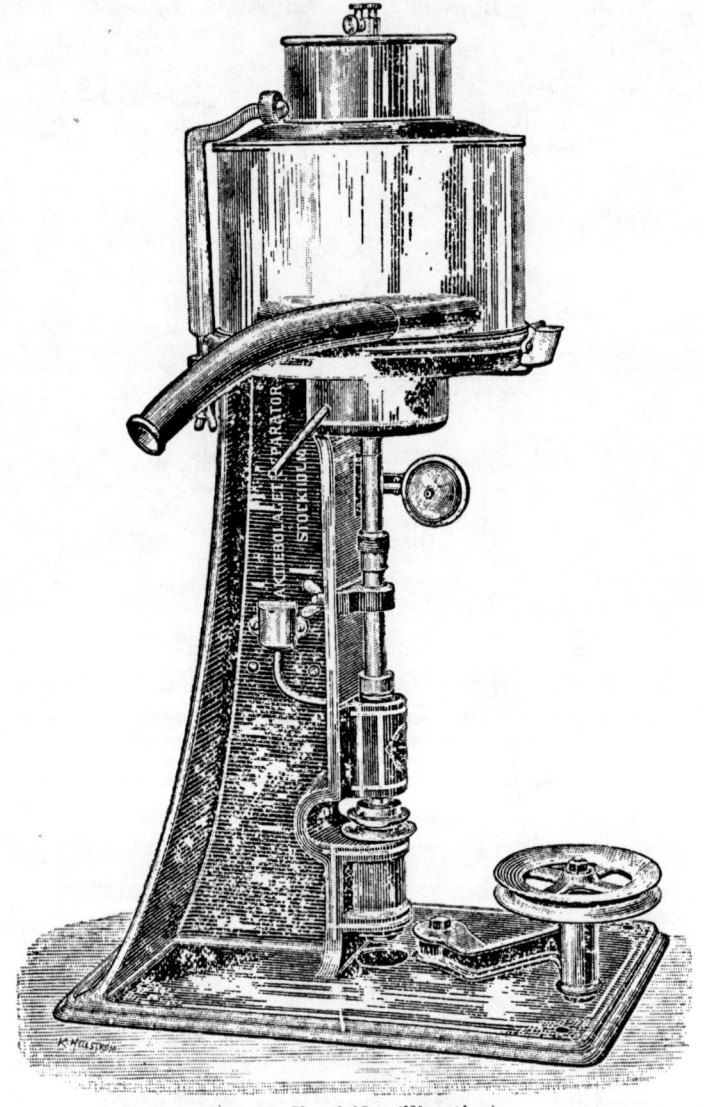

FIG. 82. Emulsifier (Elevation).

numbered by tens of thousands. Moreover, the drum of the

separator is much higher and heavier than the upper part of the emulsifier.

The capacity of the machine at the indicated speed of 7000 revolutions per minute depends on the dimensions of the space between the plates, and on the viscosity of the mixed liquids. That the capacity is great was shown by an experiment wherein, with an aperture of only 0·01 milli-metre, 700 litres of water at 16° C. were delivered in an hour. Fatty oils, melted fats, mineral oils, tar oils, etc., naturally, as a consequence of their greater viscosity, only pass through at much slower rates ; but it is not necessary to adjust the plates so close together, even for very fine emulsions, the best working apertures being in most cases between 0·05 and 1·00 millimetre.

When once properly set the apparatus works continu-ously. Before commencing, the rate of flow of the two liquids (depending on their viscosity) must be determined, once for all, by a preliminary experiment, which may easily be performed by means of the adjustable plungers in the upper feed boxes, the stems of which only require to be raised or lowered until the mixing liquids are delivered in their correct proportions. This is easily arranged after a few trials, and thereafter the work can be carried on uninter-mittently, an interruption only being necessary when oil of very different viscosity is to be treated. In order to ensure the greatest efficiency when used in the fat industry, the emulsifier should in most instances—and particularly when alkaline or neutral liquids are employed for mixing—be com-bined with the separator, which is able to rapidly dissociate emulsions otherwise of considerable stability.

The De Laval separator may be employed with advantage when the fat rises so slowly from the oil and water emulsion that the ordinary receiver, a wooden vessel with separating pipe, on the principle of the Florentine bottle, is inefficient.

These separators are made in various sizes and capacities ranging from 300 to 2000 litres per hour.

ASPINALL, HOAR AND WISE'S PROCESS OF REFINING.

In this process the oils and fats are made conductive and then traversed by an electric current. If, for instance, cotton-seed oil or olive oil is to be treated, a vat is divided into two compartments by means of a diaphragm, and an electrode placed in each, the positive pole being preferably of carbon and the negative of copper. These electrodes are connected with a direct current machine, with an EMF of not less than six volts. The positive (carbon) electrode is immersed in a solution of sodium chloride, with a density of 2° (Twad.), the oil being made conductive by mixing it with its own volume of brine of the same strength; this mixture of oil and brine is placed in the compartment containing the copper electrode. The diaphragm being porous allows the passage of the current, but retains the oil in its proper compartment. The separation of the oil and brine in the mixture is prevented by continued stirring, preferably effected by means of a mechanical agitator. The passage of the current results in the formation of caustic alkali and hydrogen, which react on the oil whilst in intimate contact with the brine solution, and cause the impurities to quickly collect in the brine. Samples are drawn from time to time, and when the operation is considered as finished, the oil is run off and left to settle. The impure brine may also be drawn off from time to time and replaced by clean water. As a rule it is not advisable to call in the aid of heat, though if the oil is hard to purify, warmth may be applied; but in such cases a temperature of about 80° C. should not be exceeded. Oil may by this method be purified with a much smaller percentage of loss than is attendant on the other usual processes. In individual instances, water strongly acidified by sulphuric acid may be substituted for the brine and electrolysed, the mixture being maintained by stirring.

The oil is frequently again refined by mixing with a solution of caustic soda at a temperature of 70° C. The process may also be advantageously applied to many other oils, such as rape oil, cocoanut oil, castor oil, and other oils and fats.

ASPINALL'S PROCESS FOR REFINING OILS.

The oil, cotton-seed oil in particular, is treated with brine and soda lye. A vessel large enough to contain double the quantity of oil to be purified is necessary for the process, and should be fitted with paddles to ensure a good mechanical stirring.

Tanks for the brine and caustic lye are situated above the oil vessel, which is also fitted with hot and cold water pipes, and surrounded by a steam jacket for warming the contents by steam heat. The vessel is emptied by way of a tap at the bottom.

The oil under treatment is run in at a temperature of about 27° C., and, the paddles being set in motion, an aqueous solution of common salt of a density of some 10° (Twad.) is added at the rate of about 360 litres per 1000 kilos. (80 gallons per ton) of oil. Stirring is continued until an intimate mixture of oil and brine is produced, and is maintained whilst the caustic soda lye of 22° (Twad.) is run in, also at a temperature of about 27° C.

According to the inventor's description of the process, the employment of sufficient caustic lye to effect by itself the purification of the oil results in considerable loss by saponification. The use of brine has been prescribed for refining oils, but with very limited and incomplete results.

According to published reports it is frequently the custom

to add brine to the oil after the purification with caustic soda, but the use of salt at this stage cannot prevent the excessive saponification which has already taken place previous to the addition of the salt. Aspinall observed that when the oil was first intimately mixed with brine, and the lye added to the mixture, the brine protected the oil from excessive attack by the caustic alkali and therefore allowed the purification to be effected with very little loss. Hence the process is based on the preliminary mixing of oil and brine by energetic agitation, and treating the resulting mixture with lye.

In carrying out this method care must be taken to use just enough caustic soda to clarify the oil.

The appearance of the oil affords a sufficient guide for the workman. A sample dropped on a glass plate should be quite clear, although it is full of little dark spots; this test being universally known in oil refineries. Immediately the oil is clarified the paddles are stopped, and water at 60° C. (or, in many instances, cold) is sprayed over the surface of the oil, whereupon the colouring matter passes into the water and sinks to the bottom, leaving the clear oil floating on the surface.

A large quantity of water is requisite, as the washing must continue until all the lumps in the oil have become dissolved, and until such of the oil that has at first been carried down mechanically along with the colouring matter has separated and reascended to the surface.

Different oils require to be treated with different quantities and strengths of lye and brine, the amount of which can be determined by preliminary tests. It is preferable to warm the oil before treatment.

After thorough washing the oil may be freed from suspended water by warming it up to 70° C. If the process is carried out in an efficient manner no saponification occurs, neither is any mucilage formed. The oil may be afterwards clarified completely in the usual manner, and cotton-seed oil so treated is marketable as olive oil. If intended for sale as bleached oil, bleaching is performed in the ordinary way. The Aspinall method is suitable for both warm and cold drawn oils, and may also be performed in a tank.

CHAPTER XIII.

PURIFYING OILS AND MECHANICAL APPLIANCES FOR REFINING.

VILLON reports as follows on the purification of oils by means of liquid sulphurous acid, which is apparently practised with success in Germany :—

"The oil is placed in a cylindrical boiling pan, with a double lead bottom and fitted with an efficient stirring apparatus. About ½ to 1 per cent. of liquid sulphurous acid, free from water, is run through a pipe into the oil, where it immediately vaporises and acts on the albuminoid and protein colouring matter. The reaction is facilitated and completed by the aid of steam heat applied by means of a coil. The resulting increase of pressure, which should not exceed 13·7 pounds per square inch, is indicated by a manometer. The mixture is allowed to cool and the reaction to continue for several hours, the oil being then washed for some time with hot water and afterwards filtered."

This process apparently yields good results; the oil is clear pale yellow and very bright, burning well without carbonising the wick, and lubricates without bletching.

Attempts have been made to combine the zinc chloride and sulphurous acid processes, and with success. When zinc chloride is used the oil needs thorough washing to remove the final traces of the reagent, otherwise the burning quality of the oil suffers. In the combined process the oil is first stirred up with a syrupy solution of zinc chloride, and the mixture then treated with sulphurous acid in the manner already described.

For clarifying and preserving fatty oils Villon employs a mucilaginous product (designated by him "Algosin") which is obtained from Algae, and, like many similar substances, is gifted with the property of clarifying turbid liquids; being, however, unique in its power of exerting the same influence on fatty oils. If a concentrated alkaline solution of this algosin be stirred up with a turbid oil, and the latter poured off and filtered after settling for twenty-four hours, a clear product is said to be obtained, which does not again become turbid even after a considerable lapse of time, and which, furthermore, has a greater power of resisting the influence of light and air than any fresh fatty oil, preserving, moreover, its pure odour and flavour for a long while. Villon treated olive oil, sesame oil and nut oil with algosin, and found that after an exposure of fifteen months to light and air in shallow basins, the percentage of acids did not exceed 0·02 to 0·03, whereas the same oils, without the algosin treatment, exhibited from 6·13 to 15·7 per cent. of acid under similar conditions.

NÖRDLINGER ON THE PURIFICATION OF VEGETABLE OILS.

Nördlinger obviates the evils attendant on the ordinary methods of purification and the use of mechanical appliances, by treating the oil with oleaginous solutions of certain reagents, certain salts of the fatty acids, resin acids, benzoic acid or their homologues being particularly suitable. So far as has hitherto been observed the solubility of the salts of fatty acids in vegetable oils increases with the molecular weight of the acids themselves, and from butyric acid upwards the majority of the salts in question dissolve in from 10 to 20 parts of vegetable oil at temperatures from 100° to 200° C. In connection with this question of solubility, the composition of the vegetable oil has but a subordinate influence, the salts dissolving almost equally in sesame oil, poppy oil, rape oil, linseed oil, ground-nut oil and cotton-seed oil.

Whereas the 5 to 10 per cent. solutions of the compounds of the alkalis with higher fatty acids, containing more than four carbon atoms, form at ordinary temperatures more or less oleaginous, viscous liquids, which do not throw down any solid deposit (the same behaviour is noticeable in the corresponding salts of oleic, abietic, and sylvic acids and their homologues), the metallic salts of these acids in oleaginous solutions at ordinary temperature have somewhat the consistency of lard, or else a portion of the salt that has been dissolved at higher temperature crystallises out again. The 5 to 10 per cent. solutions of the zinc, cadmium, iron, copper, manganese and lead salts of these acids form clear solutions at temperatures between 40° and (at highest) 100° C., the kind of vegetable oil employed as solvent being immaterial. The lime, magnesia, alumina and baryta salts are also soluble in vegetable oils, but are not—or at least not to the same extent—endowed with the peculiar property possessed by the metallic salts of throwing down mucilaginous bodies.

If small quantities (5 to 10 per cent.) of the oily solutions of the metallic salts of the aforesaid acids be introduced into vegetable oils a clear solution is at first formed, but after a little while the mixture becomes cloudy, especially in presence of air, and the mucilaginous impurities are gradually precipitated, as more or less coloured flakes, in combination with the previously dissolved metallic salts.

In Nördlinger's opinion no chemical change occurs, the probability being that the mucilaginous particles are weighted, and so brought to precipitate, by the metallic salts in the same way as is observed in the case of certain colouring matters. The turbid oil is freed from the precipitated substances by filtration.

Briefly summarised, the process is carried out as follows : The salts of heavy metals (iron, lead, copper, manganese, zinc, etc.) with higher and substituted fatty acids or benzoic acid are dissolved in about 10 to 20 parts by weight of vegetable or resin oils, at about 150° C., and the solution gradually cooled, the clear liquid being drawn off from the insoluble residue whilst still warm (51° to 80° C.). Of such solutions—so-called " purifying oils "—the following may be used for the purposes indicated, viz., a 5 per cent. solution of oleate of zinc in cotton-seed oil, or 10 per cent. solutions of oleate of lead or stearate of iron in sesame oil, or of resinate of iron or manganese in linseed oil.

These purifying oils, in so far as they are not clear and fluid at ordinary temperatures, may be rendered so by moderately warming, and are then mixed with 13 to 20 or 30 times their own weight of the vegetable oils to be refined. A clear solution forms, which after a short time becomes cloudy, especially when it has been exposed to the air. The impurities settle down to the bottom along with the metallic salts, and are removed as already described.

For refining sesame oil a purifying solution of lead oleate in sesame oil is employed ; for ground-nut oil, iron stearate in sesame oil ; for rape oil, lead oleate ; and for linseed oil, iron or manganese resinate (ferromanganic resinate).

Nördlinger has also extended the application of the process to oils and fats of animal origin in the following manner.

One of the purifying oils is mixed with about 10 to 20 volumes of the animal oil or fat under treatment (e.g., fish oil or tallow), previously liquefied by warmth if necessary. The clear liquid gradually becomes turbid by the separation of the impurities, along with the metallic salts as fine flakes. The oil is then clarified by settling, filtration or being passed through a centrifugal separator.

In order to refine crude tallow (for example), the fat is

melted and mixed with a small percentage of a solution of, say, lead oleate in tallow, and the mixture kept warm until the flocculent precipitate of impurities has formed. The clear tallow is then either poured off from the sediment, filtered or separated by the centrifugal machine. Fish oil is refined by mixing with a suitable quantity of a purifying oil, consisting of a fatty acid salt of iron dissolved in rape or any other oil.

MECHANICAL APPLIANCES FOR REFINING.

It is evident that the mixture of the oil to be refined, and the reagent which is to destroy or otherwise remove the mucilaginous or other impurities, must be very intimate indeed, and with this object mechanical appliances are used, their dimensions and capacity depending of course on the quantities of oil to be treated at any one time. These appliances are of various kinds, the following being employed :—

(a) *Stirrers*, with horizontal arms mounted on a vertical shaft, set in motion by any suitable means, and so effecting the intimate incorporation of the oil and watery fluids.

(b) *Air*, either blown into or drawn through the oil, by which means an intimate mixture is also effected. Air agitators were first successfully employed in the refining of mineral oils, and were subsequently made use of for vegetable oils. The mixture produced is extremely intimate, the operation much cleaner than when mechanical stirrers are used, and finally the air exerts a bleaching action on the vegetable oils ; the only thing to be feared is oxidation.

Rape oil, cotton-seed oil and sesame oil are not injured by air in the comparatively short time of exposure (two to three hours), but in the case of drying oils the air naturally exerts an unfavourable influence ; only, however, when they are intended for other purposes than painting or varnishing.

Injectors (for refining by exhausting air), although cheaper than air blast agitators, are very seldom used, owing to the necessity of having the refining vessel air-tight, which renders the control of the operation difficult; and indeed the mechanical stirrers with beater arms are still more generally used than any other form.

(c) *Centrifugal emulsifiers*, which at present are but little used, are nevertheless of a character to entirely supplant all other methods of mixing. The following advantages are possessed by these machines: continuous working, great capacity with little consumption of power, economy of space and sulphuric acid, better quality products, and the possibility of treating freshly pressed oil.

BLOWERS FOR MIXING ACIDS OR OTHER LIQUIDS WITH OIL.

The Körting apparatus consists of an open, trough-shaped iron vessel, at the bottom of which rests a perforated steam pipe, continued through the side of the pan and turned upwards, the outer limb being fitted with a Körting's injector. This steam blower is employed in place of a mechanical stirrer, and completely obviates the inconveniences of the latter. Its action depends on the circumstance that a current of steam, flowing from a narrow tube into a wide one, carries with it the surrounding air, and imparts to the latter sufficient speed to enable it to overcome the pressure of a column of water 2·5 metres in height. The air issues from the perforations in the pipe (Fig. 83) with such vehemence that it imparts violent motion to the surrounding liquid, and stirs up all the precipitated or added substances lying at the bottom of the vessel.

The Körting apparatus presents the following advantages over mechanical stirrers :—

1. It is cheaper and more efficient.

2. An extremely intimate mixture is produced.

3. It has no movable parts, and does not wear out in any way.

4. It can be fixed in any convenient situation, and only requires a service pipe of small diameter.

5. It requires no attention or supervision, and may be

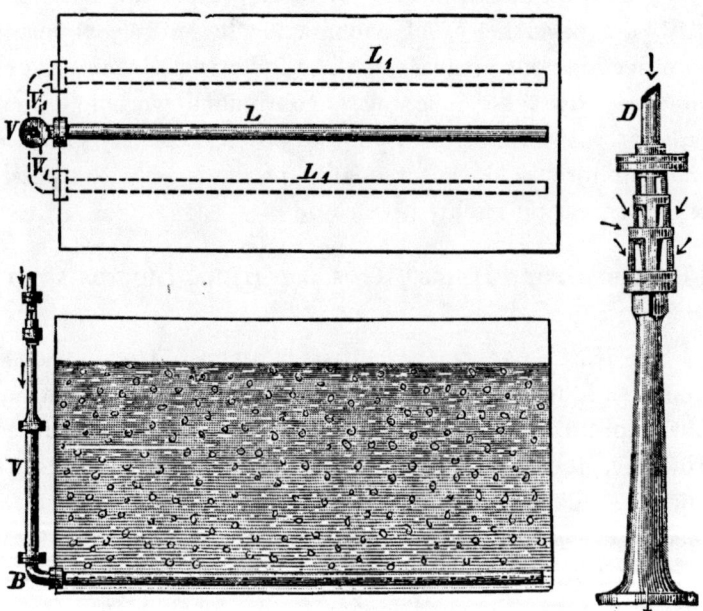

Fig. 83. Air Blast Agitator with Körting Injector.

started by simply opening a steam valve. The strength of the blast is regulated by the same means.

6. The apparatus works economically in the extreme, especially when compared with manual labour.

7. The pipe at the bottom of the vessel takes up but a small space, and does not in any way impede cleaning.

The air pipes LL are screwed on to the injector in the manner shown in the drawing. They should not be made narrower than practical experience shows to be advanta-

geous.   On either side these air pipes are fitted with sundry
tubes, 10 millimetres in diameter, projecting downwards,
their number being regulated so that the total area of
delivery is exactly double the sectional area of the air pipes
employed.   The latter are laid some $2\frac{1}{2}$ inches above the
centre of a pair of inclined boards fastened to the bottom,
and serving to lead the liquid constantly back into the sphere
of action of the compressed air.   When the vessel is over 27
inches wide, a single air pipe is no longer sufficient, and an
additional pipe must be employed for each 20 inches of

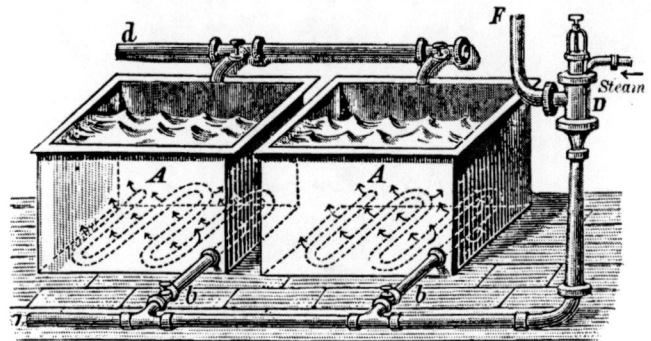

FIG. 84. Compressed Air Agitator.

width.   The diameter of the steam pipe, valve and injector
pipe must not be decreased beyond the prescribed limits.

Another apparatus for intimately mixing liquids is worked
by compressed air.

In Fig. 84 A is the tank, D the air compressor, a the air
supply pipe, with branches b in the tank.   The air escapes
through small apertures in pipes placed at the bottom of the
tank, and the ascending air bubbles set the whole liquid in
rapid motion, producing a more intimate mixture than can
be obtained by mechanical stirrers.   The air compressing
apparatus can be erected in any convenient manner, whether
vertically, horizontally or at an angle.   It is a universal rule
with air compressors that the pressure exerted by the blower

18

increases with the pressure of the steam, and the more the spindle is screwed down. In order to prevent unnecessary back pressure the air delivery aperture should not be made too small, and diminutions in the suction pipe also act unfavourably. If the delivery of the air is effected through a number of openings, the sum of their sectional areas

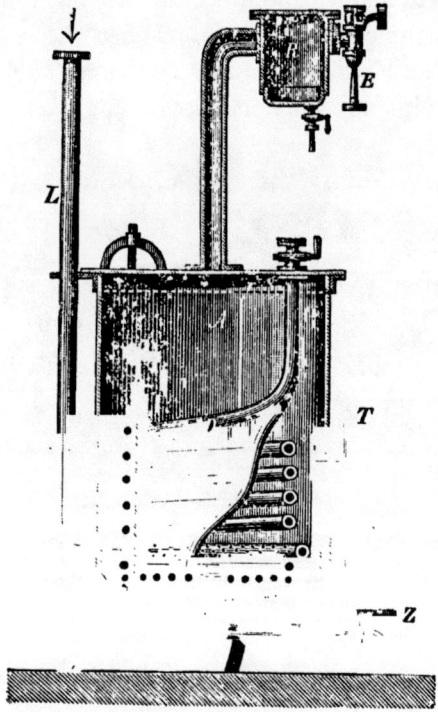

FIG. 85. Oil Refining Pan.

should not be less than $1\frac{1}{2}$ times the diameter of the pipe as given in the maker's catalogue.

OIL REFINING PANS.

The pan A (Fig. 85) is 55 inches wide and contains a steam coil D which enters through the lid, and after numerous windings makes its exit in the same way. The lid also carries a tube surmounted by a vessel R, to which an air ejector E is attached. This ejector serves, when set in motion, to produce a partial vacuum in the upper portion of the pan, the lower two-thirds of which are filled with oil. As the vacuum increases fresh air forces its way in through the tube L and causes a brisk movement in the oil, which is heated by means of the steam pipe D. Not only is any water that may be mechanically suspended in the oil removed by

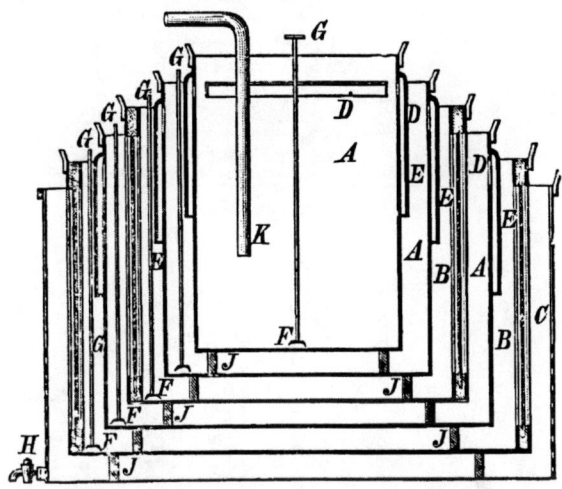

FIG. 86. Decantation and Filtering Apparatus for Palm Kernel Oil. E, Jacket Surrounding A; F, Effluent Valve; G, Valve Rods; H, Discharge Tap; K, Feed Pipe.

this movement in conjunction with the high temperature, but the oxygen of the air also acts chemically on the oil.

Oil treated in this apparatus is just as clear and pure as if purified in a refinery. Direct steam can also be employed; the precipitated matters subside quickly, and can be drawn off through the tap Z. An interesting feature about this apparatus is that the temperature of the oil is higher than can be produced by the steam coil, a circumstance explained by the internal friction of the small particles of the oil, the result being similar to that produced by shaking a liquid.

SCHNEIDER'S DECANTATION AND FILTERING APPARATUS
FOR PALM KERNEL OIL.

The apparatus is very compact in form and is easily taken
apart for cleaning. It consists of wooden and leaden boxes,
of three kinds, *viz.:* decantation boxes A, filters B, and
sifting boxes C, which latter serve to contain the two former.
The boxes A are formed of a bottom and four vertical walls

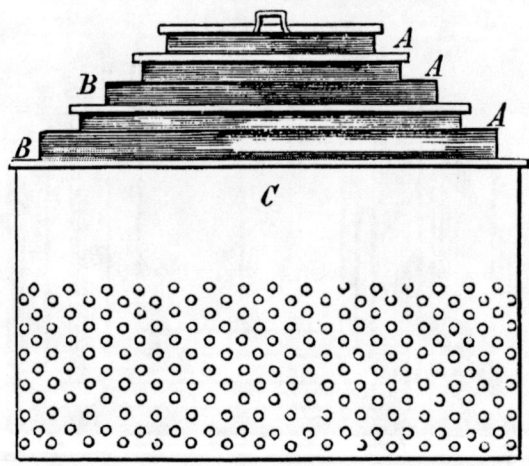

FIG. 87. Decantation and Filtering Apparatus. A, Decanting Boxes; B,
Filters; C, Sifter; D, Slits in A; J, Supports (see Fig. 86).

which, near the upper edge, are pierced by horizontal slits D.
Each box is surrounded by a jacket E, fastened on to the
walls a little above the slits. The filter boxes consist of a
bottom and frame walls, the latter being entirely covered by
linen cloth or some other filtering material. The sides of
the sifting box C are perforated with holes in the lower
half. Valves F are fitted to the filter boxes B and sifting
boxes C, and are adjusted by the valve rods G. The sifting
box has also a discharge tap H.

The apparatus is worked in the following manner: The

sifting box C is set up over a vessel which is intended to catch the clarified liquid, and the decantation boxes A and filters B are inserted, resting on supports J. The liquid to be clarified is run into the central box A through a feed pipe K, escaping thence through the slits D into the second box A, and from this passes into the filter B and through the filtering material of which the sides are composed, finally arriving at the sifting box C, which allows the liquid to escape through the lateral apertures.

The impurities are securely retained on the bottoms of the vessels and on the walls of the filters, and these must therefore be cleaned out from time to time, for which purpose the valves F and tap H are provided.

BAG FILTERS

belong to the most modern and efficient forms of apparatus for filtering oleaginous substances, and may be highly recommended, both on account of their capacity and the crystal clearness of the filtrate.

The bag filter manufactured by K. A. Stönner of Amsterdam, shown in Fig. 88, is composed of a number (corresponding to the size of the apparatus) of linen bags of about 39 × 4 inches in size, each of which contains a second bag 10 inches " in diameter ".* Each of these bags—three to nineteen in number—is fastened by cords on to a metal cone, which in turn is screwed into a receiver, serving as supply reservoir for the bags. This vessel is mounted on a metal cylinder, which encloses the bags and prevents access of air.

The apparatus—which may, for special purposes, be heated by steam or hot water—works very quickly and retains all impurities in the bags. The considerable length of the bags facilitates rapid filtration, by reason of which

* Query: 1 inch diameter or 10 inches long?

large quantities of oil can be filtered clear and bright in a short time.

THE RAYMOND-COMBRET OIL PURIFYING APPARATUS.

By this apparatus the oil is not only filtered but may also be purified by solutions of various salts, whereby the sulphuric

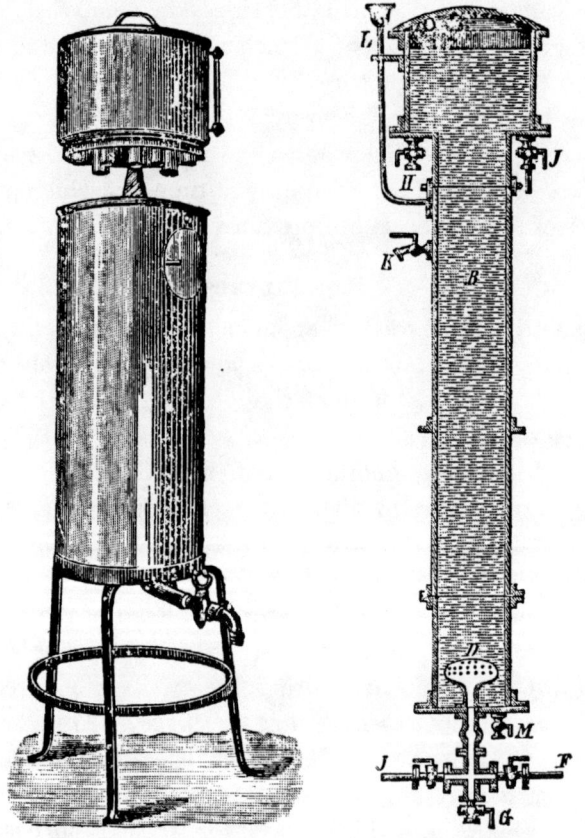

FIG. 88. Bag Filter.   FIG. 89. Raymond-Combret Oil Purifier. Purifying Cylinder.

acid can be removed from oils that have been imperfectly washed with water. The purification is effected in the purifying cylinder B, in which the oil in fine streams is brought into contact with the purifying solution. Where a series of these cylinders is present the process is continuous.

The oil is contained in a reservoir A, from whence it flows through a tube C and issues through the rose D into a tinned cylinder B, widened out at the top and closed by a lid. These cylinders are filled with water. The feed pipe C conducts

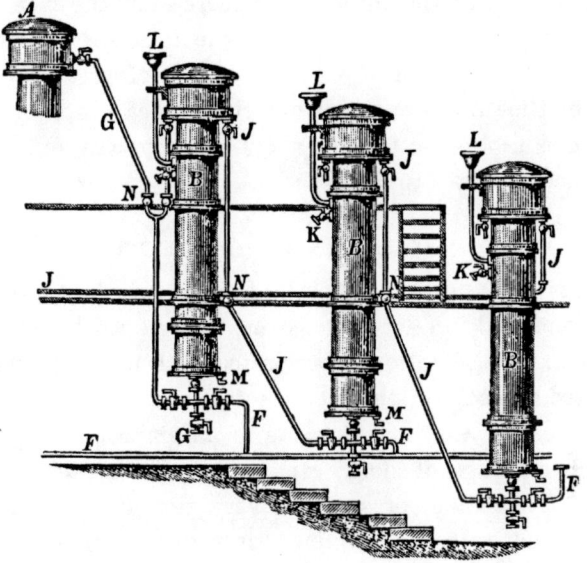

Fig. 90. Raymond Combret Oil Purifying Apparatus.

the oil into a T-shaped joint E, to which is connected the steam pipe F for heating the purifying liquid. The lower limb, fitted with a tap G, serves for cleaning out the pipes. The oil is divided equally by the rose D, and passing through the column of water—or liquid containing different acids or salts—ascends to the wide upper part of the vessel. The tap H is for drawing off the oil, and T leads it into the succeeding cylinder or apparatus. The level of the water in the cylinders can be maintained exactly on a level with the taps H and T, being added or withdrawn through the pipe L or tap K respectively. The cylinder B is emptied by means of the tap M. Where several cylinders are arranged in series the bottom of the wide part of each must be on a higher level than the top of the succeeding one, so that the oil may descend by gravity from one to the other. In this manner it passes through the entire series, and is finally discharged into the filter. For increasing the rate of flow from one cylinder to the other the introduction of small rotary pumps in the pipes N and G is of great assistance, and, by the same means, once-purified oil can be, if necessary, returned to the bottom of a cylinder by way of a pipe O attached to the tap H.

VOLLMAR'S RAPID FILTER

consists of a cylinder, which, in the case of small filters, is of glass enclosed in a tin-plate cover, larger ones being entirely of glass. False bottoms, perforated with holes, in which are inserted conical tin tubes connected with the actual filters, are fitted in the cylinder. The filters are composed of cylindrical bags of cloth, kept in position by spiral coils of wire. Their mode of action is very simple. The liquid to be clarified, on being introduced into the bottom of the filter, has to pass through the cloth walls and the conical tubes in order to reach the space between the upper bottoms, whence it flows into the outer cylinder. As may be seen from Fig. 91, the filter, which is of the same shape at both ends, may be turned upside down and worked in the reverse manner. Communication with the vessel containing the liquid to be filtered is established, as the drawing indicates, by means of a syphon and caoutchouc tube. Generally the first runnings are, as in the case of filters generally, somewhat turbid, and they are therefore collected separately and returned to the stock vessel. In a short time the pores of the filtering medium will have closed up sufficiently to prevent the passage of any solid body, and the oil will then run clear.

These filters are made in various sizes, containing from 3 to 50 filtering cylinders, and with a capacity ranging from 5 to 500 litres of liquid per hour.

UPWARD FILTER.

The upward filter shown in Fig. 92 works with linen, moss and tow. The iron filter box is lined with lead, and is fed from a reservoir at a higher level through the valve situated at the bottom, which also allows the supply to be regulated exactly in conformity with the time necessary for filtration. A

FIG. 91. Vollmar's Rapid Filter.

wooden cross piece H is placed at the bottom of the box, and supports a perforated wooden disc which is covered by two layers of linen, one coarse and the other fine in texture. Then follow in order a thin layer of tow E, a layer of moss M and linen, covered in turn by a perforated board and a second series of layers resembling the first. The screw S serves not only to assist in adjusting the filter in case the layers do not sit evenly—the central cross piece is pressed down and fixed by small wooden wedges —but also to regulate the rate of filtration, which may be altered by loosening or tightening up the screw. The moss

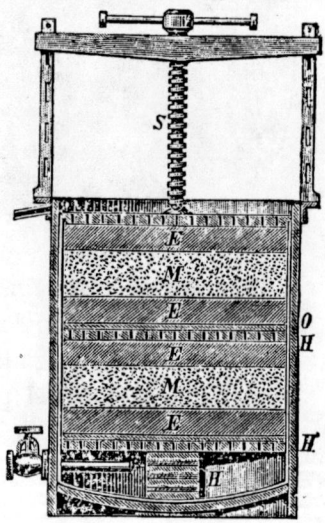

Fig. 92. Upward Filter.

used for filtering must be gathered during the dry season of the year, and sifted to free it from sand. When no other packing material is used, a suitable arrangement for pressing the loose moss must be provided. Such packing will of course require to be renewed at intervals, and the old material must then be well pressed and treated with hot water to recover all the oil retained in suspension.

Sand Filter.

According to Brunner, a sand filter is highly suitable for purifying oil. To construct this a strong sheet-iron cylinder, about $6\frac{1}{2}$ feet long and 1 foot wide, tinned inside, should be procured. At the bottom end a feed pipe is inserted, and this is connected with the oil reservoir (situated 40 to 80 inches higher than the filter) by a caoutchouc tube. The outflow pipe is at the upper end of the cylinder. About an inch above the bottom an iron ring is fixed to support a very thick perforated iron plate, on which is laid a cloth of close texture, the remainder of the cylinder being filled with perfectly pure washed sand. The lower layers of sand may be fairly coarse grained, but that in the upper layers must be progressively finer until the top stratum of finest drift sand is reached. The apparatus forms an upward filter and needs no further description. When the filtration is completed, the filtering layer remains impregnated with oil, which is recovered by introducing water through the caoutchouc tubing, and thereby driving out the oil. When the pores of the filter are clogged from having been a long time in use filtration will be sensibly retarded, and the sand will have to be cleaned, an object effected by heating up with lye to saponify the oil, and then washing repeatedly with water, whereafter the sand will be again fit for use.

URE's OIL FILTER.

Ure proposed an exceedingly practical form of filter for the mechanical purification of oil. In this apparatus the oil to be filtered is placed in a vessel fitted with a tapped side tube leading out from near the bottom and communicating with a water cistern. The filter rests on the top, and contains two perforated partitions, dividing it into three compartments, the lowest of which is connected with the oil tank by a short bent pipe, and the central division filled with coarsely powdered charcoal, cotton wool, felt, etc. The upper compartment is intended for the collection of the filtered oil, and is fitted with a draw-off tap. The cistern being filled with water and the oil tank with oil, the taps are opened and the water runs into the oil vessel, where it sinks by reason of its greater density and drives the oil over into and through the filter. When, after continued working, a mucilaginous mass is found deposited in the lower chamber of the filter, the same is drawn off by the tap. In this manner the operator is able to separate the clear oil from the deposit with ease. In former years bag filters were used for filtering oil, but the pores so soon became clogged that other materials, cotton wool, cloth, etc., were substituted. For upward filtration, sawdust was at first almost universally employed, but presented sundry disadvantages.

CHAPTER XIV.

DEODORISING OILS AND FATS.

THE object of this apparatus is to remove malodorous gases present in suspension in fats and oils. A and B (Fig. 93) represent two cylinders having an intermediate space for containing water. The cylinders are fitted on either side with circular ends dd and $d'd'$, and the inner cylinder contains a central axis, one end of which fits in a bearing f in the space between the ends d and d', and passes through a stuffing gland g affixed to the bearing. The stirrers I are mounted on this shaft in the inner cylinder, each set of paddles consisting of radial arms $j\,j'$, arranged in pairs, one outside the other, fastened together by bolts k and secured on the shaft by screws k'. As may be seen from the sketch the paddles I, which run parallel to the shaft E, are each fastened to two radial arms. Each wheel consists of four paddles l. The two pairs of radial arms, which run in the same direction and carry two paddles l, are shorter than the arms that have an opposite direction. The paddles may be either plain or perforated with holes l'.

The wheels so constituted are mounted on the shaft E, and are so arranged that the paddles of one wheel are not in the same plane as those of the adjacent wheel, this being with the object of stirring the oil and working it up thoroughly throughout, the amount of power required being at the same time reduced. The water pipe n conveys hot water to the jacketing space C, and the waste water escapes through m. Each pipe is fitted with a tap (m' and n'). By means of this water, which may be heated to any convenient temperature, the oil in the inner cylinder may be maintained at any desired degree of fluidity. The oil or fat is fed to the inner cylinder by the pipe O, which passes through the walls of both and through the block o in the jacketing space, and which can be closed by a suitable appliance. There is an inclined opening P arranged near the extremity of the upper side of the cylinders, passing through them both, and into this a pipe p^2 (with tap p^3) is fitted and connected with a rotary blower or air pump (not shown in the drawing), from which a strong current of air can be passed into the inner cylinder. This air escapes, along with the gases removed

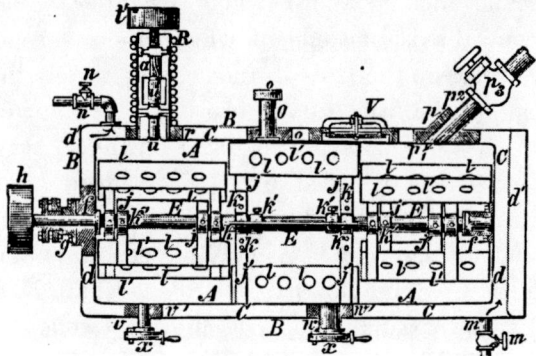

FIG. 93. John H. Filbert's Deodorising Apparatus.

from the oil, through the pipe R, which is enclosed by a steam coil S, with regulating valves S^1 and S^2, by means of which the pipe R can be warmed to any desired temperature. In R there is mounted, in a suitable manner, a vertical axis t, carrying a number of paddles u. These paddles, of which six are shown in the plan, although in practice a larger number (e.g., ten) is better, are for the following purpose: They serve to retain the particles of fat and oil carried off in suspension by the escaping air, and also to remove any fat that may settle on the inner walls of R; and as the pipe R, together with the axis and paddles, are all warmed by the steam coil, the oil and fat continually drop down into the bulk in the cylinder. The axis and its paddles are driven by means of a pully t'. v^1 and w^1 are two outlets, with valves x attached, for the removal of the deodorised oil, and there is a manhole at one side of the cylinder, closed in the usual manner by a cover y. The *modus operandi* of the apparatus is as follows: The oil or fat to be treated is introduced into the cylinder until the latter is half full, and the mass is then raised to the temperature most suitable for the operation by means of the water jacket. The paddles are set in motion, with the result that the oil is beaten up into a spray, and fills the upper part of the cylinder, where the freed gases are absorbed by the current of air admitted through P and carried away by the latter into the pipe R, wherein the suspended particles of oil are retained by the revolving paddles u, without the escape of the gaseous mixture being impeded, whilst at the same time the accumulation of fat or oil in R is prevented. The oil is by this treatment completely deodorised.

STEPHENSON'S METHOD OF DEODORISATION.

For purifying and deodorising the oil, a composition is prepared by granulating together alumina (free from lime), magnesia and iron, incorporating this mixture with imperfectly burnt charcoal containing organic matter, and the whole heated in closed retorts, which are then allowed to cool down before being opened.

DEODORISING WITH GASES.

It is well known that oils, fats, waxes and other similar bodies can be deprived of smell by the action of steam. Nevertheless, it has not, so far, been possible to prepare by this means fats of unimpeachable quality for alimental purposes, since, although the smell of the fat is removed, the subsequent development of a rancid flavour cannot be prevented. However, since the opinion has been formed that rancidity is caused by the action of the atmospheric oxygen mixed with the steam, the possibility of combating this evil by treating the oil with superheated steam in the absence of air has become apparent. The fat is melted or heated in suitable vessels, in which a vacuum may be produced, or through which an inert gas (nitrogen, carbon monoxide, carbonic acid, hydrogen, etc.) is passed, and, as soon as the air is removed, the temperature is raised to between 110° and 220° C. according to circumstances, and a current of super-heated steam passed through the melted mass until the condensed water is perfectly inodorous. As soon as this is accomplished the steam is shut off and the oil cooled in presence of an atmosphere of the gas employed before.

In treating solid fats, *e.g.*, oleomargarin or other solid animal fat, ordinary steam is admitted, and the odoriferous matter driven off by means of an inert gas. To increase the purification, saponification may be effected by 2 to 10 per cent. by weight of a 40° B. solution of sodium bisulphite, drawing off the solution, which contains the greater part of the malodorous impurities in a state of combination, and washing the fat thoroughly with water.

DEODORISING BY AGITATION.

The method of agitating rancid or evil-smelling fats (removing the fatty acids) with amyl alcohol (90, 88 and 86 per cent. strength) gives very good results. As a rule an 85 to 87 per cent. pure spirit is sufficient, since it dissolves most of the fatty acids. Experiments made with this reagent were performed in glass cylinders, 1 to $1\frac{1}{4}$ volumes of the spirit being poured over 1 volume of rancid oil warmed to 35° C., and the two well shaken up together three times in the course of half a day, an emulsion being produced on each occasion. On the second day the mixture, at 20° to 24° C., had separated into two clear liquids, the upper of spirit and

the lower one of oil. The spirit being removed by decantation and syphoning, a further ½ volume of 85 to 90 per cent.
spirit was poured on to the oil, and the shaking up and
subsidence repeated ; in this latter instance the separation
required two or three days at 20° to 24° C.

A third agitation was necessary for complete purification.
The oil was of an extremely pale yellow colour, and both
smell and rancid taste had completely disappeared. In order
to approximate the colour to that of Provence oil, an addition
of fresh Provence oil is recommended. The process costs
but very little, as the spirit can be recovered by distillation,
leaving a residue composed of fatty acids. In the case of
another experiment with very old rape oil, satisfactory results
were also obtained.

CHAPTER XV.

BLEACHING WITH HYDROGEN PEROXIDE.

PURE hydrogen peroxide is a syrupy liquid, colourless and perfectly transparent, of a faint bitter (but at the same time irritating) flavour. When applied to the skin it causes considerable itching and produces white spots. The commercial preparation contains about $1\frac{1}{2}$ volumes of available oxygen, corresponding to about $\frac{1}{2}$ per cent. of H_2O_2. A little hydrochloric or sulphuric acid is added to increase its stability, so that in certain cases this addition must be borne in mind.

The high price of H_2O_2 has retarded its application to technical purposes; and for fats and oils intended for technical uses its employment is very limited. The case is, however, different with regard to fats and oils for consumption, for which, *e.g.*, olive oil, cocoanut butter, etc., chemical bleaching agents, such as potassium bichromate, " chloride of lime " (bleaching powder) and similar bodies are unsuitable, and where, in consequence of their higher price, a little extra expense in bleaching is immaterial. Hydrogen peroxide solution of usual (4 to 5 per cent.) commercial strength is added to the fat and well stirred or shaken up with it. The action may be facilitated by the addition of a little alkali, which promotes decomposition and assists the bleaching effect. Without this addition of alkali the action of the peroxide may be protracted for several days without the reagent being completely exhausted; so that, in such cases, it will be found advantageous to keep the water deposited during clarification for use in subsequent operations. The clarification of the oil is unattended with difficulty, because it must have been thoroughly purified before the bleaching process is performed. In this method there is no loss of oil from muddy deposits, such as occur in other processes of bleaching, and it may be characterised as a very clean operation.

BLEACHING WITH SODIUM PEROXIDE.

The sodium peroxide discovered by Castner, which in its chemical characteristics recalls hydrogen peroxide, is, according to its discoverer, calculated to supersede the latter preparation. Sodium peroxide combines cheapness with stability and ease of application. For the fat and oil industry, however, it cannot be regarded as presenting any advantage, in view of the unfavourable results it has been found to produce, even under the most favourable conditions imaginable. After many fruitless trials the hope of finding a way to utilise this preparation to advantage was finally abandoned.

BLEACHING WITH POTASSIUM BICHROMATE AND HYDROCHLORIC ACID.

This method is fully described in treating of the bleaching of palm oil—page 293—and the directions there given apply to all other fats and oils.

BLEACHING WITH POTASSIUM PERMANGANATE.

The permanganate is dissolved in water and decomposed by sulphuric acid. The bleaching process is identical with that for bichromate. At the end of the operation it is advisable to blow in sulphurous acid to remove the final traces of permanganate adhering to the oil. By re-melting the bleached fat along with magnesia and leaving it to stand exposed to the air, any residual taste may be dissipated.

Bleaching with Chlorine.

Bleaching with chlorine is comparatively inexpensive, and should be kept in view when the finding of a cheap and good process is in question for any particular oil. The bleaching powder mostly used in chlorine bleaching is simply mixed with water, the necessary quantity of hydrochloric acid added, and the whole stirred in with the fat or oil. The washing of the fat is easier to accomplish in this process than in others, on account of the ready solubility of the $CaCl_2$ formed. It must, however, be borne in mind that, as with other processes wherein chlorine is produced, chlorination of the fat readily occurs. The substitution of manganese dioxide for bleaching powder in the production of the chlorine is irrational, since the full effect cannot be got out of the former body owing to its insolubility, and, in fact, large quantities must be employed in order to get any action at all.

The direct employment of hypochlorites—Javelle and Larabaque lyes—is not advantageous. On the other hand these compounds may be used in the following manner: The fats are melted in a 10 per cent. soda bath, and a solution of bleaching powder added with continued stirring, the mixture being then heated to boiling and mixed with sufficient dilute sulphuric acid to produce a weak acid reaction. The whole is then left to settle, and finally well washed repeatedly with hot water.

Bleaching with Nitric Acid and Nitrates.

Nitric acid and nitrates also exerts a bleaching action, but Solly's method for bleaching wax is the only one finding practical application. He proceeds by adding 10 per cent. of sodium nitrate and 5 per cent. of dilute (1 : 8) sulphuric acid, which are stirred into the melted wax. The layer of wax resulting on the completion of the process is re-melted several times, and is said to be not inferior to sun-bleached wax.

BLEACHING WITH SULPHUROUS ACID.

Sulphurous acid, so greatly appreciated in the textile industry, has not yet been made available for the purposes of the fat industry. The objections raised against it are : First, that it only masks but does not completely destroy colouring matter; so that the colour may be caused to reappear by the action of dilute acids, nitrous fumes, chlorine, bromine, and iodine; secondly, it has been ascertained that the yellow vegetable colours are precisely those towards which sulphurous acid is more or less inert.

A proof that the action of sulphurous acid is very slight, if exerted at all, is afforded in the course of the method of refining by sulphuric acid, the free sulphurous acid produced therein, and disseminated through the oil, exhibiting no bleaching properties.

BLEACHING BY COMMON SALT AND ELECTRICITY.

Herzog mixes the fat, at ordinary temperatures, with 2·3 per cent. of common salt and then stirs up energetically for five to ten minutes along with water at 25° to 30° C. Whilst this is going on an electric current is passed through the oil, causing the evolution, at the positive pole, of chlorine (from the salt) which bleaches by indirect oxidation.

BLEACHING PALM OIL.

The operation is performed by heating the fat up to 190° C. and then pumping it up and allowing it to fall back into the vessel in thin streams—that is to say, the de-coloration is effected by the action of light and air. Nowadays this method of bleaching is no longer employed, being too expensive and taking too much time, more especially since a simpler method has been found, consisting in heating the palm oil up to 240° C.

To bleach palm oil by heat some 10 to 12 cwts. of the fat are melted in a large tank, and after the impurities have subsided the clarified oil is transferred to the bleaching pan. The impurities are cleared out of the melting tank at intervals.

The bleaching pan—which, on account of the high rate of expansion on heating exhibited by palm oil, is only filled to about two-thirds of its capacity—is heated rapidly, and the oil begins to throw up bubbles at between 115° and 130° C. as though it were about to boil, an effect due to the evolution of the mechanically suspended water. At about 140° C. strongly acid vapours begin to come off, which powerfully affect the eyes, so that the bleaching pan has to be covered by a tight-fitting lid, with a pipe to convey the vapours away to the furnace. At 240° C. the bleaching is complete; the solidified oil is beautifully white, but has a peculiar empyreumatic smell, which, however, in a short time gives place to the original odour of violets.

It is desirable to utilise the heat contained in the palm oil at the temperature to which it is raised (240° C.), and with this object the oil is passed through a coiled cooler surrounded by the batch of palm oil to be bleached next.

Pohl's proposition to heat the palm oil in closed pans from which air is excluded, and to maintain it at this temperature for fifteen minutes, was tried a short time since, but abandoned owing to the danger of fire.

The chemical bleaching process, wherein potassium bichromate and hydrochloric acid are used, is preferable to all others. Manganese dioxide and sulphuric acid, potassium permanganate, hydrogen peroxide, and all other bleaching agents necessitate very careful supervision in the performance of the process, otherwise the wished-for effect is not produced in the right direction. Even potassium bichromate and sulphuric acid do not react so powerfully as when this acid is replaced by hydrochloric. The reason for this is to be sought in the evolution of chlorine gas, which indirectly liberates oxygen, the active bleaching agent.

$$K_2Cr_2O_7 + 14HCl = 7H_2O + 2KCl + Cr_2Cl6 + 6Cl.$$
$$3H_2O + 6Cl = 6HCl + 3O.$$

It would seem as though this indirectly produced oxygen exerts a more powerful bleaching action than the same body liberated direct, for, as already stated, potassium bichromate and sulphuric acid bleach

$$K_2Cr_2O_7 + 4H_2SO_4 = K_2SO_4 + Cr_23SO_4 + 4H_2O + 3O$$

less effectively although the same amount of oxygen, the bleaching agent, is liberated.

In the first stage of this bleaching process the oil is clarified, i.e., freed from water, dirt, particles of vegetable matter, etc., by melting and leaving to settle. The clarified palm oil is then ladled over into a strong wooden vat, which in large works is fitted with mechanical stirrers, and there left to cool down to 31°-32° R. (39°-40° C.). Meanwhile a solution of potassium bichromate in three to four times its weight of water has been prepared, and a quantity equivalent to 1 part by weight of chrome salt per 100 parts of oil is taken and mixed with 4 per cent. (also reckoned on the weight of the oil) of hydrochloric acid, the mixture being then well stirred into the contents of the vat. Decoloration begins in one or two minutes, the thermometer quickly rises some 8° to 10° C., and the mass, which must consist of an intimate emulsion of the palm oil and bleaching liquid, becomes dirty, turbid, then brown, and finally bluish green.

In about ten to fifteen minutes the decoloration is complete. The oil is then left at rest for a few hours to allow the watery lye, composed of potassium chloride and chromium chloride, to settle out and be drawn off through the outflow tap, the oil being thereafter washed with hot water to completely remove the chromium salts and any hydrochloric acid left.

At the end of six hours the palm oil, now very pale in colour, is quite clear and may be taken out of the pan.

The accurate maintenance of the requisite temperature plays an important part in chemical bleaching. Reports in the trade journals and handbooks of the fat industry mostly give 50° C. as the correct temperature, but this is certainly some 10° too high, since the emulsion, necessary for the performance of the reaction, does not occur above 40° C., the chromic acid solution floating about as little globules in the oil and effecting merely an imperfect bleaching even in the most favourable instances. The sodium bichromate recently introduced into commerce may be advantageously used to replace the potassium salt, being much cheaper, and furthermore because, on account of its greater solubility in water, it, unlike the latter, does not require to be used boiling hot.

The chemical process of bleaching is practised in many works both large and small, although the largest prefer air-bleaching. Among the advantages possessed by the chemical method, employing potassium or sodium bichromate and acids, may be mentioned :—

1. It will completely decolorise even the worst grades of palm oil ;

2. No special appliances are necessary, and the operation can be performed even in very small works ;

3. The agreeable odour of violets is completely preserved to the oil.

A disadvantage is certainly caused by the somewhat high cost of the operation, which in the case of air-bleaching is hardly estimable.

Air-bleaching consists in forcing a constant stream of warm air through the oil heated to between 70° and 80° C. At present the process is employed for the treatment of large quantities at a time and necessitates the use of special appliances and the more expensive grades of palm oil. The fat is melted by steam heat in a large tank and left at rest for some hours, so that the dirt and other impurities may settle down. As these bodies exert a highly unfavourable influence during the bleaching process it is necessary to draw off the clarified oil with great care into the spacious wooden or iron bleaching vat. This vessel is fitted with a system of perforated pipes placed in the bottom, warm air being blown through them into the oil for several hours by means of a blower. A constant temperature of 75° C. is maintained by the aid of a steam coil, the bleaching being perfect at this temperature. After the blower has been at work for twenty to twenty-one hours the oil will have become yellowish white in colour, and the operation may be considered at an end.

These installations are capable of treating enormous quantities of oil, and as the only expense to be considered is the steam required for the blower, the cost is very low. The warming of the oil, melting (clarifying), and maintaining the proper temperature during the bleaching process, are all effected by the waste steam, which would otherwise escape into the air and be lost.

CHAPTER XVI.

PRACTICAL EXPERIMENTS ON THE TREATMENT OF OILS, WITH REGARD TO REFINING AND BLEACHING.

A NUMBER of experiments have been made in the laboratory of an Austrian oil refinery, with processes recently patented for the refining and bleaching of oils, the results of which are now given.

PURIFYING COTTON-SEED OIL.

According to the American patent taken out by Scyolla, cotton-seed or similar oil is refined by admixture with ochre, followed by filtration.

Result.—In the case of oils containing a large proportion of impurities, mere settling would be equally efficient. When the impurities are few the results are, as may be anticipated, satisfactory. Of course, fine dry sea sand, etc., would do just as well.

BLEACHING COTTON-SEED OIL.

According to A. Jolles and E. Wild, 100 kilos. of oil are warmed to 60° C., and stirred up with a solution of 0·5 kilo. of potassium bichromate in 5 kilos. of water, to which is added 1 kilo. of sulphuric acid. The stirring is continued for one to one and a half hours and the oil then left to settle, being afterwards washed with warm water until the bitter taste has disappeared; then heated to 100° C., stirred up well with 1 kilo. of bone black and filtered.

Result.—The method proved satisfactory.

PURIFYING COCOANUT OIL.

In the process patented in America by Weiss, carbon bisulphide vapour is passed into the oil, driven off again, and the oil washed with alcohol.

Result.—The oil was not altered in the least, but tenaciously retained the carbon bisulphide when subjected to distillation, and could not be completely freed therefrom even by washing with alcohol. The process is moreover too expensive.

BLEACHING LINSEED OIL.

(*a*) According to the "Seifenfabrikant" 100 kilos. of linseed oil should be intimately mixed with 5 kilos. of hot 30° B. potash. After thorough crutching, a white flocculent precipitate should ensue, the flakes becoming progressively larger and finally sinking to the bottom along with the lye, the operation lasting one half to three quarters of an hour.

Result.—Beyond the anticipated saponification, no appreciable bleaching of dark oils could be detected.

(*b*) In the English patent of Hermite, Patterson and Cooper, palm oil and other vegetable oils may be bleached by treatment with electrolysed chlorides. The fat is melted in a steam jacketed pan, and treated with magnesium chloride and sea salt, or by sodium chloride and calcium chloride. The frothing tendency exhibited by the oil may be removed by washing with acidified water.

Result.—No bleaching effect was produced in dark linseed oil.

BLEACHING RAPE OIL AND OLIVE OIL.

The same process applied to rape oil and olive oil also gave no satisfactory result.

BLEACHING PALM OIL.

In the case of palm oil, for which the process was specially elaborated, a bleaching action is observed.

CHAPTER XVII.

OIL-CAKE AND MEAL—TESTING OILS AND FATS.

OIL-CAKE and oil-meal are the solid residue of pulverised seeds or nuts from which the oil has been removed by pressure or extraction. Oil-cake contains the whole of the woody fibre and mineral matters of the seeds or nuts, together with the residual unextracted fat and the protein or nitrogenous constituents. The latter substances determine the value of the cake, on account of their importance as cattle food or as a basis for artificial manure.

The composition of the most important oil-cakes is given in the following table :—

Oil-cake.	Water.	Nitrogenous Matter.	Crude Fat.	Non-nitrogenous Extractive Matter.	Crude Fibre.	Ash.
Rape cake (Brassica napus oleifera) . . .	11·72	30·78	9·80	28·18	11·58	7·94
Rape meal (extracted) . .	9·95	33·80	5·01	30·75	12·86	7·63
Rubsen cake	10·72	32·73	9·97	31·07	7·78	7·73
Linseed cake . . .	11·95	28·56	10·60	32·09	9·48	7·32
Linseed meal . . .	11·02	33·25	3·59	36·78	9·15	6·21
Poppy-seed cake . . .	11·42	36·40	9·76	19·37	11·84	11·21
Sunflower-seed cake . .	9·24	34·66	14·53	22·29	12·60	6·68
Beech-mast cake . . .	14·93	18·74	8·54	31·41	21·62	4·76
Sesame cake . . .	10·92	37·25	13·46	20·64	7·28	10·45
Palm cake . . .	10·09	16·20	10·98	37·38	21·45	3·90
Palm meal	10·87	16·43	4·45	38·07	25·92	4·26
Ground-nut cake (undecorti-cated)	10·47	46·85	7·88	24·35	5·29	4·89
Ground-nut cake (decorticated)	11·11	30·71	9·04	19·38	23·43	6·33
Cotton cake (decorticated) .	8·62	44·09	14·23	20·85	5·16	7·05
Cocoanut cake . . .	10·56	19·51	10·90	40·26	14·17	4·60
Maize-germ cake . . .	11·43	16·60	8·00	57·37	4·68	1·92

As may be seen from this table, the oil-cakes differ from each other very much in their content of protein substances. Being all, however, too rich in protein and fatty matter to be used as food in an unmixed condition, they are therefore mixed with cereals, hay or straw, and in this condition constitute a valuable fodder. The ash, being very rich in phosphoric acid and potash, accounts for the value of the cakes in the preparation of artificial manures. Thus, for example, 1 ton of cotton-seed ash has the same manurial value as $4\frac{1}{2}$ tons of the ash of hard wood or 15 tons of lixiviated wood ashes.

As a rule, oil-cakes are not directly employed for manure, their utilisation in the bodies of animals, whence the ground derives its supply of fertilisers, being much more profitable, and it therefore does not seem rational to employ as manure good oil-cakes which are sound and constitute a good feeding material. Nevertheless, in cases where the cake, by reason of unsoundness, bad flavour or very low percentage of fat, is unsuitable for feeding purposes, its direct application for manurial purposes becomes advisable.

Both theoretical and practical opinions are in favour of the use of oil-cakes as an addition to cattle foods and for fattening purposes. All oily seeds contain a not unimportant amount of nitrogenous (protein) matter which in characteristics and composition is the equivalent of milk casein. The residual cake in the press contains the whole of this nitrogenous matter, this valuable nutritive material being associated with up to 10 per cent. of fat or oil, which is directly assimilable, forming fat, and indirectly generating warmth in the body of the animal. Moreover, oil-cakes contain phosphatic salts, which serve to build up the substance of bone.

The price of oil is frequently influenced by the oil-cake. In years when green fodder is plentiful and of good quality oil-cake is in less demand than when the fodder harvest is bad, the price of the cake falling in the former case and rising in the latter, so that when oil-cake goes off readily oil is cheaper, and *vice versa.*

Oil-meal is the residue remaining from the partial or total extraction of oil seeds and oil fruits, and its value as a feeding material is very low, the percentage of oil being very small. This circumstance, together with its mealy condition and the ease with which it may be adulterated, causes oil-meal to be held in little estimation for cattle food, the cake form being widely preferred.

PERCENTAGE COMPOSITION OF OIL-CAKES.

Oil-cake.		Dry Matter.	Albuminoids.	Fat.	Non-nitrogenous Extractive Matter.	Woody Fibre.	Ash.
Cocoanut .	Minimum	86·8	19·0	2·3	39·6	5·9	
	Maximum	87·7	21·1	10·0	44·5	20·9	6·6
	Mean	87·2	20·0	6·2	42·0	13·4	
Linseed .	Minimum	83·8	24·9	0·7	24·5	6·2	
	Maximum	90·3	35·1	4·4	39·9	10·8	8·0
	Mean	88·0	32·7	2·5	36·4	8·6	
Palm kernel	Minimum	81·9	4·7	1·1	22·4	11·7	
	Maximum	93·4	23·9	7·3	52·5	39·7	4·0
	Mean	89·2	18·5	3·3	41·7	21·7	
Rape . .	Minimum	85·5	21·8	0·8	26·9	11·1	
	Maximum	96·1	36·8	6·8	38·9	20·3	8·0
	Mean	91·5	33·2	2·5	34·3	13·5	
Rubsen		92·8	36·8	2·4	26·9	19·1	8·6

TESTING OILS AND FATS.

The physical constants regarded as characteristic for oils and fats are: Specific gravity, and, in the case of solid fats, melting point. On the other hand the boiling points are unreliable, the oils being partly decomposed on heating.

The specific gravity of fluid oils may be determined by means of the pyknometer, the Sprengel tube or the West-phal hydrostatic balance. The Sprengel tube consists of a

U-tube, both ends of which are drawn out as capillaries and bent at right angles to the limbs of the tube. The tube is completely filled with oil by dipping the one end into the liquid and exhausting the air, by suction, through the other end. The excess of oil overflowing is removed by wiping with filter paper, and when the oil has ceased to expand the tube is removed from the flask, cooled and weighed, the specific gravity being calculated from the known weights of the tube empty and filled with water.

The Westphal balance is shown in Fig. 94; the thermometer displaces a definite volume of oil, so that the loss in weight represents the weight of this quantity of oil.

The melting point of the solid fats may be determined by the usual methods. A capillary tube is filled with the melted fat and, after the latter has set on cooling, fastened on to the tube of a sensitive thermometer, the two being immersed in a beaker of water, which is then slowly heated until the melting point of the fat is reached and the latter liquefies; the temperature at which this occurs is read off on the thermometer. The accuracy of the determination is increased by placing the beaker in a second vessel of water, heat being applied to the latter.

A number of chemical reactions have been proposed for distinguishing the various vegetable and animal fats from each other. Many of these reactions, being dependent on special conditions, are unreliable and yield contradictory results, and therefore cannot have much value attached to them. This is particularly the case with the majority of the colour reactions resulting from the action of sulphuric and nitric acids on the various oils. In the same way, the differences noticeable in the increase of temperature resulting when concentrated sulphuric acid is added to fatty oils, are not a sufficiently certain guide.

On the other hand, different quantitative methods of

testing may be successfully employed for the differentiation of the various fats and oils. These serve to estimate quantitatively different classes of substances in a fat, and for the identification of the individual fats, the content of these substances often differing characteristically therein.

To these quantitative tests belong the acid number, saponification value, ether number, Reichert-Meissl number, Hehner number, acetyl number, bromine and iodine numbers, the meaning of which will be now explained.

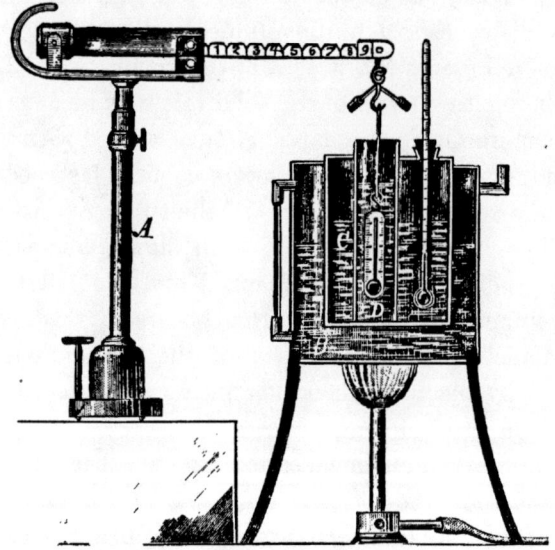

FIG. 94. Westphal Balance.

1. The *acid number* represents the number of milligrams of potassium hydroxide required to neutralise the free fatty acids contained in a fat, and is determined by titrating the fat dissolved in alcohol, etc., with an alcoholic or aqueous solution of caustic potash.

2. The *saponification value* test, which was originated by Köttstorfer, and is also called the "Köttstorfer number," is performed in the following manner: 1·5 to 2 grams of

the fat are treated with 25 cc. of $\frac{1}{2}$-normal alcoholic caustic potash for fifteen minutes on the water bath; when saponification sets in 1 cc. of alcoholic phenolphthalein solution is added, and the liquid titrated by the aid of $\frac{1}{2}$-normal hydrochloric acid, a blank experiment being made by titrating another 25 cc. of the potash solution. The difference between the number of milligrams of potassium hydroxide originally taken and the quantity found by titrating back, is calculated to 1 gram of fat, the result being the saponification value. The term "saponification equivalent," used in England and America, means the quantity of fat saponified by one equivalent (56·1 parts) of KHO. The saponification values of a number of oils and fats are given on page 308.

3. The *ether number* (ester number) refers to the number of milligrams of potassium hydroxide required for the saponification of the neutral fat in 1 gram of the sample.

4. The *Reichert-Meissl number* indicates the percentage of volatile fatty acids in a fat. It represents the number of cubic centimetres of $\frac{1}{10}$-normal caustic potash requisite to neutralise the volatile fatty acids (soluble in water) obtained from 5 grams (formerly 2·5 grams) of a fat.

Five grams of fat are saponified on the water bath in a 200 cc. flask with 2 grams of solid alkali and 60 cc. of 70 per cent. alcohol. The alcohol is driven off and the solution obtained by dissolving the mass in 100 cc. of water and adding 40 cc. of (1 : 10) sulphuric acid distilled. 110 cc. of distillate are caught in a graduated flask, 100 cc. of which are filtered into a second graduated flask, and titrated by $\frac{1}{10}$-normal potash with litmus or phenolphthalein as indicator.

5. The *Hehner number* gives the percentage of insoluble fatty acids present. 3 to 4 grams of fat are saponified by 50 cc. of alcohol and 1 to 2 grams of caustic potash. After

20

the alcohol has been driven off, the soap is dissolved in 100 to 150 cc. of water, a little hydrochloric or sulphuric acid is added and, after melting, the recovered fatty acids are passed through a filter dried at 100° C. The washing with water is continued until the filtrate ceases to have an acid reaction.

6. The *acetyl number* shows the quantity of oxy-fatty acids or fatty alcohols in a fat. 20 to 50 grams of the non-volatile fatty acids are acetylised by two hours' boiling with acetic anhydride, the product of the reaction being extracted several times with 500 to 600 cc. of boiling water, and the acids, which now have a neutral reaction, are filtered in the air bath. The acetyl number is then determined by titrating with $\frac{1}{2}$-normal aqueous potash.

7. *Bromine and iodine absorption.*—The methods of estimating these reactions give the percentage of bromine or iodine absorbed by the oils under conditions conducive to the formation of addition products exclusively. The fatty acids of the acetic or stearic series are saturated compounds forming no addition products, whereas the acids of the acetyl or oleic acid series combine with two, and those of the propyl or linolic series with four atoms of a halogen.

The glycerides of the acids of these three series behave exactly like the free acids, so that the percentage of iodine absorbed forms a guide to the ratio of olein to palmitin and stearin in a fat, and also the content of linolein in a drying oil compared with the oil content of a non-drying oil.

The estimations of bromine absorption give no reliable values, whereas Hübl's method of determining the iodine number yields more constant results. Hübl employs an alcoholic mixture of iodine and mercuric chloride containing 25 grams of iodine dissolved in $\frac{1}{2}$ litre of 95 per cent. alcohol (free from fusel oil), and 30 grams of mercuric chloride dissolved in the above quantity of spirit.

The solution is ready for use after twelve hours' standing, but must be tested before use to determine its composition. For estimating the iodine number, 0·2 to 0·4 gram of fluid, or 0·8 to 1 gram of solid fat must be weighed out, and dissolved in 10 cc. of chloroform. 20 cc. of the iodine solution are added at first, then successively 5 to 10 cc. until the solution at the expiration of two hours has assumed a dark brown colour. Hereupon 10 to 15 cc. of a 10 per cent. aqueous solution of potassium iodide are added, together with 150 cc. of water, the free iodine being titrated by sodium thiosulphate (20 grams per litre). The absorbed iodine is then referred to percentage units of the fat, the value so obtained being designated the iodine number (Hübl number). The number appears to be nearly constant for each oil or class, and is highest in the case of vegetable drying oils. The Hübl method has proved particularly applicable for the detection of cotton-seed oil in tallow and lard. Pure cotton-seed oil has the iodine number 109·1; pure tallow, 40·8; tallow with 5 per cent. of cotton-seed oil, 44; with 10 per cent., 47·1; with 15 per cent., 49·7; with 20 per cent., 52·9; with 25 per cent., 56·1; with 30 per cent., 59·2; and with 40 per cent., 66·2. In the case of lard the detection of cotton-seed oil is rendered difficult when beef stearin is present. The iodine number of pure lard is 57 to 63, that of beef stearin 23 to 28. The various constants of the oils and fats are as follows :—

TABLE OF CONSTANTS OF OILS AND FATS.

Oil.	Specific Gravity at 15° C.	Saponification Value.	Iodine Number.	Hehner Number.	Reichert Number.	Acid Number.	Acetyl.
Apricot-kernel oil	0·915	192·9	100	...	...	...	...
Arachis oil	0·9163	193·5	193	95·86	...	...	....
Cotton-seed oil	0·922	195·5	106	95·87	...	...	16·65
Curcas oil	...	230·5	...	...	...	...	...
Dolphin oil	...	197·3	...	...	...	...	...
Shark oil	...	84·5	...	...	...	...	...
Hemp oil	0·9255	193·1	143	...	...	...	...
Radish oil	0·9175	174·0	105	...	...	...	...
Pumpkin-seed oil	...	189·5	...	...	...	...	...
Gundschitt oil	0·9336 (at 20°)	185·0	162·1	93·3	1·55	...	...
Fish-liver oil	...	185·0	...	...	...		
Linseed oil	0·9347	193·0	170	...	...	...	...
Maize oil	0·9215	188·6	119·5	94·7	0·66	...	...
Almond oil	0·9186	192·0	89·4	96·2	2·08	...	....
Porpoise oil	0·9260	143·9	76·8	96·5	...	...	...
Menhaden oil	0·9320	192·0	147·9	...	...	...	...
Poppy oil	0·924	193·7	136	95·38	...	...	...
Niger oil	0·9270	190·0	132·9	...	...	...	..
Nut oil	0·926	196·0	143	...	...	...	...
Oil-cake oil	...	183·6	...	...	...	...	...
Olive-kernel oil	0·9202	188·5	81·8	...	...	90·1	2·5
Olive oil	0·9178	193·0	82·8	95·43	0·3	...	...
Pilchard oil	...	186·7	...	...	...	...	...
Rape oil (Raps)	...	177·0	...	...	...	...	...
Ricinus oil	0·960	180·0	84·4	...	...	...	152·4
Seal oil	0·9153	193·5	93	...	...	...	...
Rape oil (Rüböl)	0·9112—0·9175	177·0	100	95·10	0·25	...	...
Sesame oil	0·9225	190·0	106	95·86	0·35	...	....
Sunflower oil	0·9262	193·0	129	95·00	...	...	....
Lard oil	...	193·5	...	...	...	...	...
Spermaceti oil	0·875	132·2	84	...	...	...	...
Whale oil	0·9307	190·5	80·9	...	3·7	...	...
Neatsfoot oil	0·914	...	70	...	...	...	...
Palm oil	0·945	202·0	51·5	95·6	0·5	...	...
Cocoanut oil	0·925 (at 18°)	261·3	89	...	3·70	...	...
Cacao butter	0·950—0·952	200·0	34	94·59	...	10	...
Japanese wax	0·977—0·978	222·0	4·2	...	...	20	...
Beef tallow	0·943—0·952	195·7	40·0	95·8	0·25	...	...
Lard	0·931—0·932	195·8	59·0	95·6	...	...	...

According to Becchi the presence of cotton-seed oil in lard can be qualitatively determined by the brown coloration which it gives with an alcoholic solution of silver nitrate. Bizio, however, avers that other vegetable oils, *e.g.*, olive oil, also give the same reaction.

In examining fats it is not sufficient to identify a certain fat and determine its purity: the presence of soaps, free fatty acids and extraneous non-fatty substances, such as resins or hydrocarbons, has also to be borne in mind. The soaps may be removed by extracting, with water, the solution of the fat in carbon bisulphide. The presence of free fatty acids cannot always be regarded as indicative of adulteration, since they exist in many vegetable oils. It sometimes, however, points to a decomposed condition of the fat (rancidity), whereas for certain purposes (lubrication) the fats should be neutral. In the absence of free fatty acids resin is detectable by shaking up the oil with moderately strong alcohol and evaporating the solvent. The separation of the resin acids from free fatty acids is most conveniently effected by the method described by T. S. Gladding. This method is based on the ready solubility of silver resinate in ether, the nitrate, etc., of silver being almost totally insoluble in this solvent. Hydrocarbons can generally be recognised by saponifying the sample with alcoholic caustic potash (5 grams of oil, 2 grams of potassium hydroxide, 25 cc. of 90 per cent. alcohol), mixing the resulting soap with clean sand, evaporating the alcohol on the water bath at a temperature not exceeding 50° C., and extracting the residue with ether or petroleum ether. The hydrocarbons are obtained by concentrating the resulting solution.

SCHEME OF ANALYSIS FOR ADULTERATED OILS (ALLEN).

Five to ten grams of the sample (previously melted if necessary) are filtered through a dry filter if not initially clear.

The *RESIDUE* may contain common salt, water, sand, and any other insoluble matter present in the oil. Wash with ether; calcine and reweigh; dry and weigh. The difference represents organic matter.

The *CLEAR OIL* is shaken up in a separating funnel with water, ether or freshly distilled carbon bisulphide. (If an aliquot part of the solution of oil is not blackened by ammonium sulphide or leaves no ash behind on combustion, so that metallic compounds do not appear to be present, the treatment with water and sulphuric acid may be omitted.) The aqueous solution is drawn off, and the oil solution again shaken up with water, provided anything was taken up by the preliminary treatment.

The *AQUEOUS LIQUID* may contain soaps of the lighter metals. Evaporate to dryness at 100° C. and weigh the residue, which may be further investigated if desired.

The solution is agitated along with dilute sulphuric acid, and the liquids separated. The residual oil is washed with water until the washings no longer redden litmus paper.

The *ACID LIQUID* may contain the sulphates of aluminium and the heavy metals, which were present as soaps.

THE SOLUTION OF OIL IN ETHER OR CARBON BISULPHIDE.—The solvent is distilled off, and the residual oil heated with alcohol and a few drops of phenolphthalein solution. Add carefully filtered caustic soda, and shake after each addition until a red coloration results, appearing after the shaking. The quantity of soda used indicates the amount of free fatty acids and resin acids present. After removing any insoluble oil, the alcoholic solution is diluted and the alcohol driven off by moderate heat. Shake up with petroleum ether, separate, evaporate the solvent, and unite any resulting oil to the main body.

OIL. — Saponify with alcoholic caustic potash. Evaporate the alcohol, dissolve the residual soap in warm water, and shake up the cold solution repeatedly with ether.

The ETHEREAL LIQUID on distillation at 100° C. —the final traces of the solvent being removed by a current of air— leaves behind hydrocarbons.

The AQUEOUS LIQUID contains glycerin and the soaps resulting from the saponification of the neutral fats. If the solution be treated with hydrochloric acid and extracted by ether, the weight of the residual fatty acids (left after evaporating the ethereal layer) multiplied by 1·055 will give the approximate weight of the neutral oil.

AQUEOUS LIQUID. —Add hydrochloric acid and shake up with ether or carbon bisulphide. Evaporate the ethereal solution at 100° C. and weigh the residue. This contains the free fatty acids and resin acids of the original sample, together with the fatty acids of any aluminium or metallic soaps originally present in the oil.

APPENDIX A.

MAIZE OIL OR OIL OF CORN.

Mr. C. G. Hopkins' paper on corn oil, as follows, was published in 1900 by the American Chemical Society.

The presence of oil in the corn kernel was discovered by Bizio in 1823. A partial analysis by Hoppe-Seyler gave the following as the percentage composition of the oil:—

Cholesterol	2·65
Protogon	3·95
Saponifiable fats, etc.	93·40

The statement is made that the oil contains stearin, palmitin, and much olein, and the melting-point of the fatty acids is given as 51° to 54° F. (11° to 12° C.).

Some of the so-called physical and chemical "constants," which have been determined by several investigators, are given below:—

	Specific gravity of oil at 15° C.	Unsaponifiable substance. Per cent.	Iodine absorption. Per cent.
Spüller	—	1·35	119·7
Smith	0·9244	—	122·9
Hart	0·9239	1·55	117·0
Rokitianski	0·8360	—	75·8

The oil used by Spüller was the ordinary ether extract. Rokitianski used a petroleum ether extract. Hart worked with a "dark brown" sample, presumably found on the market. Smith's material was obtained on the market, but was of a "bright golden colour" and was probably a fair sample of corn oil.

Spüller observed that the oil absorbed no oxygen from the air even after fourteen days' exposure. Smith states that the freezing-point of the oil is below −20°. Hart gives the melting-point of the fatty acids as 25°. Rokitianski reports further qualitative chemical work which showed the oil to contain oleic and linolic

acids. It is evident from the specific gravity and the iodine absorption that the material with which he worked was not ordinary
corn oil.

Wiley and Bigelow have recently found the heat of combustion
of oil of corn to be 9280 calories per gram.

In a preliminary study a small amount of oil was obtained by
collecting the ether extract from a large number of proximate
analyses of corn. In this advantage was taken of the fact that
the oil is moderately soluble in alcohol when hot and but slightly
so at ordinary temperatures.

The oil was transferred from the small flasks, used in its
extraction, by means of hot alcohol to a single vessel. On cooling
the oil precipitated and settled to the bottom, the alcohol being
each time decanted from the collected oil, and used in transferring
the next lot. Finally the alcohol was evaporated, and the oil
dried to constant weight in a water oven. When freshly obtained
from white dent corn the oil is nearly colourless, but on standing
a pale yellow and finally a deep golden colour develops, plainly
indicating a gradual change in its condition, presumably due to
absorption of oxygen. This was confirmed by determining the
iodine absorption which was found to be 115·5 per cent.

A large quantity of corn oil, including samples from four
different sources, was then secured in order to make a more
thorough investigation. The oil is obtained as a bye-product in
the manufacture of corn-starch and glucose-sugar, and all of the
samples secured were of a pale straw colour and evidently fresh
and pure.

Three of these samples of corn oil were sufficient in quantity
to enable me to make determinations of their specific gravity by
means of a delicate Westphal balance which by trial gave the
specific gravity of pure water at 15° as 1·000. The samples of
oil gave the following results :—

	I.	II.	III.
Specific gravity at 15° . . .	0·9245	0·9262	0·9258

Preliminary experiments confirmed the observation of Smith
that the oil is still fluid at − 20°, a temperature of − 23° (obtained
with snow and concentrated sulphuric acid) failing to solidify the
oil. It was found, however, that the oil became hard and solid
at about − 36°.

The melting-point was determined by a modification of the method of the Association of Official Agricultural Chemists.

In a tall beaker of about $2\frac{5}{10}$ litres' capacity was placed a small quantity of concentrated sulphuric acid (to absorb water vapour so that the apparatus would remain transparent at low temperatures). A second beaker of about 2 litres' capacity was placed in the first, being supported by the rim without touching the bottom. A 1 litre beaker, taller than the second, was placed in the latter and filled with alcohol, the space between the two being filled with solid carbon dioxide. A glass tube 30 mm. in diameter, and closed at the bottom, was fitted into the inner beaker with a large cork, the tube being about one-third filled with a mixture of 1 volume of concentrated sulphuric acid and 3 volumes of absolute alcohol, and then nearly completely filled with absolute alcohol. The temperature of the alcohol in the beaker was kept uniform throughout by constant stirring with a wire which passed through the cork and terminated in a ring surrounding the glass tube. A heavy glass spoon and a glass spatula were placed in the alcohol.

When the temperature reached $-50°$, the spoon was removed and a drop of the oil at once let fall upon it. A thin, solid, white, opaque disc formed, and was quickly made to drop into the inner tube by using the glass spatula. The disc of solidified oil settled through the absolute alcohol to the denser liquid below and there remained in suspension.

The beaker which had contained carbon dioxide was replaced by another and the temperature allowed to slowly rise. An alcohol thermometer was used for reading the temperatures below the freezing-point of mercury. Above $-38°$ a delicate mercury thermometer was employed.

As the temperature rose the disc remained unchanged, until at $-19°$ it began to lose its opacity. At $-14°$ it had become perfectly transparent, but no change in shape could be detected below $-7°$. The disc was much contracted and thickened at $-5°$ and became entirely symmetrical in form at $-2·3°$. A second determination gave practically the same results, the final reading being $-2·4°$. The change in temperature (when near the melting-point) required five to six minutes for $1°$.

To determine the change in the consistency of the oil, a

thin-wall tube of 8 mm. diameter, closed at the bottom and containing 1 cm. of the oil, was placed in alcohol at − 45°. After the oil had become solid a glass rod 20 cm. long and 2 mm. thick (the lower end being widened to 5 mm. diameter) was placed in the tube so that its weight was entirely supported by the solidified oil. At − 13° the oil had become transparent but still supported the rod. At − 10° the rod began to settle appreciably and at − 9° it had passed through the centimetre of oil to the bottom, although a disc of oil suspended beside the tube in the same liquid had not changed appreciably in shape. The change of temperature from − 10° to − 9° required five minutes.

Iodine Absorption.—The method of Hübl was employed for this determination, except for certain details of the process.

Standard sodium thiosulphate solution was prepared by dissolving 47·2 grams of the crystallised salt ($Na_2S_2O_35H_2O$) in water and diluting to 2 litres. From theory 1 cc. of this solution should be equivalent to 12·06 milligrams of iodine if the salt were pure. The solution was standardised with re-sublimed iodine with the following results :—

Iodine taken	0·5160	0·5574 gram.
Thiosulphate solution required 42·9		46·4 cc.
Iodine equivalent to 1 cc. . 12·03		12·01 milligrams.

The average of these results, 12·02, was used in the following work :—

The iodine solution, containing 50 grams iodine, and 60 grams mercuric chloride in two litres of alcohol, was standardised whenever used.

Little pipettes of about $\frac{5}{10}$ cc. capacity were placed in 5 cc. vials nearly filled with the corn oil, the bulb of the pipette being immersed, and the whole weighed. The measure of oil was then transferred to a 500 cc. glass-stoppered bottle, the pipette returned to the vial, and the exact weight of oil taken determined by difference. The duplicate is taken immediately and necessitates only one more weighing. Ten cc. of chloroform and 40 cc. of iodine solution were added to the oil. After two hours 25 cc. of 10 per cent. potassium iodide solution and about 125 cc. of water were added and the excess of iodine determined by titrating with the sodium thiosulphate solution, starch indicator being added near the close of the reaction.

Duplicate determinations of four different samples of oil from as many different sources gave the following results:—

	Oil taken. Gram.	Iodine absorbed. Gram.	Iodine absorbed. Per cent.
1	0·3473	0.4255	122·5
	0·3844	0·4729	123·0
2	0·4251	0·5179	121·8
	0·4714	0·5729	121·5
3	0·4281	0·5212	121·7
	0·4742	0·5772	121·7
4	0·4326	0·5324	123·1
	0·5168	0·6351	122·9

In order to afford a large surface for the absorption of oxygen, the oil was placed in a large crystallising dish of 75 mm. diameter. This was allowed to stand at the room temperature, the weight of the oil being determined from time to time as follows:—

	Grams.
Weight of oil taken	2·1732
„ after 1 day	2·1722
„ „ 7 days	2·1718
„ „ 11 „	2·1718
„ „ 12 „	2·1718

These results confirm those of Spüller, showing that the oil does not take up oxygen under these conditions.

The dish was then placed in a water-oven and the following data obtained:—

	Grams.
Weight after 1 hour	2·1726
„ „ 1 day	2·1996
„ „ 2 days	2·2488
„ „ 3 „	2·2590
„ „ 4 „	2·2588
„ „ 5 „	2·2558
„ „ 6 „	2·2513
„ „ 7 „	2·2448

The first action of air upon the hot oil is evidently the direct addition of oxygen; but after two or three days the oil began to turn noticeably darker in colour and finally to lose weight, evidently due to a secondary reaction which effects some decomposition of the oil with formation of volatile products.

A weighed quantity of oil was mixed with potassium nitrate and sodium carbonate in a platinum dish and ignited until the carbon was completely burned. The fused mass was dissolved in dilute hydrochloric acid, and the total phosphoric acid determined. The amount of lecithin was calculated by multiplying the weight of magnesium pyrophosphate obtained by the factor 7·25. Duplicate determinations gave the following results :—

	Grams.	Grams.
Oil taken	10·728	6·435
KNO_3 used	10·0	35·0
$Mg_2P_2O_7$ obtained	0·0221	0·0132
Lecithin	0·1602	0·0957
	Per cent.	Per cent.
Lecithin in oil	1·49	1·49

Cholesterol.—To determine cholesterol about 50 grams of the oil was saponified on the water-bath with 20 grams of potassium hydroxide and 100 cc. of 70 per cent. alcohol. The soap was transferred to a large separatory funnel with 200 cc. of water and shaken first with 500 cc. of ether and then three times with 250 cc. of ether. The four portions of separated ether were combined, and the ether distilled, the residue being resaponified with 2 grams of potassium hydroxide and 10 cc. of 70 per cent. alcohol. The solution was then transferred to a small separatory funnel with 20 cc. of water and shaken with 100 cc. of ether. After separating the aqueous layer the ether solution was washed four times with 10 cc. of water, the ether solution being finally transferred to a weighed flask, the ether distilled and the weight of the dry residue (cholesterol) determined. Three determinations gave the following results :—

	Grams.	Grams.	Grams.
Oil taken	50·16	53·50	54·24
Cholesterol obtained	0·7002	0·7114	0·7512
	Per cent.	Per cent.	Per cent.
Cholesterol in oil	1·40	1·33	1·38

The cholesterol was recrystallised from absolute alcohol in characteristic glistening plates, melting at 137° to 137·5°. It also gave the characteristic colour reactions from cholesterol : (1) when shaken with chloroform and sulphuric acid ; (2) when evaporated to dryness with nitric acid ; (3) when warmed with hydrochloric acid and ferric chloride.

After removing the cholesterol from about 50 grams of oil the remaining soap solution (about 500 cc.) was acidified with

hydrochloric acid and shaken in a separatory funnel. An ethereal
layer of about 150 cc. at once separated. After adding 100 cc.
more ether and thoroughly shaking, the aqueous layer was drawn
off, the ether solution of the fatty acids washed with several portions
of water and then transferred to a weighed flask, the ether distilled
off, a few cubic centimetres of absolute alcohol dissolved in the
residue and evaporated to remove traces of water, and the weight
of the total fatty acids determined :—

	Grams.
Oil taken	50·160
Fatty acids obtained	46·935
	Per cent.
Fatty acids in oil	93·57

The fatty acids form a solid mass at 15°, but melt nearly completely at one or two degrees above, the last particles of solid
disappearing at 23°. Prepared as described the fatty acids absorbed
only 126·4 per cent. of iodine instead of 130·7 per cent., as calculated
from the iodine absorption of the oil. This indicates that oxygen
had been absorbed by the acids during the process of separation.
It was found that oxygen is slowly absorbed by the fatty acids
while standing in a desiccator at the ordinary temperature. At
100° the absorption is much more rapid, although, as with the oil,
secondary reactions soon begin at the higher temperature. The
change in weight was found to be as follows :—

Time. In days.	In desiccator. Grams.	In water-oven. Grams.
0	1·9685	2·2740
1	1·9692	2·3106
2	1·9717	2·3366
3	1·9777	2·3366
4	1·9847	2·3282
8	2·0231	—
12	2·0665	—
16	2·0911	—
22	2·1157	—
28	2·1293	—
34	2·1297	—

All action apparently ceased after about one month's time.
A considerable portion of the fatty acids had separated in the solid
form and of a pure white colour, while the other portion remained
a colourless, oily liquid.

It is of interest to note the apparent relation between the iodine absorption and the oxygen absorption by the fatty acids. As already shown the fatty acids as prepared absorbed 126·4 per cent. of iodine. If an equivalent amount of the bivalent oxygen may be absorbed instead of the univalent iodine then 8 per cent. of oxygen should be taken up. The results show that 1·9685 grams of the fatty acids absorbed 0·1612 gram of oxygen, an amount equal to $8\frac{2}{10}$ per cent.

Time would not permit the preparation of the fatty acids in a manner which would prevent the absorption of oxygen during the process, and then a repetition of the quantitative determination of the absorption. This is especially desirable in order to confirm the results as given above, and the writer expects to investigate this point more fully in the future.

About 5 grams of oil were saponified in a 500 cc. flask with 2 grams of potassium hydroxide and 40 cc. of 80 per cent. alcohol. After evaporating the last of the alcohol, 100 cc. of recently boiled water was added, the soap solution acidified with 40 cc. of dilute sulphuric acid (1 : 10), a few pieces of freshly ignited pumice-stone added, the flask connected with a condenser by means of a safety bulb tube, and 110 cc. of distillate collected. After mixing 100 cc. was passed through a dry filter and titrated with $\frac{1}{25}$ normal barium hydroxide solution.

Four determinations gave the following results :—

	Grams.	Grams.	Grams.	Grams.
Oil taken	4·506	5·894	5·671	5·718
	cc.	cc.	cc.	cc.
N/25 barium hydroxide required .	1·3	1·5	1·4	1·3

As two blank determinations required $1\frac{3}{10}$ and $1\frac{5}{10}$ cc., respectively, of the barium hydroxide solution, it is evident that the oil contains no volatile acids.

It has been found, especially by Hazura and his associates, that the oxidation of unsaturated fatty acids by alkaline potassium permanganate serves as a basis for the approximate separation of several fatty acids. Under proper conditions the oxidation is chiefly confined to the direct addition of the hydroxyl group (OH) wherever " free valences " exist. The following shows the relations among several acids in the series containing 18 atoms of carbon in the molecule :—

Unsaturated acids.		Saturated acids. Stearic $C_{18}H_{36}O_2$.
Oleic, $C_{18}H_{34}O_2$,	oxidises to dihydroxy stearic,	$C_{18}H_{34}(OH)_2O_2$.
Linolic, $C_{18}H_{32}O_2$,	oxidises to tetrahydroxy stearic,	$C_{18}H_{32}(OH)_4O_2$.
Linolenic, $C_{18}H_{30}O_2$,	oxidises to hexahydroxy stearic,	$C_{18}H_{30}(OH)_6O_2$.

After removing the cholesterol from 53·5 grams of oil, the combined soap solution was heated till the dissolved ether was distilled, cooled, and diluted to 2 litres. Two litres of a $1\frac{5}{10}$ per cent. potassium permanganate solution was then gradually added with constant stirring. After ten minutes the precipitated manganese hydroxide was filtered off, and the clear filtrate acidified with hydrochloric acid. The precipitate thus formed was filtered off, washed, air-dried, and then extracted with ether. The residue insoluble in ether weighed, after drying, 18 grams. It was extracted with boiling water until but 2 grams remained, which, when again extracted with ether, left a residue of $\frac{6}{10}$ gram and soluble in boiling water.

The substance dissolved in hot water was practically completely precipitated as the solution cooled and proved to be sativic acid (tetrahydroxystearic acid), as is indicated by the method of formation and by its solubility in hot water. The melting-point of the dried substance was 157°-159°.

The quantitative synthesis of the potassium salt was effected by dissolving a weighed amount of the acid in warm alcohol and titrating with standard alcoholic potassium hydroxide solution :—

Sativic acid taken.	Potassium hydroxide required.	Per cent. potassium in product.	Per cent. potassium (theory).
1·000	0·1604	10·08	10·14

The ether solutions obtained as described above were combined and the ether distilled. The residue was solid at the room temperature, melted gradually as the temperature rose from 40° to 60°, and was found to absorb 79·2 per cent. of iodine, thus showing very incomplete oxidation of the unsaturated acids.

A second lot of corn oil (54·24 grams) was oxidised by alkaline permanganate, the cholesterol and then the dissolved ether having been previously removed. The soap was diluted to 2 litres and cooled to 0° by ice kept in the solution. A solution of potassium permanganate containing 80 grams in 2 litres of water was slowly added with constant stirring. After thirty minutes pre-

cipitated matter was filtered off and washed; the clear filtrate
was acidified with 150 cc. of concentrated hydrochloric acid; the
precipitated acids were filtered off, dried, and extracted with ether.
The residue insoluble in ether (17·7 grams) was dissolved in
boiling 95 per cent. alcohol. On cooling the sativic acid separated
in the crystalline form, melting at 161°-163°.

By distilling the ether from the solution obtained as above
described, a brown residue ($9\frac{5}{10}$ grams) was obtained which melted
at 55° to 60° and showed an iodine absorption of only $9\frac{2}{10}$ per cent.

The aqueous acid solution from which the insoluble organic
acids had been precipitated by hydrochloric acid was evaporated
nearly to dryness, a black tarry mass gradually separating, showing
that, although a small amount of unsaturated acids had been
unacted upon, the oxidation had gone far beyond the simple
addition of hydroxyl groups to the unsaturated compounds.

To further investigate the fatty acids, a method essentially
that of Muter was tried for their separation and determination.
It is based upon the fact that the lead salts of the unsaturated
acids, oleic, linolic, etc., are soluble in ether; while the lead salts
of the saturated acids, stearic, palmitic, etc., are not.

About $1\frac{5}{10}$ grams of the oil were saponified with alcoholic
potash and the soap dissolved in water, the unsaponifiable
substance (cholesterol) being separated from the soap solution
by shaking with ether. The solution was then neutralised with
acetic acid, and the fatty acids precipitated with lead acetate,
a slight excess being added. The lead salts were washed with
water, and then transferred with 50 cc. of ether to a glass
cylinder of about 60 cc. capacity, which was stoppered and
then violently shaken for five to ten minutes. The small quantity
of matter insoluble in ether was then allowed to settle. A stopper
carrying two glass tubes similar to those used in the ordinary
washing bottle was placed in the cylinder, the long tube reaching
nearly to the undissolved sediment. By blowing in the short
tube the clear solution is transferred almost completely without
disturbing the sediment. The undissolved substance was then
shaken with more ether, allowed to settle, and the ether transferred
as before as completely as possible. This treatment was twice
more repeated. The undissolved lead salt was then warmed with
about 25 cc. of dilute hydrochloric acid, till the fatty acid separ-

ated; and, after cooling sufficiently, the whole was transferred to a 250 cc. graduated bulb tube, ether being used to complete the transfer. The portion of the tube below the bulb contained 50 cc. and was graduated to $\frac{2}{10}$ cc. A small glass tube carrying a stopcock was sealed in just below the 50 cc. mark. The tube was filled to the 250 cc. mark (above the bulb) with ether, and thoroughly shaken. The aqueous layer, containing the excess of hydrochloric acid and the precipitated lead chloride was allowed to separate.

The volume of ether solution was observed, and 200 cc. of it was drawn off into a weighed flask, evaporated to dryness, and the weight of the residue determined.

Duplicate determinations gave the following :—

	Grams.	Grams.
Oil taken	1·60	1·610
	cc.	cc.
Volume of ether solution	222·4	221·0
Ether solution taken	200·0	200·0
	Gram.	Gram.
Saturated acids obtained	0·0670	0·0648
	Per cent.	Per cent.
Saturated acid in oil	4·66	4·44

The residue of saturated acids formed a white solid mass. It was dissolved in hot alcohol and allowed to crystallise. The melting-point was 57°. The quantity of the saturated acids thus obtained was considered too small for further satisfactory examination.

Before the lead salts of the saturated acids were completely washed by decantation the clear ether solution of the lead salts of the unsaturated acids absorbed oxygen, and became cloudy, a white precipitate forming in considerable amount. Two samples of the atmosphere in the cylinders above the solutions were drawn off in gas burettes; and, after removing the ether vapour, the residual air was found to contain only 15·3 per cent. and 13·9 per cent., respectively, of oxygen instead of 20·8 per cent. as found in the air of the laboratory.

By subtracting the percentage (4·55) of saturated acids found in the oil from that of the total fatty acids (93·57) the amount of total unsaturated acids is found to be 89·02 per cent., consisting of oleic and linolic acids. (The melting-point of the sativic acid obtained and the composition of its potassium salt prove the absence of linusic acid in the products of oxidation, and, hence, of linolenic acid in the total fatty acids.)

From the iodine absorption the amounts of oleic and linolic acids can be accurately determined. Thus :—

Oleic acid, $C_{18}H_{34}O_2 + I_2 = C_{18}H_{34}I_2O_2$, diiodostearic acid.
Linolic acid, $C_{18}H_{32}O_2 + 2I_2 = C_{18}H_{32}I_4O_2$, tetraiodostearic acid.

As 89·02 grams of these unsaturated acids in the ratio in which they exist in corn oil absorb 122·3 grams of iodine, the following equation can be stated, x being the number of grams of oleic acid :—

$$x \frac{254}{282} + (89 \cdot 02 - x) \frac{508}{280} = 122 \cdot 3$$

The oleic acid is found to be 42·92 grams and the linolic acid 46·10 grams.

By subtracting from the amount of saturated acids the equivalent of the stearic acid contained in the lecithin, and calculating to the respective glycerol esters the remaining saturated acids (as stearic acid), the oleic acid and the linolic acid, the following summary is obtained as the composition of the oil of corn :—

Cholesterol	1·37
Lecithin	1·49
Stearin (?)	3·66
Olein	44·85
Linolin	48·19
Total	99·56

APPENDIX B.

THE FATTY ACIDS OF COCOANUT OIL.*

Two commercial refined cocoanut oils—known as "palmin" and "kunerol" respectively—examined by Ulzer, gave the following constants :—

	Saponification value.	Iodine value.	Reichert-Meissl value.
Palmin	259·9	9·1	8·5
Kunerol	258·8	9·2	8·3

the values in the last column being thus a little in excess of the figure (7·5) generally given as the highest limit.

The determination of the quantity and mean molecular weight of the readily volatile fatty acids was effected by the method employed by Henriques, *viz.*, evaporating, drying, and weighing the neutralised soap solution, the solution from two Reichert-Meissl determinations (corresponding to 10 grams of fat) being taken in each case, in order to have a sufficiently large amount of soap for this test. The mean molecular weight of the volatile fatty acids distilled in making the Reichert-Meissl estimation was found to be 123·3 in the case of palmin, and 121·5 in the case of kunerol, the quantities present being therefore calculated as 2·09 and 2·02 per cent. respectively. To facilitate the investigation of the insoluble fatty acids of the palmin a quantity was prepared by saponification and decomposing the soap with dilute sulphuric acid, 100 grams of the product being then distilled in fractions, in a partial vacuum (15 mm. pressure). The first 50 grams of distillate gave the acid value 273·9, corresponding to a mean molecular weight 204·5. The second fraction, constituting about 30 per cent. of the total fatty acids, gave the acid value 261·1, and the mean molecular weight 214·5, whilst the acid value of

* Translated from the *Chemische Revue Fett u. Harz-Industrie.*

the residue—about 20 per cent. of the total—was 257·1, and the mean molecular weight 217·8. To separate the palmitic acid assumed to be present in cocoanut oil, the above-named residue was subjected to repeated recrystallisations from a mixture (first proposed by David) of 300 vols. of alcohol and 220 vols. of dilute acetic acid (50 per cent. vol. water), a mixture wherein palmitic acid and stearic acid are only sparingly soluble. After three recrystallisations the residue amounted to only 2·5 grams. The acid value of this portion of the fatty acids was 253·8, the mean molecular weight 220·6, and the melting-point of the mixture 34° C. From these data—and especially in view of the circumstance that the result of the distillation in partial vacuum, and at a temperature not exceeding 190° C., was the production of a residue having a mean molecular value between that of lauric acid (200) and myristic acid (228)—it appears certain that the amount of palmitic acid (if any) present in cocoanut fat is merely small, otherwise the acid value of the fatty acids prepared by the David method would have been lower, and the mean molecular weight of same greater. Contrary to Görey's report, the percentage of myristic acid in the fatty acids from cocoanut oil is considerable. A portion of the residue obtained by the above-named method of distillation—whereby a large proportion of the lauric and myristic acids was removed—was converted into lead soap in the usual manner, the lead salts of the liquid fatty acids being then separated from those of the solid fatty acids by digestion with ether. The ethereal solution of the liquid fatty acids was decomposed by agitation with dilute sulphuric acid, and the ether distilled off. A comparatively small quantity of fatty acids was obtained, exhibiting a salve-like consistency at 15° C., and therefore containing solid fatty acids, as well as liquid acids. This mixture gave the iodine value 66·5. To definitely ascertain whether the unsaturated acid in this mixture is oleic acid or not, 2 grams of the mixture was oxidised in alkaline solution by potassium permanganate, the excess of oxidising agent being destroyed by sulphurous acid, and the manganese oxide eliminated. On acidifying, an abundance of solid fatty acids was isolated and washed with ether to extract the saturated fatty acids. The residue, after being washed with boiling water, formed a white powder, which, on recrystallisation from alcohol, yielded small plates melting at 132° C.—*i.e.*, imperfectly purified dioxystearic acid. The difference between this melting-point and that of pure dioxystearic acid (136·5° C.) is explained by the circumstance that the melting-point of fatty acids undergoes considerable modification, if even only a very small percentage of impurities is present, and is therefore unimportant. The presence of oleic acid, converted into dioxystearic acid by oxidation, is therefore regarded as proved, the actual proportion determined from the iodine value by calculation being about 10 per cent.

Accordingly, the cocoanut fat examined (palmin) contains about 3·2 per cent. of triglycerides of readily volatile fatty acids (mainly caproic and caprylic acids) and about 10·45 per cent. of triolein, the remainder of the bulk consisting of trilaurin and trimyristin, in addition to which is a little of the glycerides of capric acid. It is doubtful whether tripalmitin is present in cocoanut oil.

APPENDIX C.

VEGETABLE TALLOWS FROM THE DUTCH EAST INDIES.

Two samples of vegetable tallow, received from the Hamburg Museum of Applied Botany, have recently been examined by Heim, who reports them to be suitable for the same industrial applications as Piney tallow. The samples were obtained from Borneo, where both the fats themselves and the trees from whence they are derived are known as "Menyak Tangkawang" (says the *Revue Prod. Chim.*).

The one sample, from *Shorea aptera* (Burch), is of a faintly yellowish-white colour, and slight taste and smell. It melts at 31° C., and exhibits the following composition and constants:— Saponification value, 191·2; Hehner value, 95·5; oleic acid, 16·7 per cent.; fatty acids, solid at the ordinary temperature, 78·8 per cent.; fusing-point of the total fatty acids, 55° C.; fusing-point of the solid fatty acids, 63° C.; solidification-point of the solid fatty acids, 61° C.; glycerin content, 10·9 per cent.

The second sample, which is derived from *Isoptera borneensis* (Scheff), has the same organoleptic characteristics as the first, but the colour is slightly tinged with green. The saponification value is 192·2; Hehner value, 95·3; fusing-point of the total fatty acids, 55° C.; fusing-point of the solid fatty acids, 63° C.; solidification-point of the solid fatty acids, 61° C.; percentage of oleic acid, 18·0 per cent.; fatty acids, solid at the ordinary temperature, 77·3 per cent.; glycerin, 11·4 per cent.

Provided they can be obtained at a suitable price, there should be a market for these fats, in connection with the soap and stearin industries.

INDEX.

A.

LaVergne, TN USA
01 August 2010
191600LV00004B/252/A